C.S. PACAT   JOHANNA THE MAD   JOANA LAFUENTE

VOLUME TWO

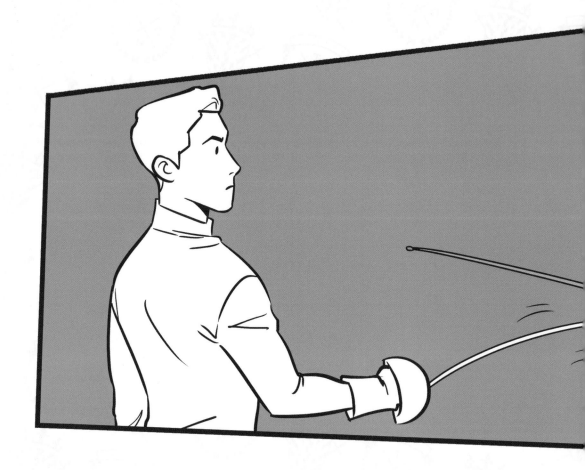

ROSS RICHIE	CEO & Founder	GWEN WALLER	Assistant Editor
JOY HUFFMAN	CFO	AMANDA LaFRANCO	Executive Assistant
MATT GAGNON	Editor-in-Chief	JILLIAN CRAB	Design Coordinator
FILIP SABLIK	President, Publishing & Marketing	MICHELLE ANKLEY	Design Coordinator
STEPHEN CHRISTY	President, Development	KARA LEOPARD	Production Designer
LANCE KREITER	Vice President, Licensing & Merchandising	MARIE KRUPINA	Production Designer
ARUNE SINGH	Vice President, Marketing	GRACE PARK	Production Designer
BRYCE CARLSON	Vice President, Editorial & Creative Strategy	CHELSEA ROBERTS	Production Design Assistant
SCOTT NEWMAN	Manager, Production Design	SAMANTHA KNAPP	Production Design Assistant
KATE HENNING	Manager, Operations	JOSÉ MEZA	Live Events Lead
SPENCER SIMPSON	Manager, Sales	STEPHANIE HOCUTT	Digital Marketing Lead
SIERRA HAHN	Executive Editor	ESTHER KIM	Marketing Coordinator
JEANINE SCHAEFER	Executive Editor	CAT O'GRADY	Digital Marketing Coordinator
DAFNA PLEBAN	Senior Editor	AMANDA LAWSON	Marketing Assistant
SHANNON WATTERS	Senior Editor	HOLLY AITCHISON	Digital Sales Coordinator
ERIC HARBURN	Senior Editor	MORGAN PERRY	Retail Sales Coordinator
CHRIS ROSA	Editor	MEGAN CHRISTOPHER	Operations Coordinator
MATTHEW LEVINE	Editor	RODRIGO HERNANDEZ	Mailroom Assistant
SOPHIE PHILIPS-ROBERTS	Associate Editor	ZIPPORAH SMITH	Operations Assistant
GAVIN GRONENTHAL	Assistant Editor	BREANNA SARPY	Executive Assistant
MICHAEL MOCCIO	Assistant Editor		

BOOM! BOX™

FENCE Volume Two, April 2019. Published by BOOM! Box, a division of Boom Entertainment, Inc. Fence is ™ & © 2019 C.S. Pacat. Originally published in single magazine form as FENCE No. 5-8. ™ & © 2018 C.S. Pacat. All rights reserved. BOOM! Box™ and the BOOM! Box logo are trademarks of Boom Entertainment, Inc., registered in various countries and categories. All characters, events, and institutions depicted herein are fictional. Any similarity between any of the names, characters, persons, events, and/or institutions in this publication to actual names, characters, and persons, whether living or dead, events, and/or institutions is unintended and purely coincidental. BOOM! Box does not read or accept unsolicited submissions of ideas, stories, or artwork.

For information regarding the CPSIA on this printed material, call: (203) 595-3636 and provide reference #RICH – 844866.

BOOM! Studios, 5670 Wilshire Boulevard, Suite 400, Los Angeles, CA 90036-5679. Printed in USA. Second Printing.

ISBN: 978-1-68415-297-1 eISBN: 978-1-64144-150-6

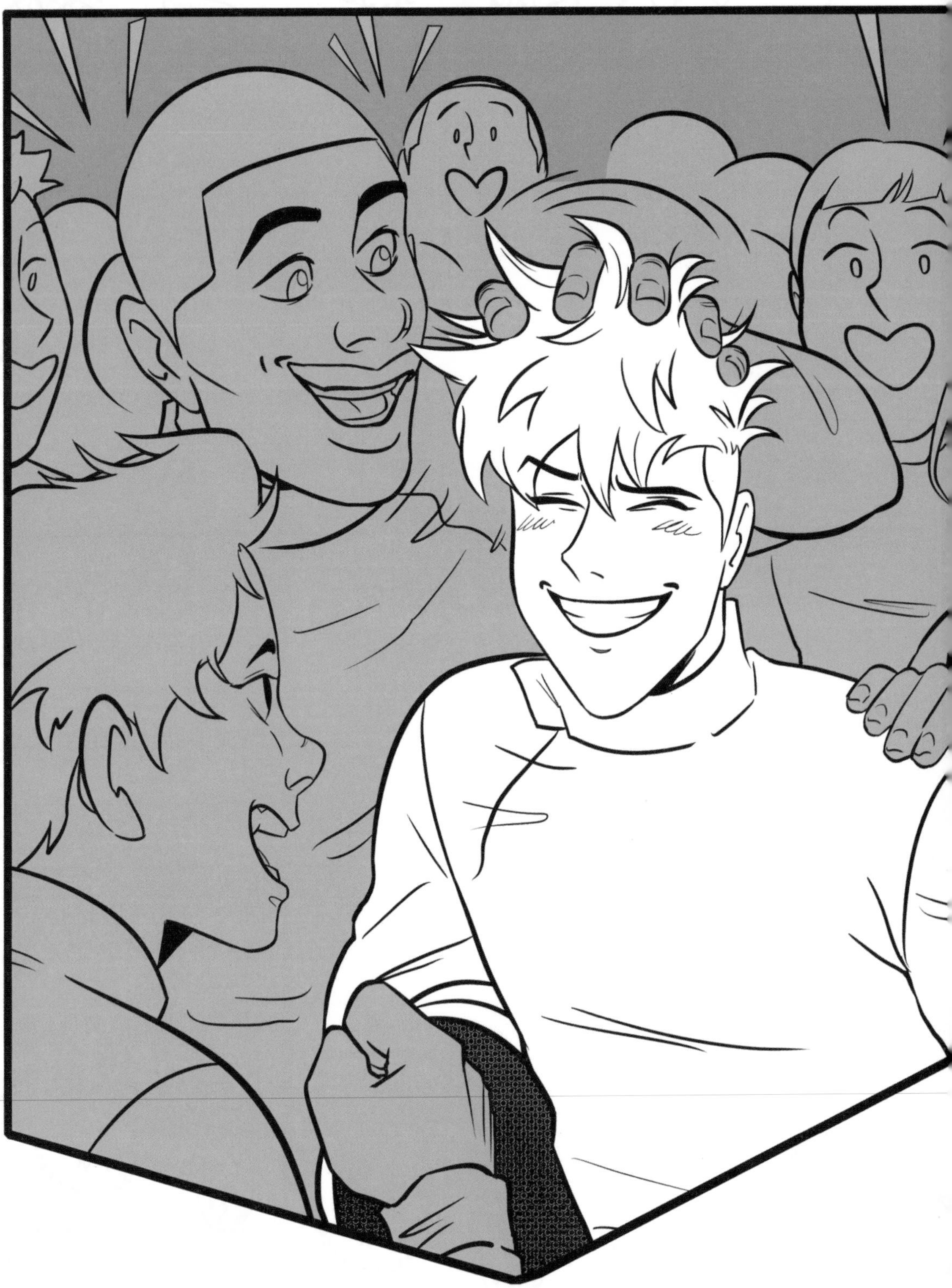

WRITTEN BY
C.S. Pacat

ILLUSTRATED BY
Johanna the Mad

COLORS BY
Joana LaFuente

LETTERS BY
Jim Campbell

TECHNICAL CONSULTANT
Pieter Leeuwenburgh

SCHOOL LOGO DESIGNS
Fawn Lau

COVER BY
Johanna the Mad

SERIES DESIGNER
Marie Krupina

COLLECTION DESIGNER
Kara Leopard

ASSISTANT EDITOR
Sophie Philips-Roberts

EDITORS
Shannon Watters & Dafna Pleban

CREATED BY
C.S. Pacat & Johanna the Mad

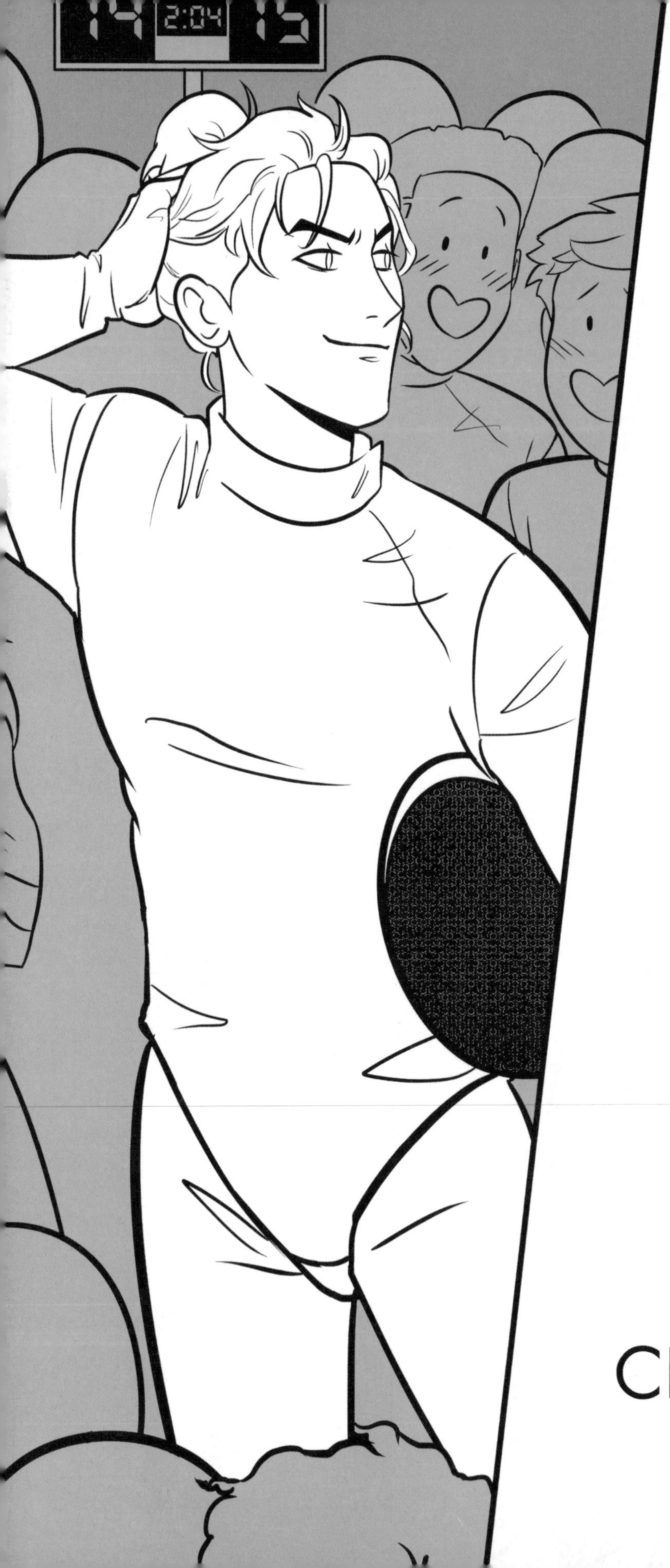
2:04

CHAPTER
Five

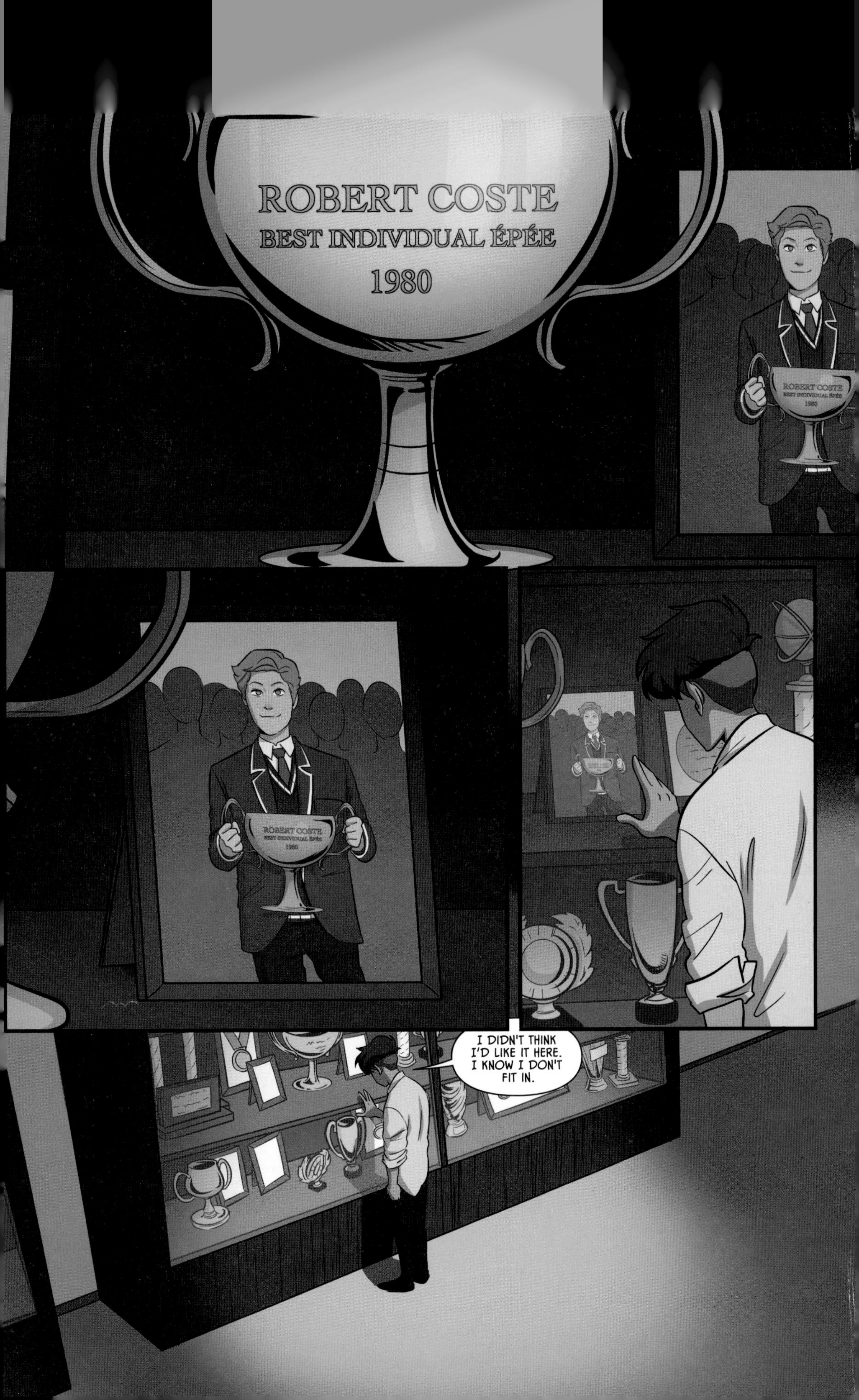
ROBERT COSTE
BEST INDIVIDUAL ÉPÉE
1980
I DIDN'T THINK I'D LIKE IT HERE. I KNOW I DON'T FIT IN.

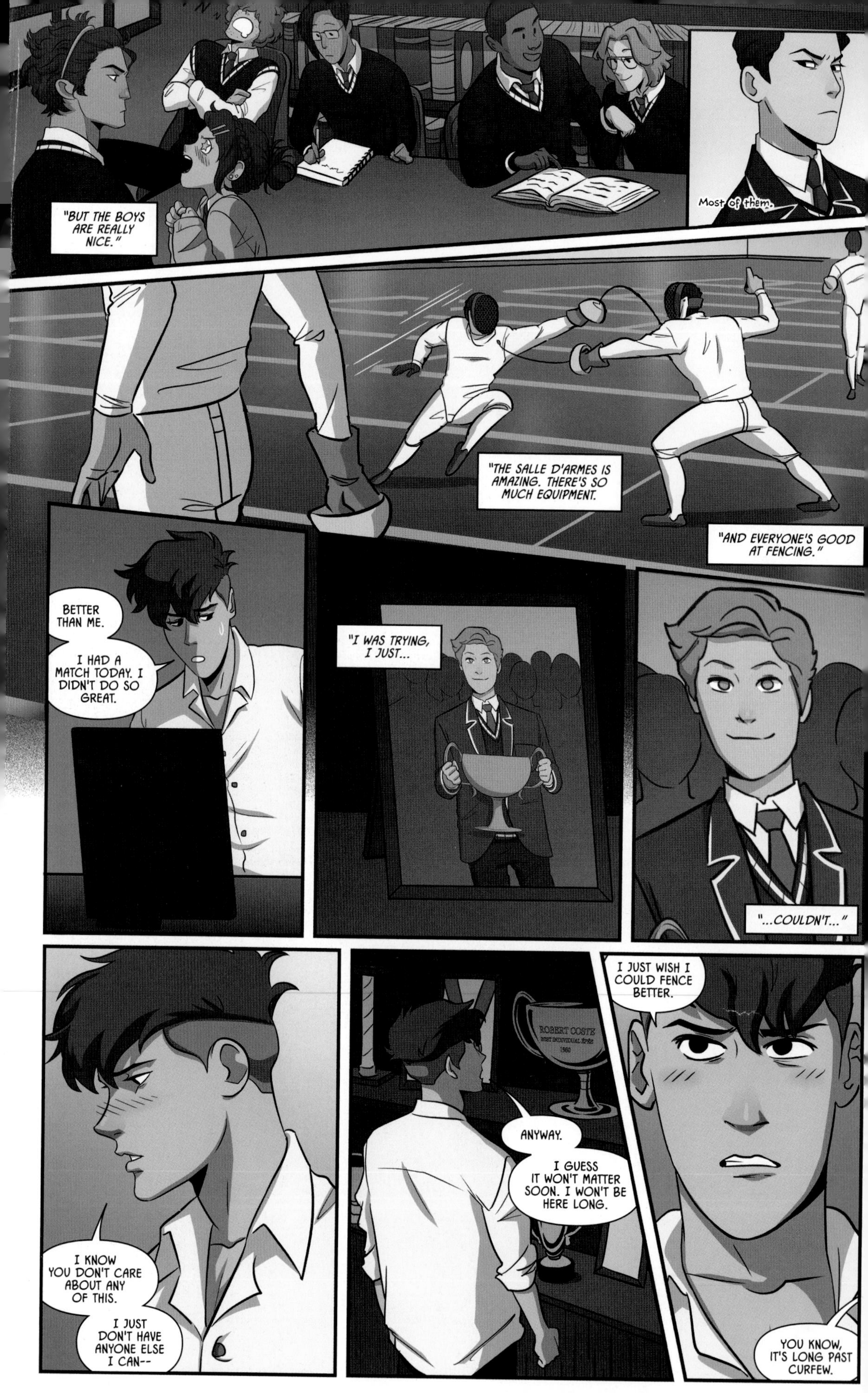
"BUT THE BOYS ARE REALLY NICE."
Most of them.
"THE SALLE D'ARMES IS AMAZING. THERE'S SO MUCH EQUIPMENT.
"AND EVERYONE'S GOOD AT FENCING."
BETTER THAN ME.
I HAD A MATCH TODAY. I DIDN'T DO SO GREAT.
"I WAS TRYING, I JUST...
"...COULDN'T..."
I KNOW YOU DON'T CARE ABOUT ANY OF THIS.
I JUST DON'T HAVE ANYONE ELSE I CAN--
ROBERT COSTE
ANYWAY.
I GUESS IT WON'T MATTER SOON. I WON'T BE HERE LONG.
I JUST WISH I COULD FENCE BETTER.
YOU KNOW, IT'S LONG PAST CURFEW.

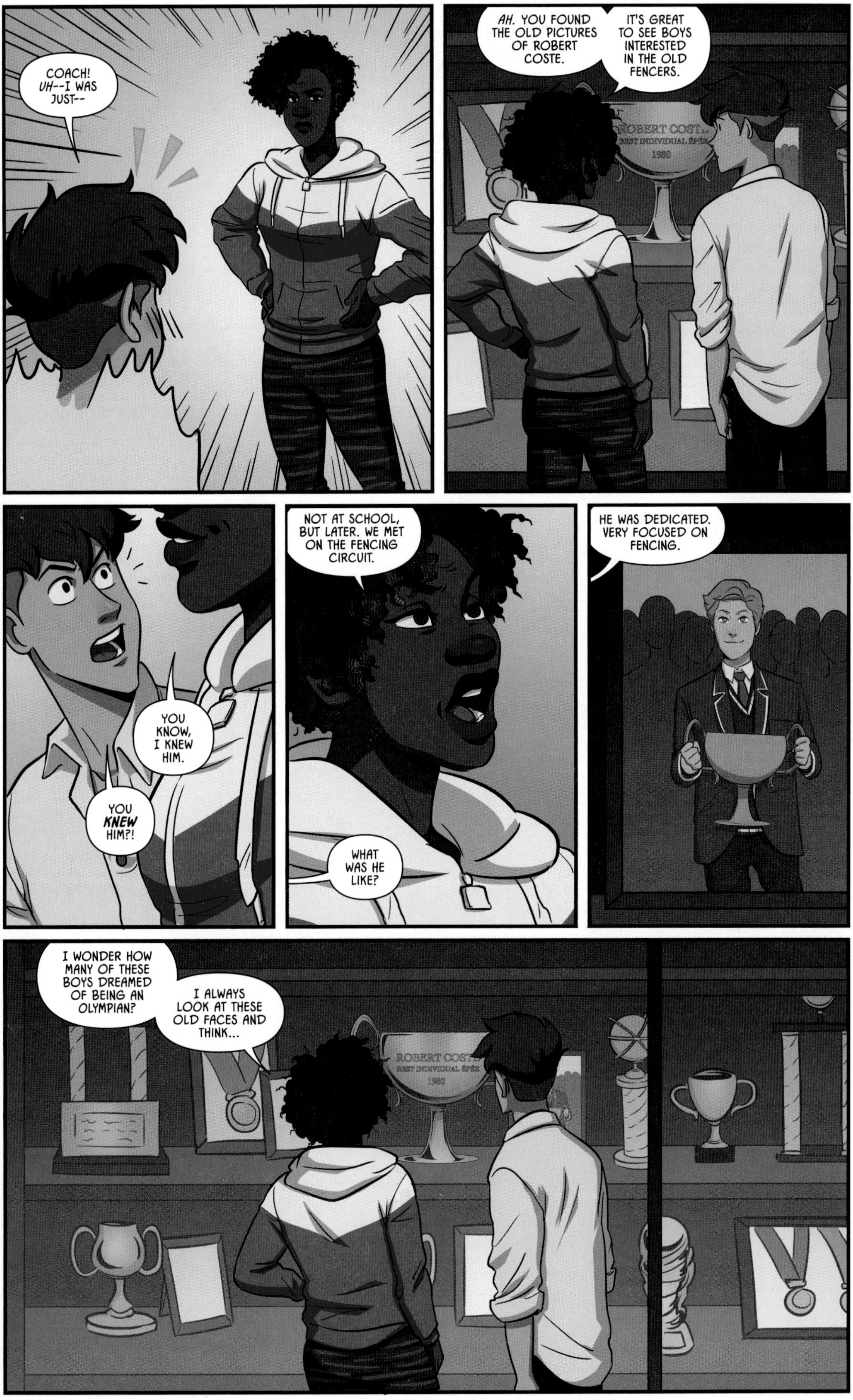
COACH! UH--I WAS JUST--
AH. YOU FOUND THE OLD PICTURES OF ROBERT COSTE.
IT'S GREAT TO SEE BOYS INTERESTED IN THE OLD FENCERS.
ROBERT COSTE
BEST INDIVIDUAL ÉPÉE
1980
YOU KNOW, I KNEW HIM.
YOU KNEW HIM?!
NOT AT SCHOOL, BUT LATER. WE MET ON THE FENCING CIRCUIT.
WHAT WAS HE LIKE?
HE WAS DEDICATED. VERY FOCUSED ON FENCING.
I WONDER HOW MANY OF THESE BOYS DREAMED OF BEING AN OLYMPIAN?
I ALWAYS LOOK AT THESE OLD FACES AND THINK...
ROBERT COSTE
BEST INDIVIDUAL ÉPÉE
1980

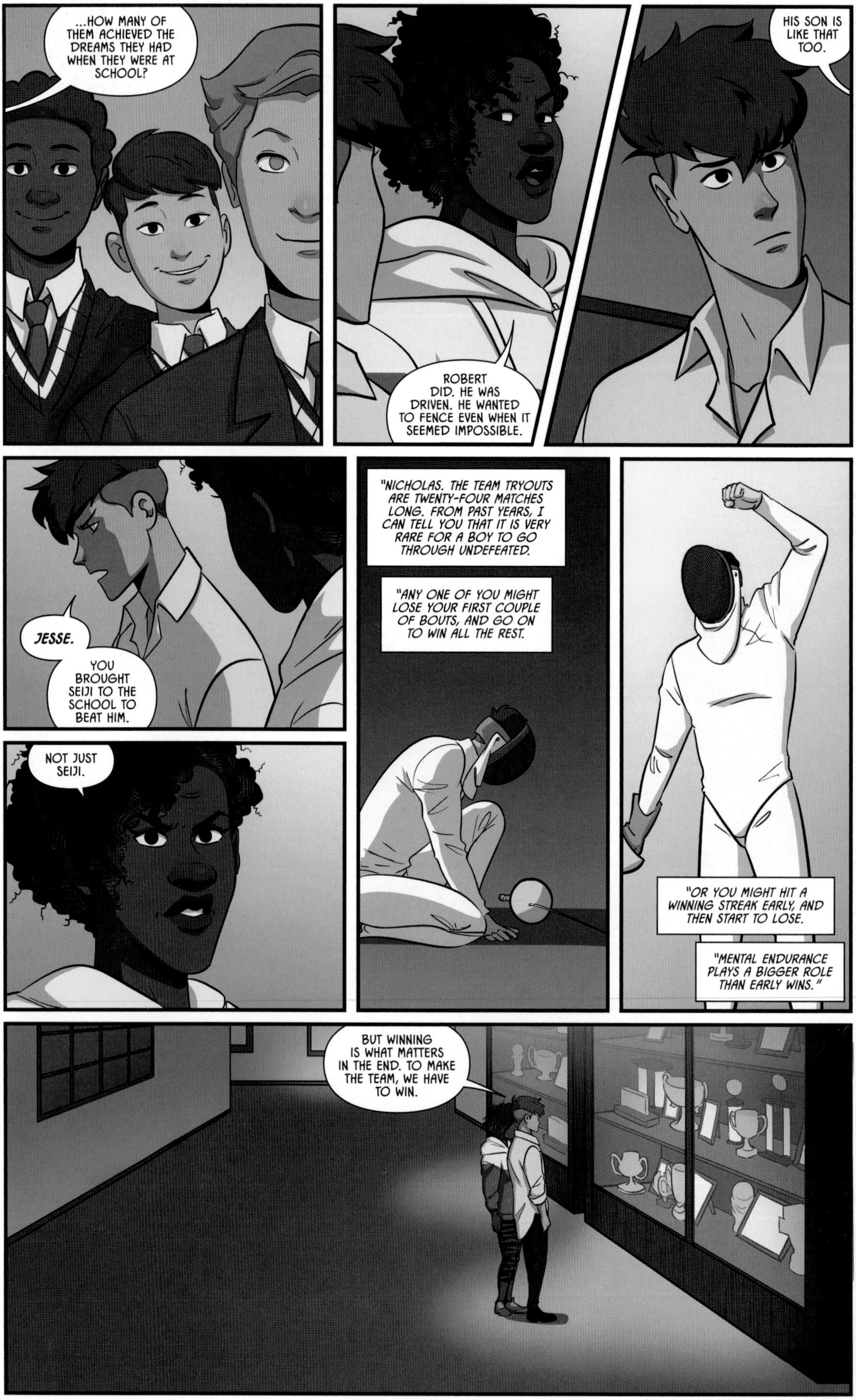
...HOW MANY OF THEM ACHIEVED THE DREAMS THEY HAD WHEN THEY WERE AT SCHOOL?
ROBERT DID. HE WAS DRIVEN. HE WANTED TO FENCE EVEN WHEN IT SEEMED IMPOSSIBLE.
HIS SON IS LIKE THAT TOO.
JESSE.
YOU BROUGHT SEIJI TO THE SCHOOL TO BEAT HIM.
NOT JUST SEIJI.
"NICHOLAS. THE TEAM TRYOUTS ARE TWENTY-FOUR MATCHES LONG. FROM PAST YEARS, I CAN TELL YOU THAT IT IS VERY RARE FOR A BOY TO GO THROUGH UNDEFEATED.
"ANY ONE OF YOU MIGHT LOSE YOUR FIRST COUPLE OF BOUTS, AND GO ON TO WIN ALL THE REST.
"OR YOU MIGHT HIT A WINNING STREAK EARLY, AND THEN START TO LOSE.
"MENTAL ENDURANCE PLAYS A BIGGER ROLE THAN EARLY WINS."
BUT WINNING IS WHAT MATTERS IN THE END. TO MAKE THE TEAM, WE HAVE TO WIN.

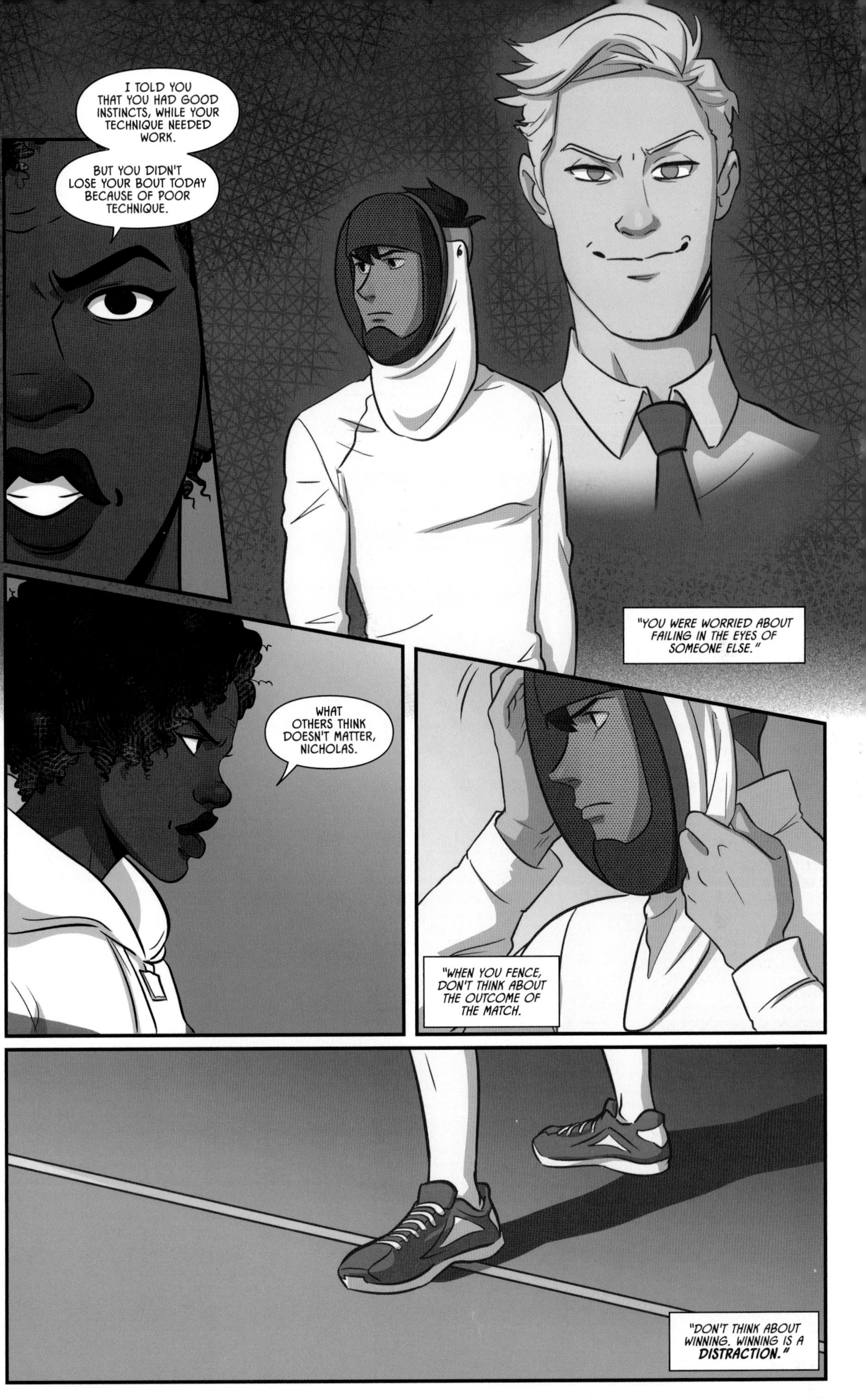

I TOLD YOU THAT YOU HAD GOOD INSTINCTS, WHILE YOUR TECHNIQUE NEEDED WORK.
BUT YOU DIDN'T LOSE YOUR BOUT TODAY BECAUSE OF POOR TECHNIQUE.
"YOU WERE WORRIED ABOUT FAILING IN THE EYES OF SOMEONE ELSE."
WHAT OTHERS THINK DOESN'T MATTER, NICHOLAS.
"WHEN YOU FENCE, DON'T THINK ABOUT THE OUTCOME OF THE MATCH.
"DON'T THINK ABOUT WINNING. WINNING IS A **DISTRACTION.**"

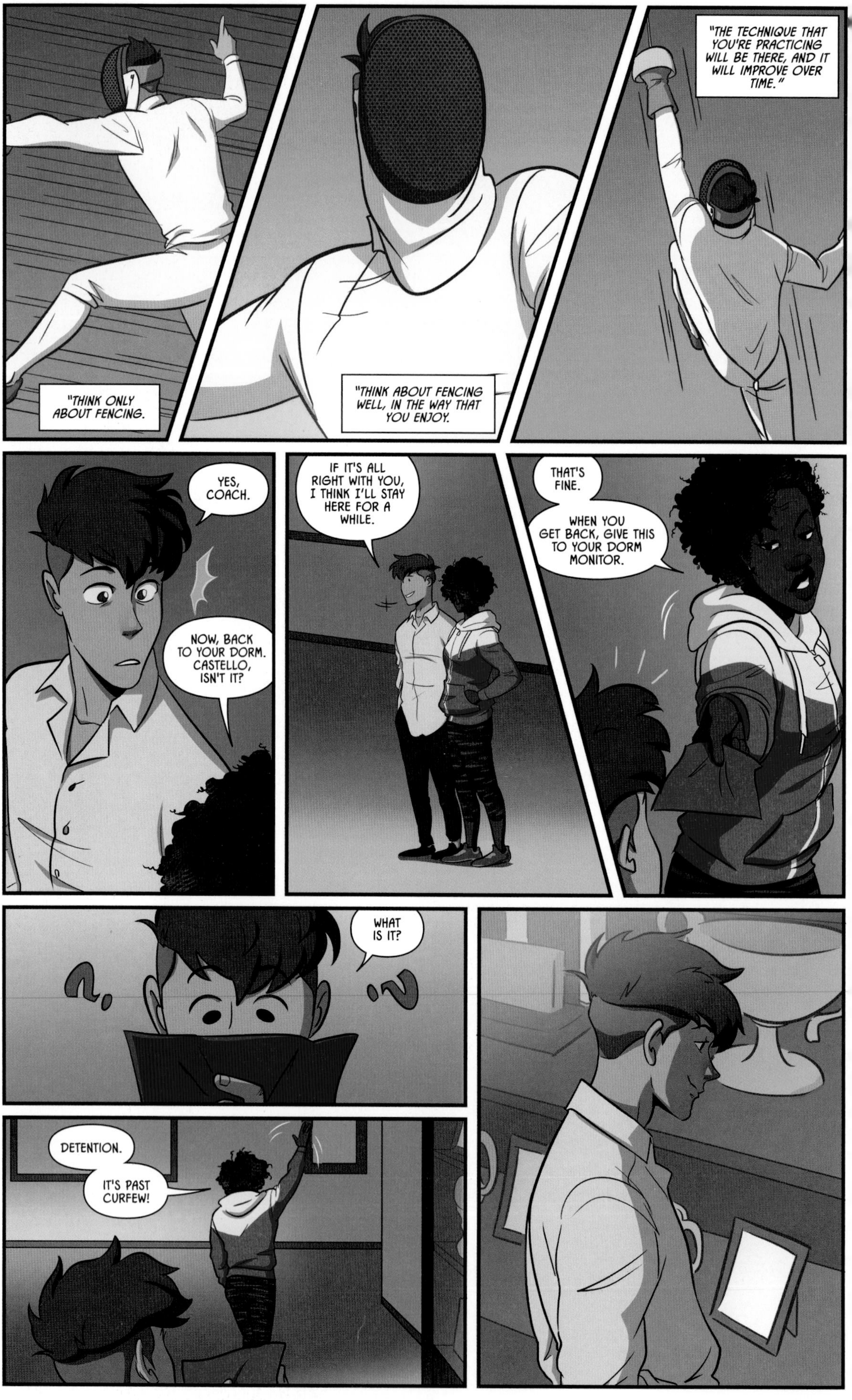
"THINK ONLY ABOUT FENCING.
"THINK ABOUT FENCING WELL, IN THE WAY THAT YOU ENJOY.
"THE TECHNIQUE THAT YOU'RE PRACTICING WILL BE THERE, AND IT WILL IMPROVE OVER TIME."
YES, COACH.
NOW, BACK TO YOUR DORM. CASTELLO, ISN'T IT?
IF IT'S ALL RIGHT WITH YOU, I THINK I'LL STAY HERE FOR A WHILE.
THAT'S FINE.
WHEN YOU GET BACK, GIVE THIS TO YOUR DORM MONITOR.
WHAT IS IT?
DETENTION.
IT'S PAST CURFEW!

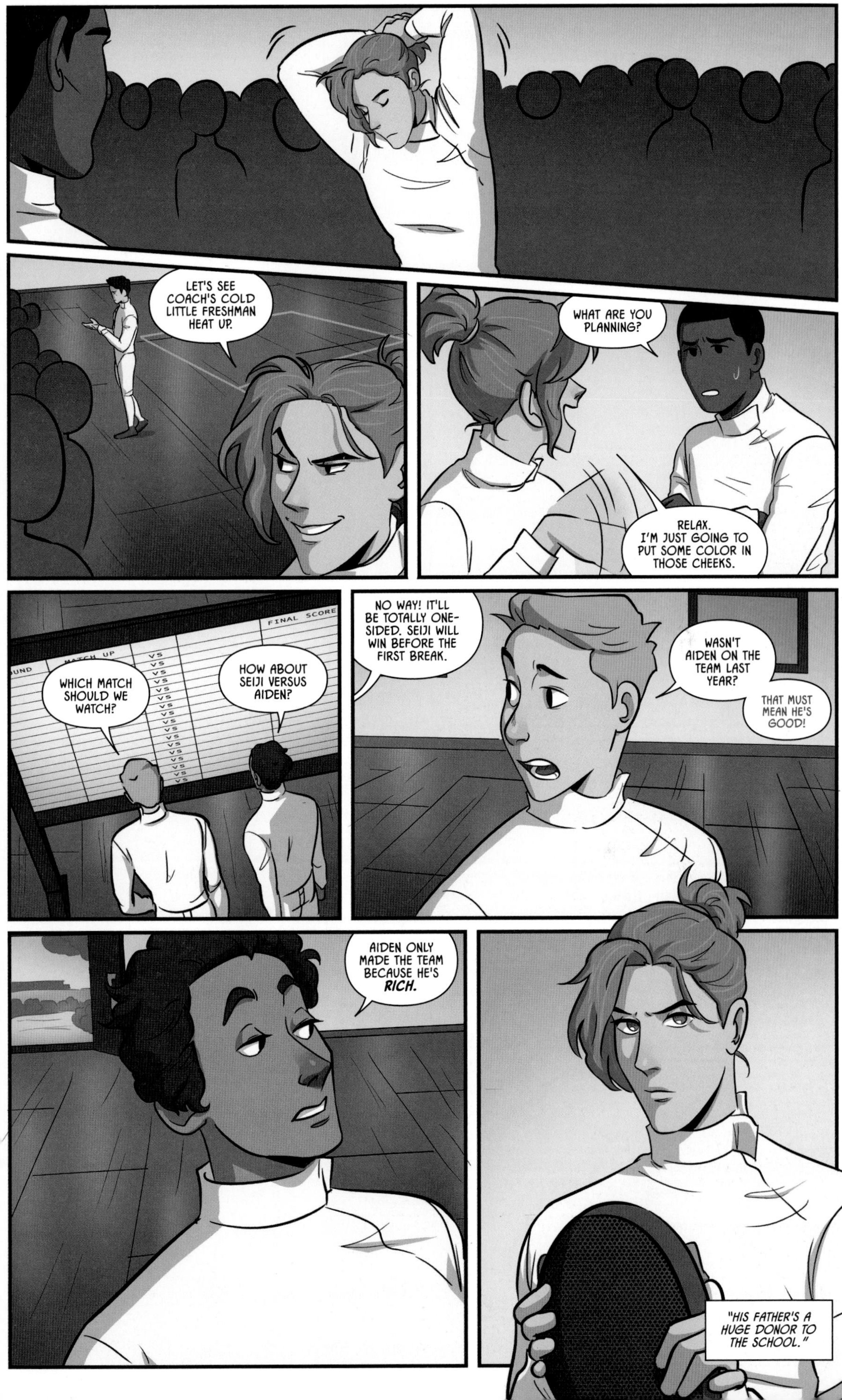
LET'S SEE COACH'S COLD LITTLE FRESHMAN HEAT UP.
WHAT ARE YOU PLANNING?
RELAX. I'M JUST GOING TO PUT SOME COLOR IN THOSE CHEEKS.
FINAL SCORE
WHICH MATCH SHOULD WE WATCH?
HOW ABOUT SEIJI VERSUS AIDEN?
NO WAY! IT'LL BE TOTALLY ONE-SIDED. SEIJI WILL WIN BEFORE THE FIRST BREAK.
WASN'T AIDEN ON THE TEAM LAST YEAR?
THAT MUST MEAN HE'S GOOD!
AIDEN ONLY MADE THE TEAM BECAUSE HE'S *RICH.*
"HIS FATHER'S A HUGE DONOR TO THE SCHOOL."

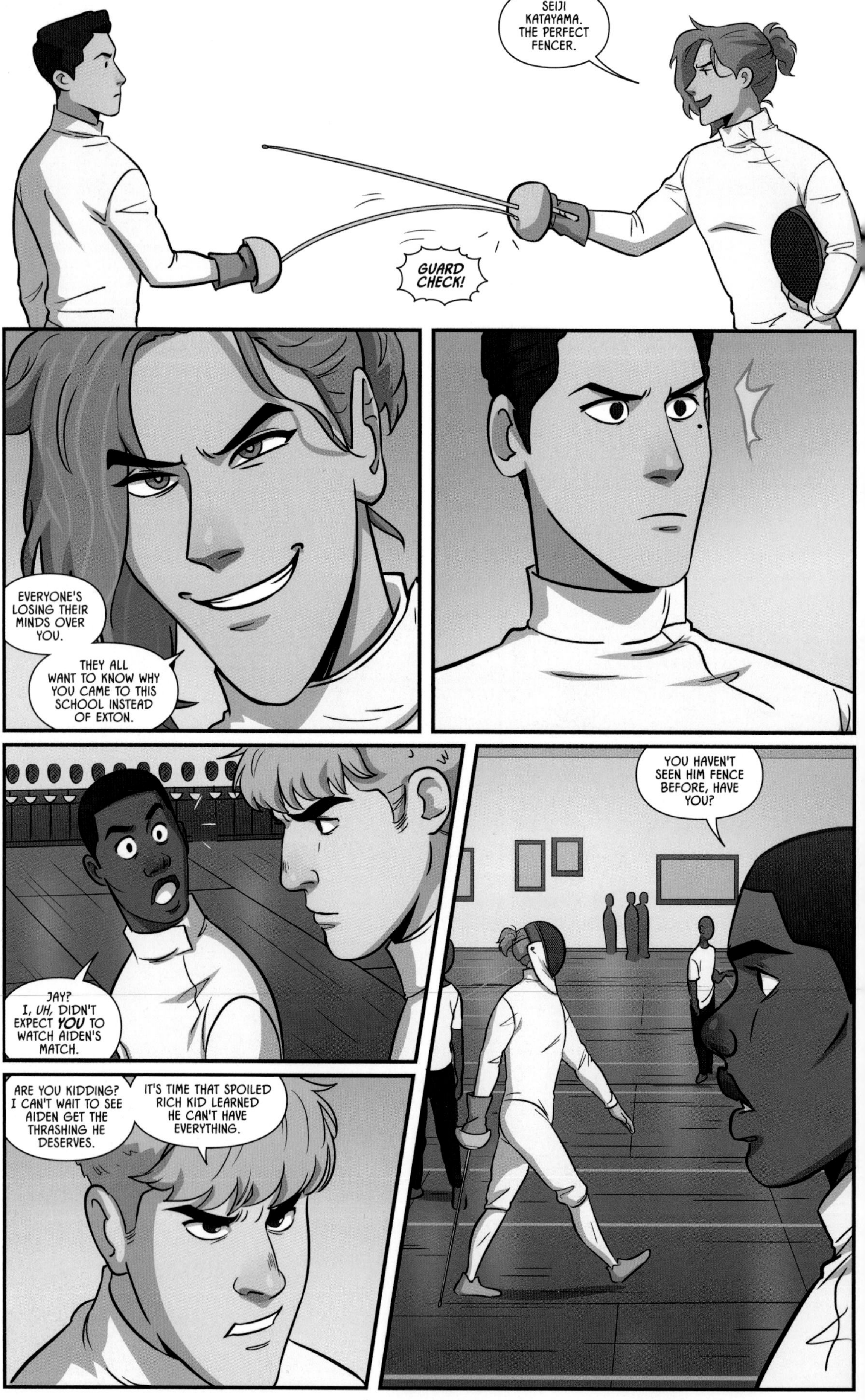

SEIJI KATAYAMA. THE PERFECT FENCER.
GUARD CHECK!
EVERYONE'S LOSING THEIR MINDS OVER YOU.
THEY ALL WANT TO KNOW WHY YOU CAME TO THIS SCHOOL INSTEAD OF EXTON.
JAY? I, *UH,* DIDN'T EXPECT ***YOU*** TO WATCH AIDEN'S MATCH.
YOU HAVEN'T SEEN HIM FENCE BEFORE, HAVE YOU?
ARE YOU KIDDING? I CAN'T WAIT TO SEE AIDEN GET THE THRASHING HE DESERVES.
IT'S TIME THAT SPOILED RICH KID LEARNED HE CAN'T HAVE EVERYTHING.

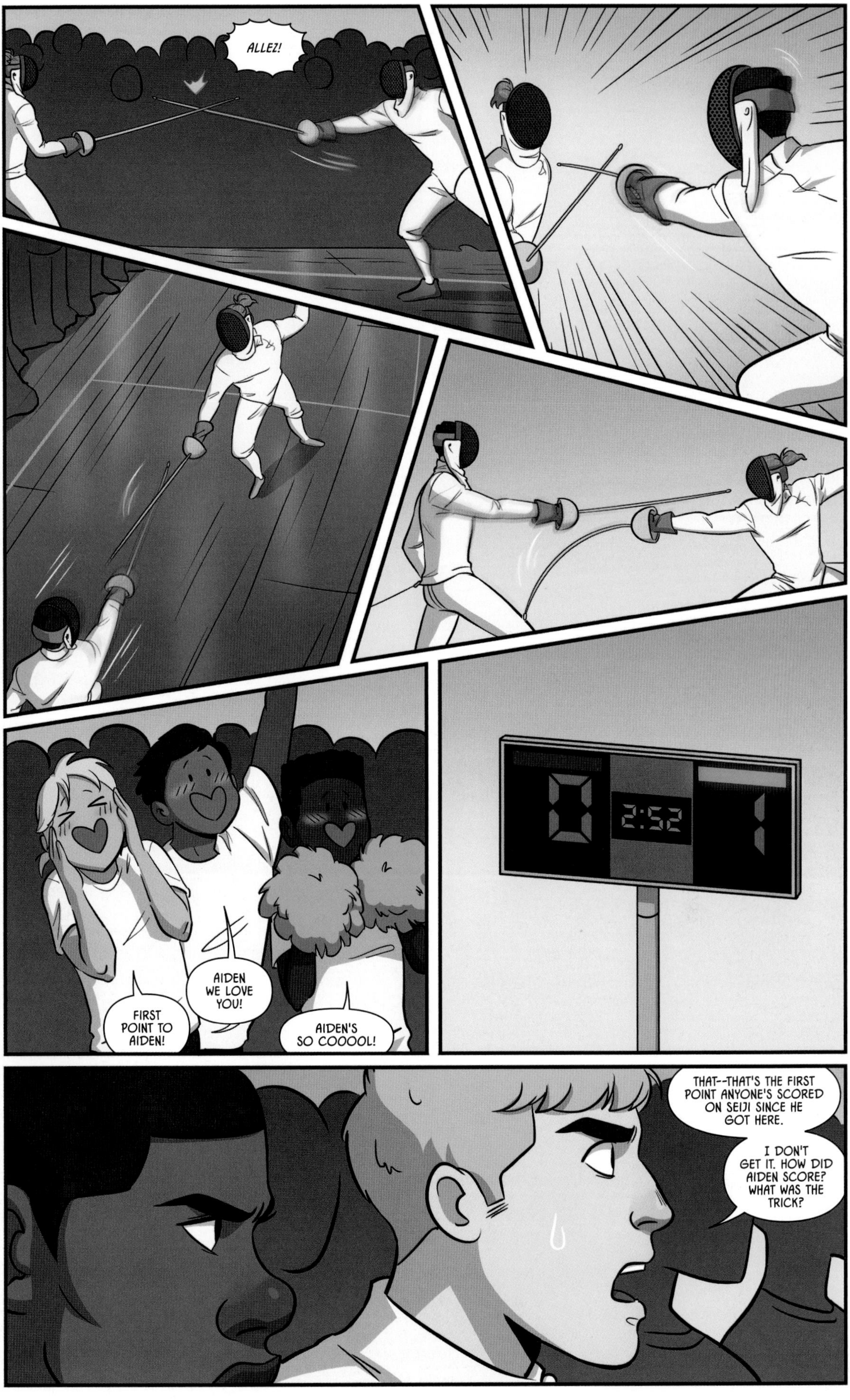
ALLEZ!
FIRST POINT TO AIDEN!
AIDEN WE LOVE YOU!
AIDEN'S SO COOOOL!
2:52
THAT--THAT'S THE FIRST POINT ANYONE'S SCORED ON SEIJI SINCE HE GOT HERE.
I DON'T GET IT. HOW DID AIDEN SCORE? WHAT WAS THE TRICK?

IT'S NOT A TRICK. AIDEN'S JUST GOOD.

"BUT FOR A FENCER LIKE SEIJI...

"...IT DOESN'T TAKE LONG TO GET THE MEASURE OF AN OPPONENT.

"PLUS, HE'S SEEN SEIJI FENCE BEFORE.

"WHEREAS SEIJI DOESN'T KNOW AIDEN AT ALL SINCE AIDEN'S UTTERLY LAZY AND NEVER COMES TO PRACTICE.

"THE SAME TACTIC WON'T WORK ON HIM TWICE."

YES! SEIJI, WIPE HIM OUT!

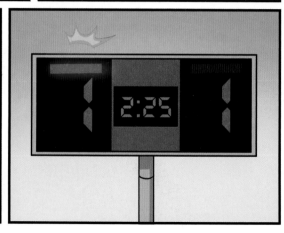

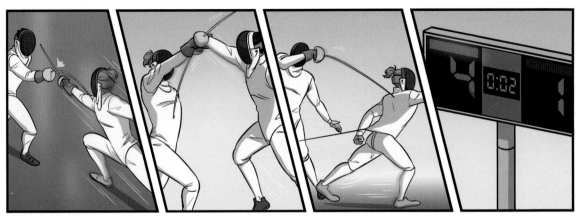

HALT!

BREAK FOR ONE MINUTE!

AIDEN SHOULD ENJOY THAT POINT BECAUSE IT'S THE ONLY ONE HE'S GOING TO GET.

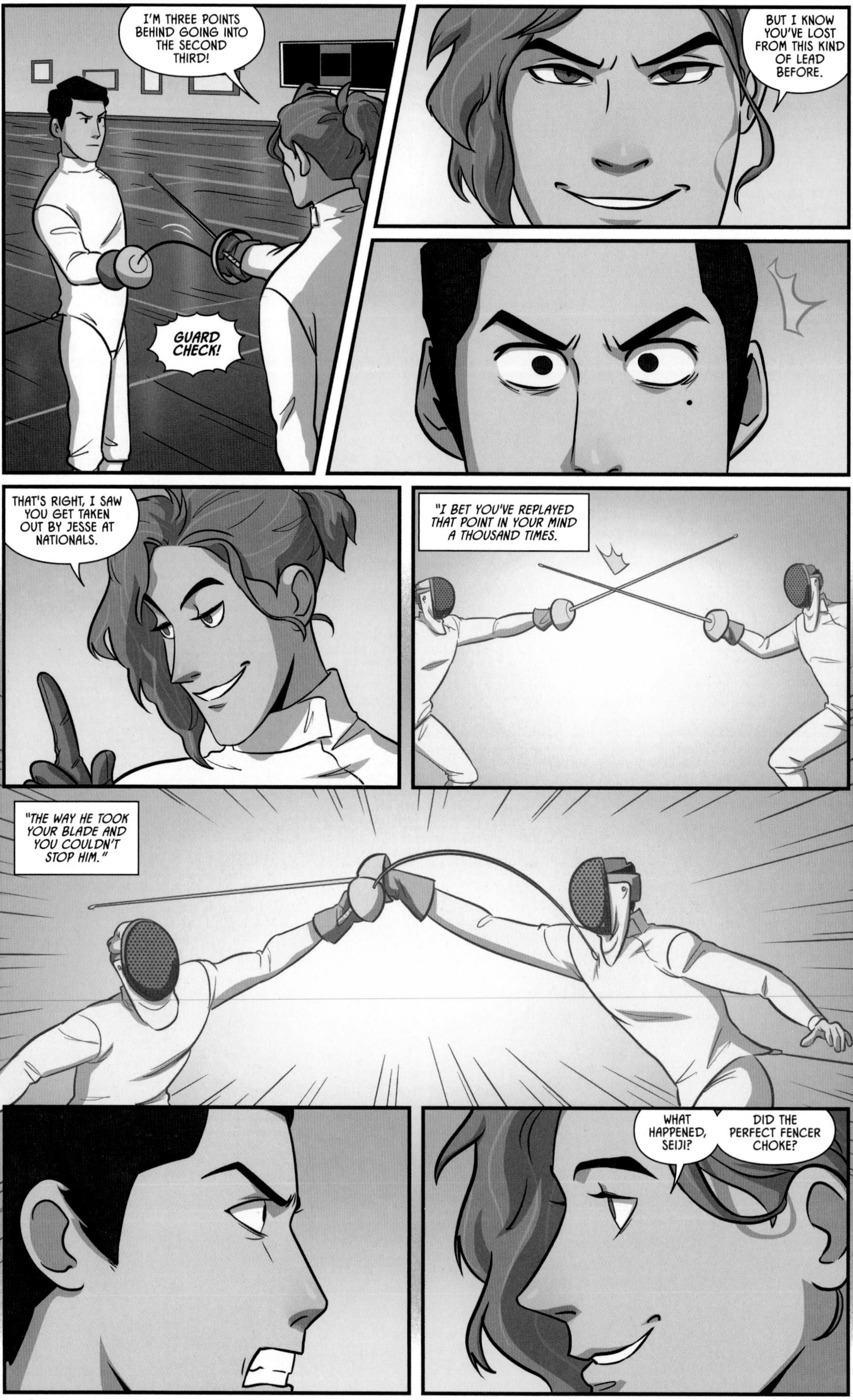
I'M THREE POINTS BEHIND GOING INTO THE SECOND THIRD!
GUARD CHECK!
BUT I KNOW YOU'VE LOST FROM THIS KIND OF LEAD BEFORE.
THAT'S RIGHT, I SAW YOU GET TAKEN OUT BY JESSE AT NATIONALS.
"I BET YOU'VE REPLAYED THAT POINT IN YOUR MIND A THOUSAND TIMES.
"THE WAY HE TOOK YOUR BLADE AND YOU COULDN'T STOP HIM."
WHAT HAPPENED, SEIJI?
DID THE PERFECT FENCER CHOKE?

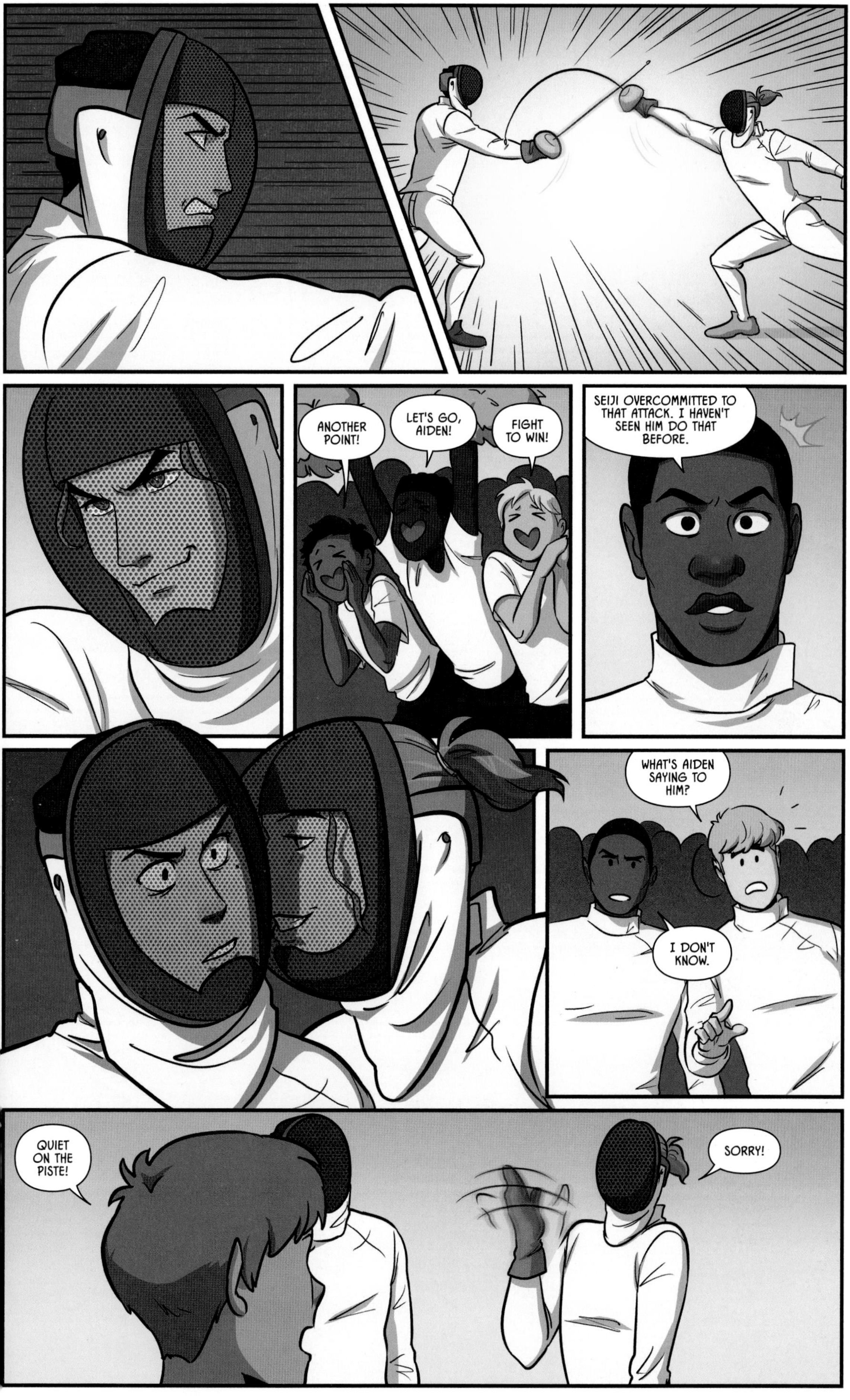
ANOTHER POINT!
LET'S GO, AIDEN!
FIGHT TO WIN!
SEIJI OVERCOMMITTED TO THAT ATTACK. I HAVEN'T SEEN HIM DO THAT BEFORE.
WHAT'S AIDEN SAYING TO HIM?
I DON'T KNOW.
QUIET ON THE PISTE!
SORRY!

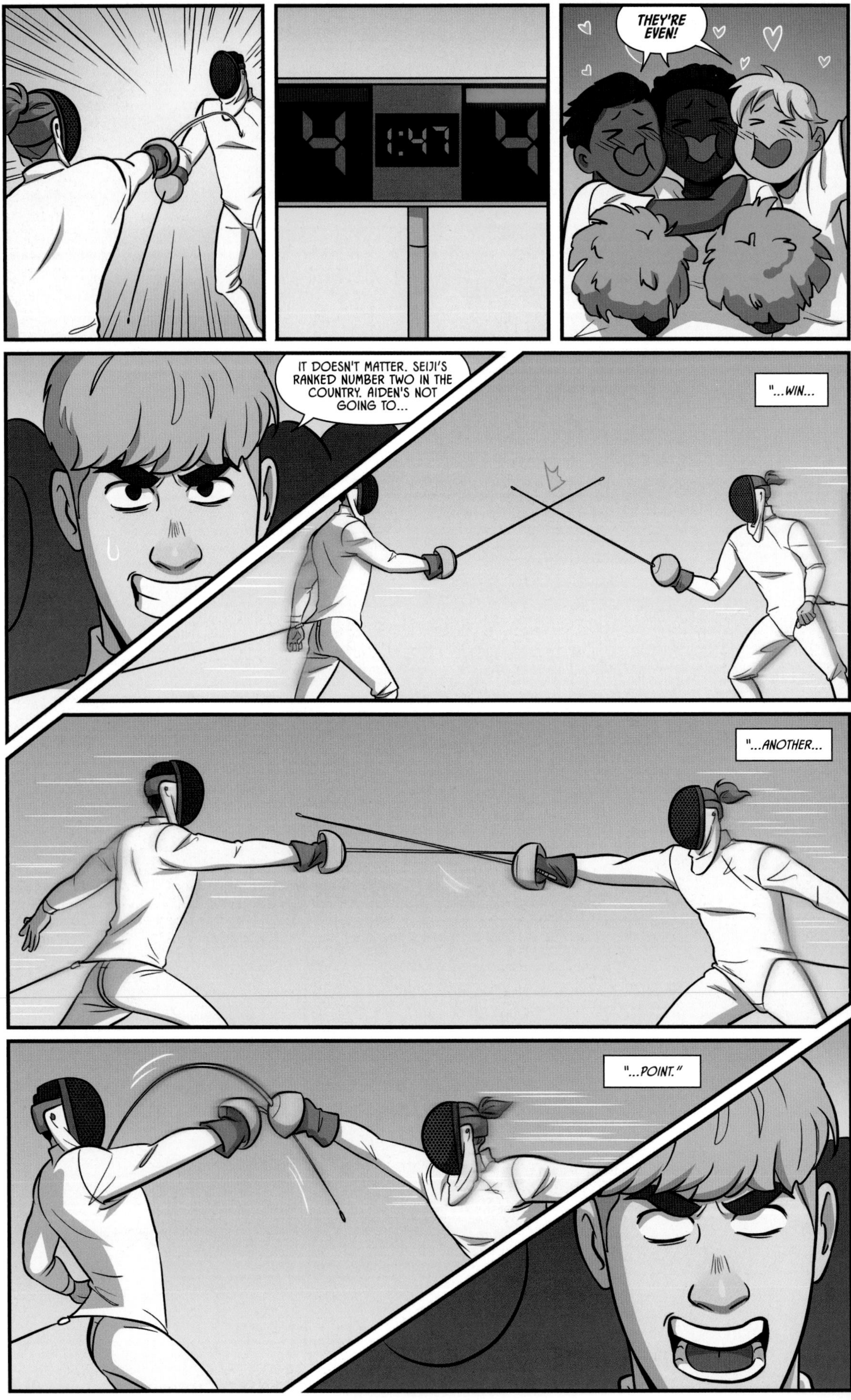
4
1:47
4
THEY'RE EVEN!
IT DOESN'T MATTER. SEIJI'S RANKED NUMBER TWO IN THE COUNTRY. AIDEN'S NOT GOING TO...
"...WIN...
"...ANOTHER...
"...POINT."

FINISHED! I CAN'T WAIT TO WATCH THE END OF SEIJI'S MATCH. SEIJI!

I'M SURPRISED IT'S STILL GOING. SEIJI USUALLY WINS SO QUICKLY.

BOBBY! YOU'RE JUST IN TIME! AIDEN'S BEATING SEIJI!

HUH? AIDEN'S... AIDEN'S WINNING?

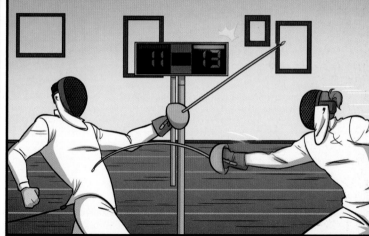

AIDEN'S ONLY TWO POINTS AWAY FROM A WIN!

SEIJI IS BARELY HOLDING ON.

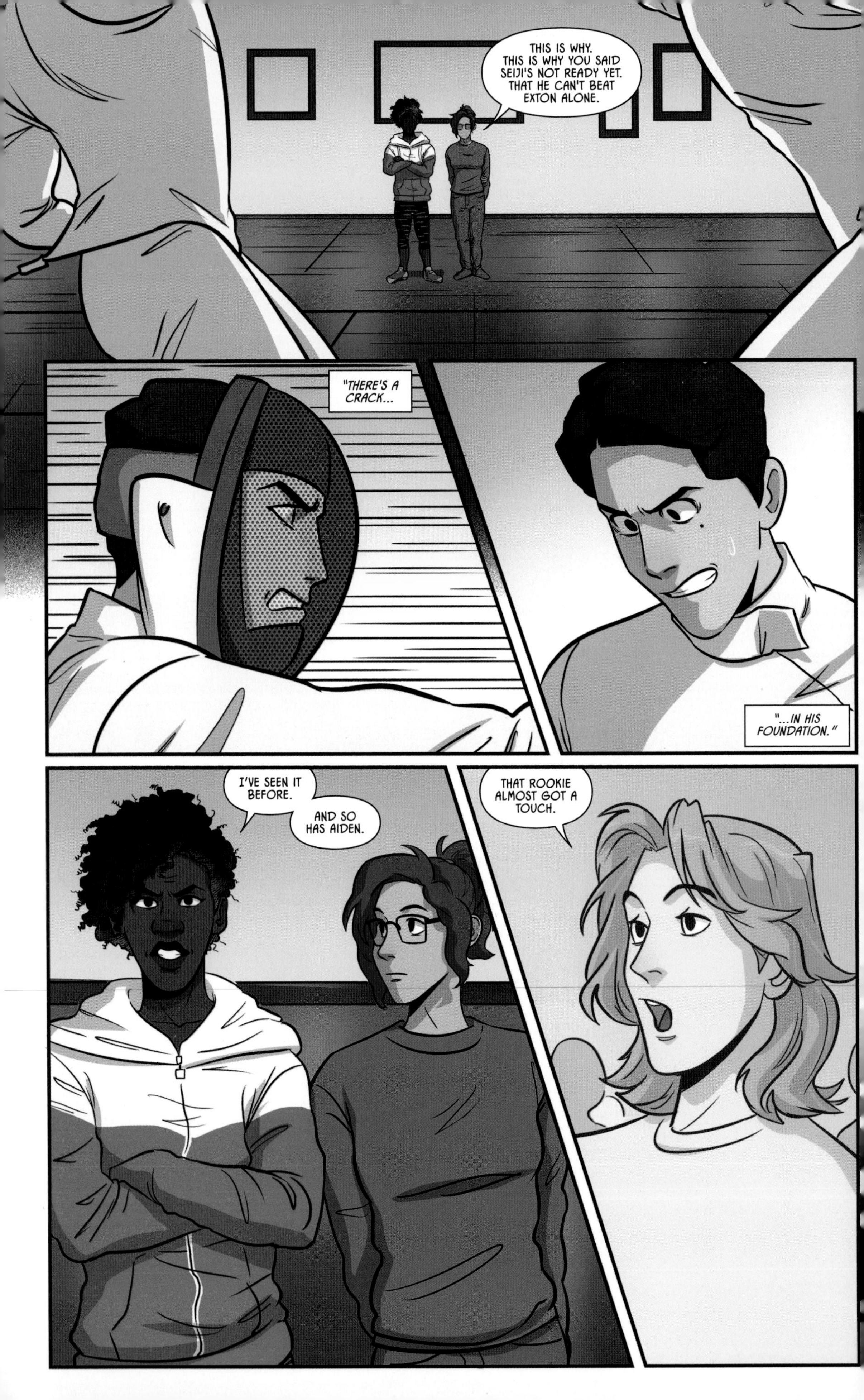
THIS IS WHY. THIS IS WHY YOU SAID SEIJI'S NOT READY YET. THAT HE CAN'T BEAT EXTON ALONE.
"THERE'S A CRACK...
"...IN HIS FOUNDATION."
I'VE SEEN IT BEFORE.
AND SO HAS AIDEN.
THAT ROOKIE ALMOST GOT A TOUCH.

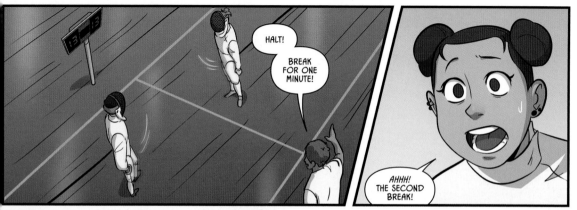

HALT!

BREAK FOR ONE MINUTE!

AHHH! THE SECOND BREAK!

TO THE AVERAGE PERSON, COMING SECOND AT NATIONALS WOULD BE AN EXTRAORDINARY ACCOMPLISHMENT.

"BUT FOR AN ELITE ATHLETE LIKE SEIJI...

"...WINNING IS EXPECTED.

"IT'S A DISTORTED MINDSET, IN WHICH WINNING ISN'T AN ACCOMPLISHMENT..."

...BUT LOSING IS FAILURE.

LOSING IS UNTHINKABLE.

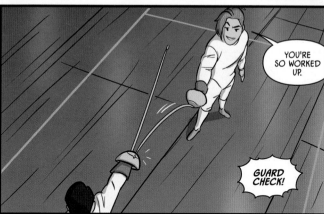

YOU'RE SO WORKED UP.

GUARD CHECK!

WHAT MAKES COACH'S LITTLE PRODIGY LOSE HIS COOL?

YOU NEVER TOLD ANYONE WHY YOU'RE HERE, SLUMMING ON A THIRD-RATE TEAM.

IS IT BECAUSE YOU CAN'T FACE JESSE?

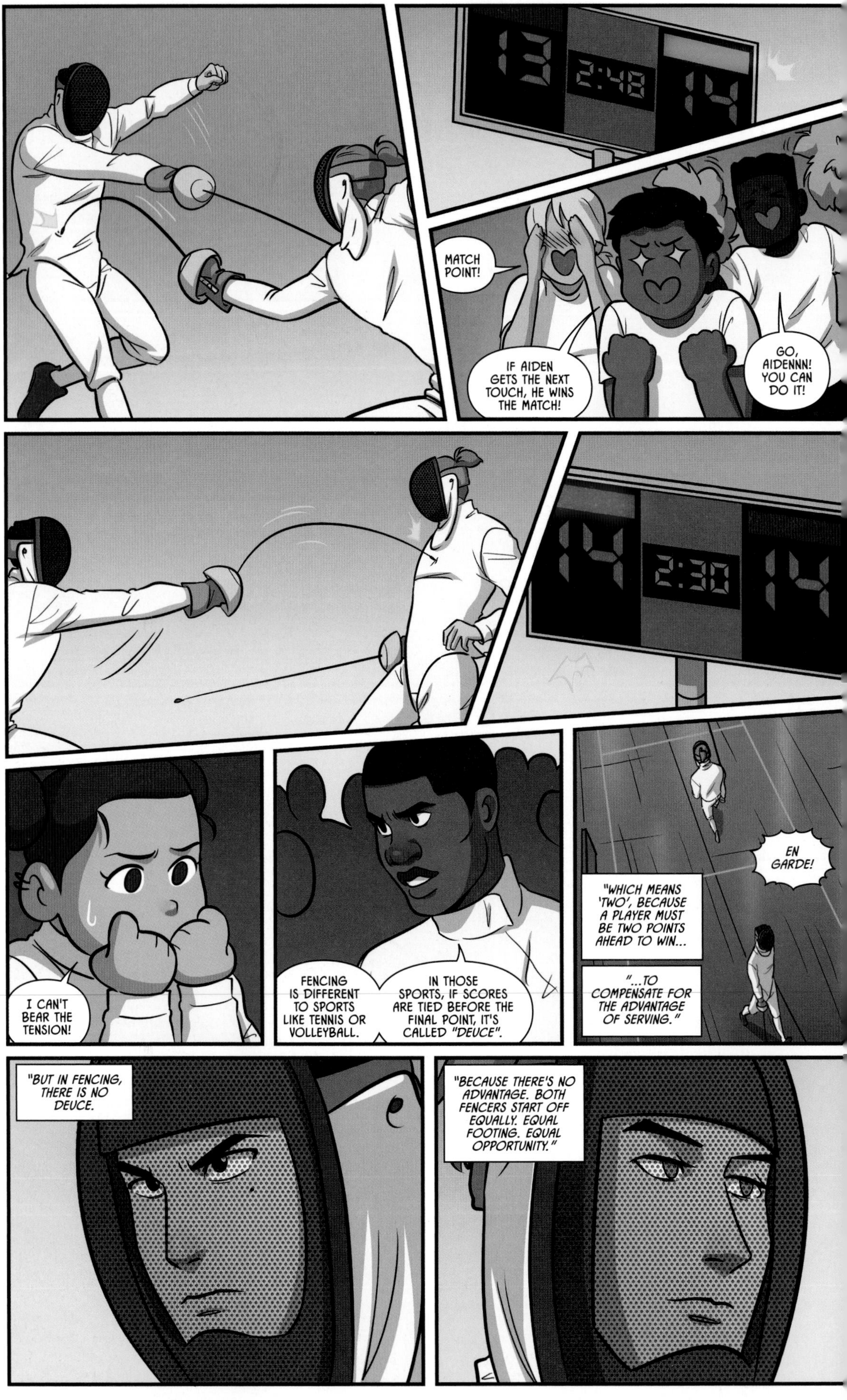

13
2:48
14
MATCH POINT!
IF AIDEN GETS THE NEXT TOUCH, HE WINS THE MATCH!
GO, AIDENNN! YOU CAN DO IT!
14
2:30
14
I CAN'T BEAR THE TENSION!
FENCING IS DIFFERENT TO SPORTS LIKE TENNIS OR VOLLEYBALL.
IN THOSE SPORTS, IF SCORES ARE TIED BEFORE THE FINAL POINT, IT'S CALLED "DEUCE".
EN GARDE!
"WHICH MEANS 'TWO', BECAUSE A PLAYER MUST BE TWO POINTS AHEAD TO WIN...
"...TO COMPENSATE FOR THE ADVANTAGE OF SERVING."
"BUT IN FENCING, THERE IS NO DEUCE.
"BECAUSE THERE'S NO ADVANTAGE. BOTH FENCERS START OFF EQUALLY. EQUAL FOOTING. EQUAL OPPORTUNITY."

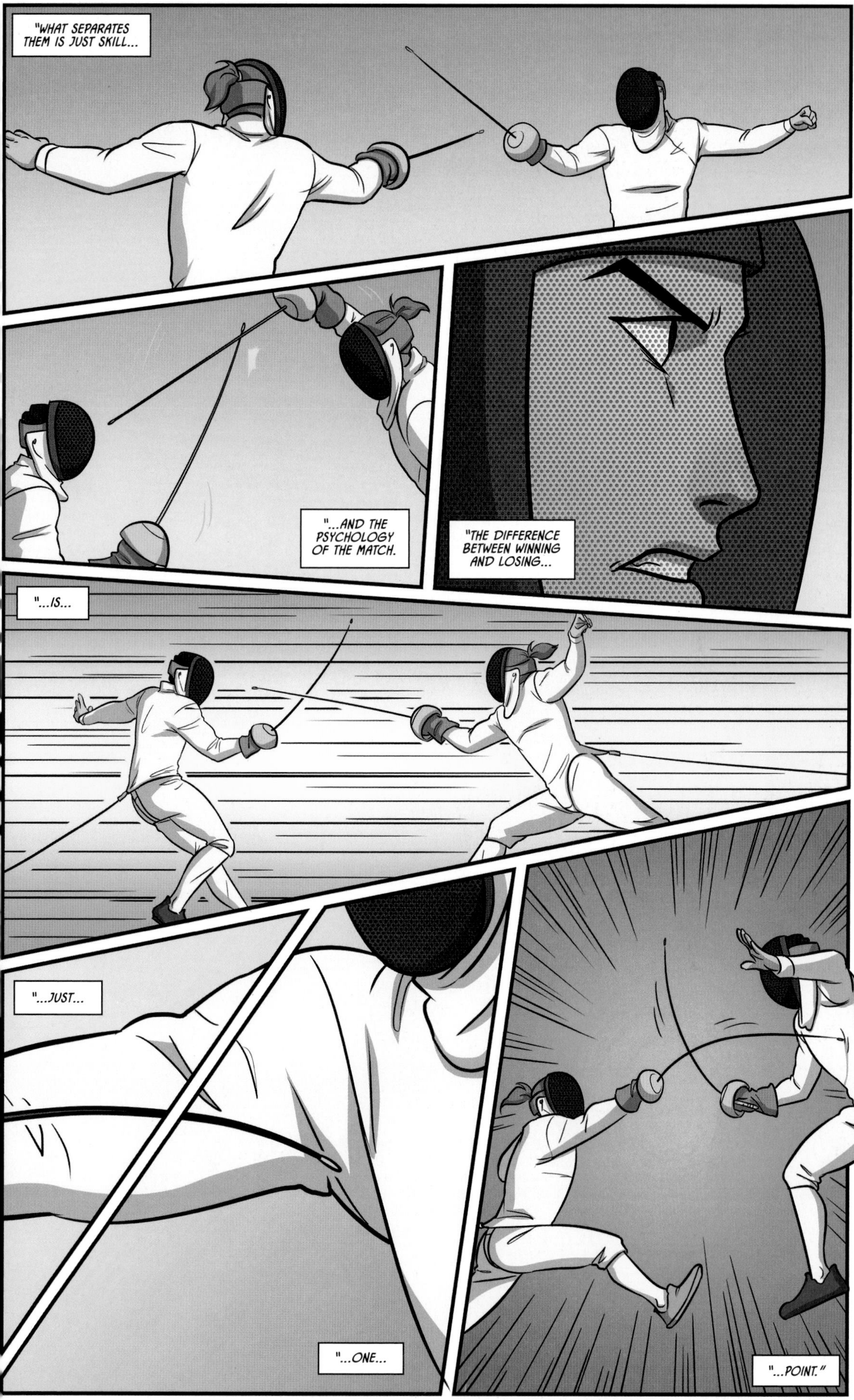
"WHAT SEPARATES THEM IS JUST SKILL...
"...AND THE PSYCHOLOGY OF THE MATCH.
"THE DIFFERENCE BETWEEN WINNING AND LOSING...
"...IS...
"...JUST...
"...ONE...
"...POINT."

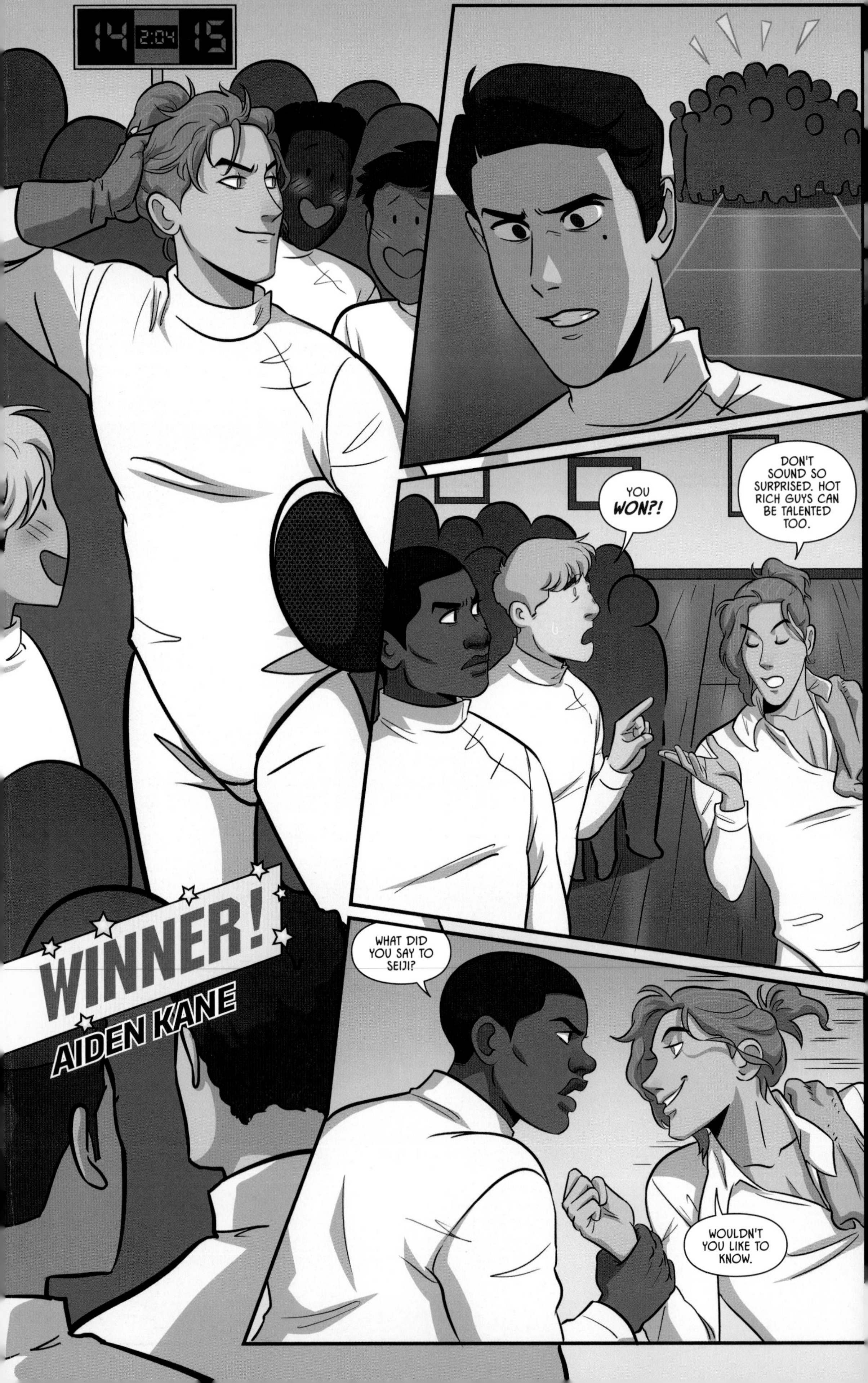

14 2:04 15
WINNER!
AIDEN KANE
YOU WON?!
DON'T SOUND SO SURPRISED. HOT RICH GUYS CAN BE TALENTED TOO.
WHAT DID YOU SAY TO SEIJI?
WOULDN'T YOU LIKE TO KNOW.

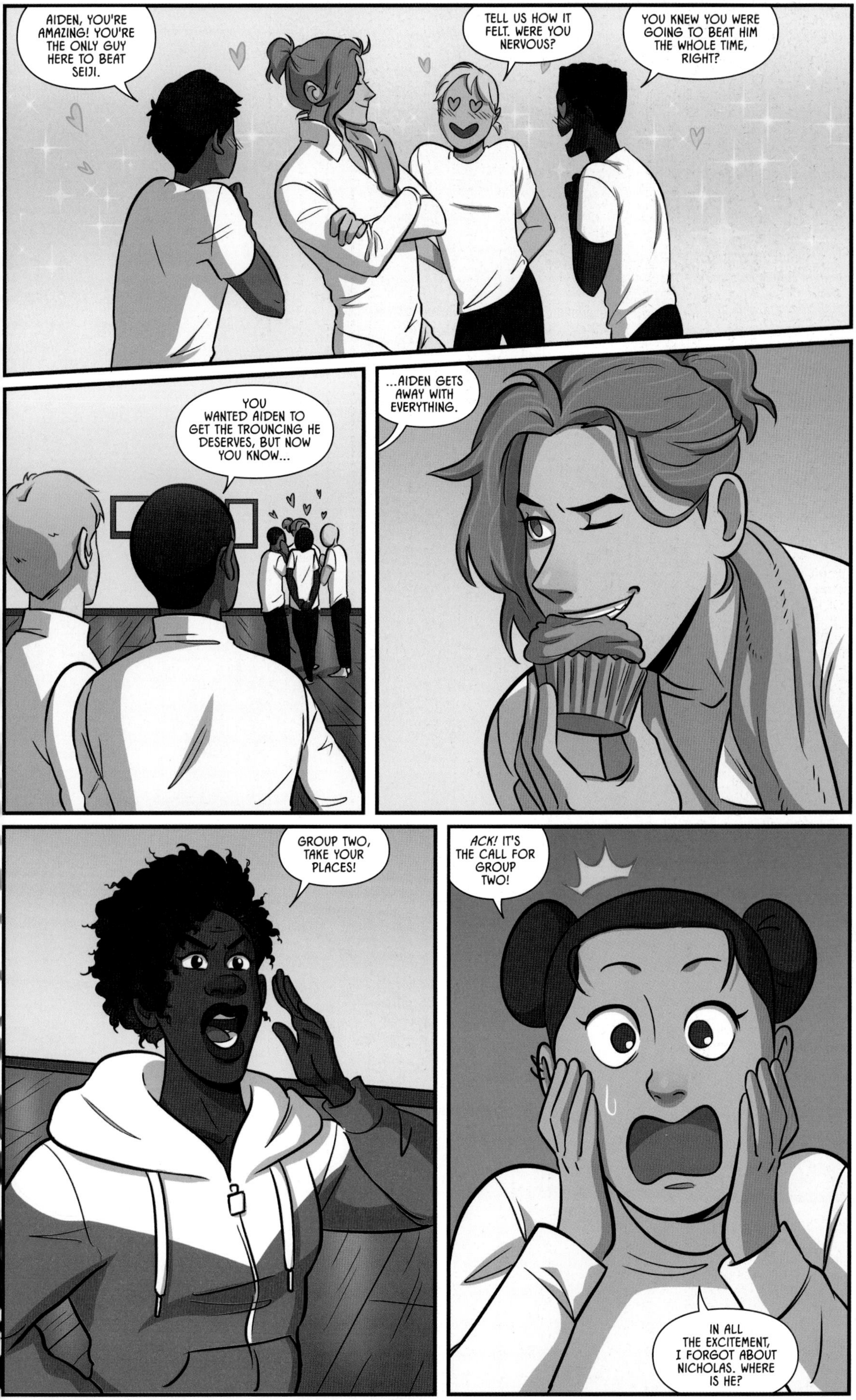
AIDEN, YOU'RE AMAZING! YOU'RE THE ONLY GUY HERE TO BEAT SEIJI.
TELL US HOW IT FELT. WERE YOU NERVOUS?
YOU KNEW YOU WERE GOING TO BEAT HIM THE WHOLE TIME, RIGHT?
YOU WANTED AIDEN TO GET THE TROUNCING HE DESERVES, BUT NOW YOU KNOW...
...AIDEN GETS AWAY WITH EVERYTHING.
GROUP TWO, TAKE YOUR PLACES!
ACK! IT'S THE CALL FOR GROUP TWO!
IN ALL THE EXCITEMENT, I FORGOT ABOUT NICHOLAS. WHERE IS HE?

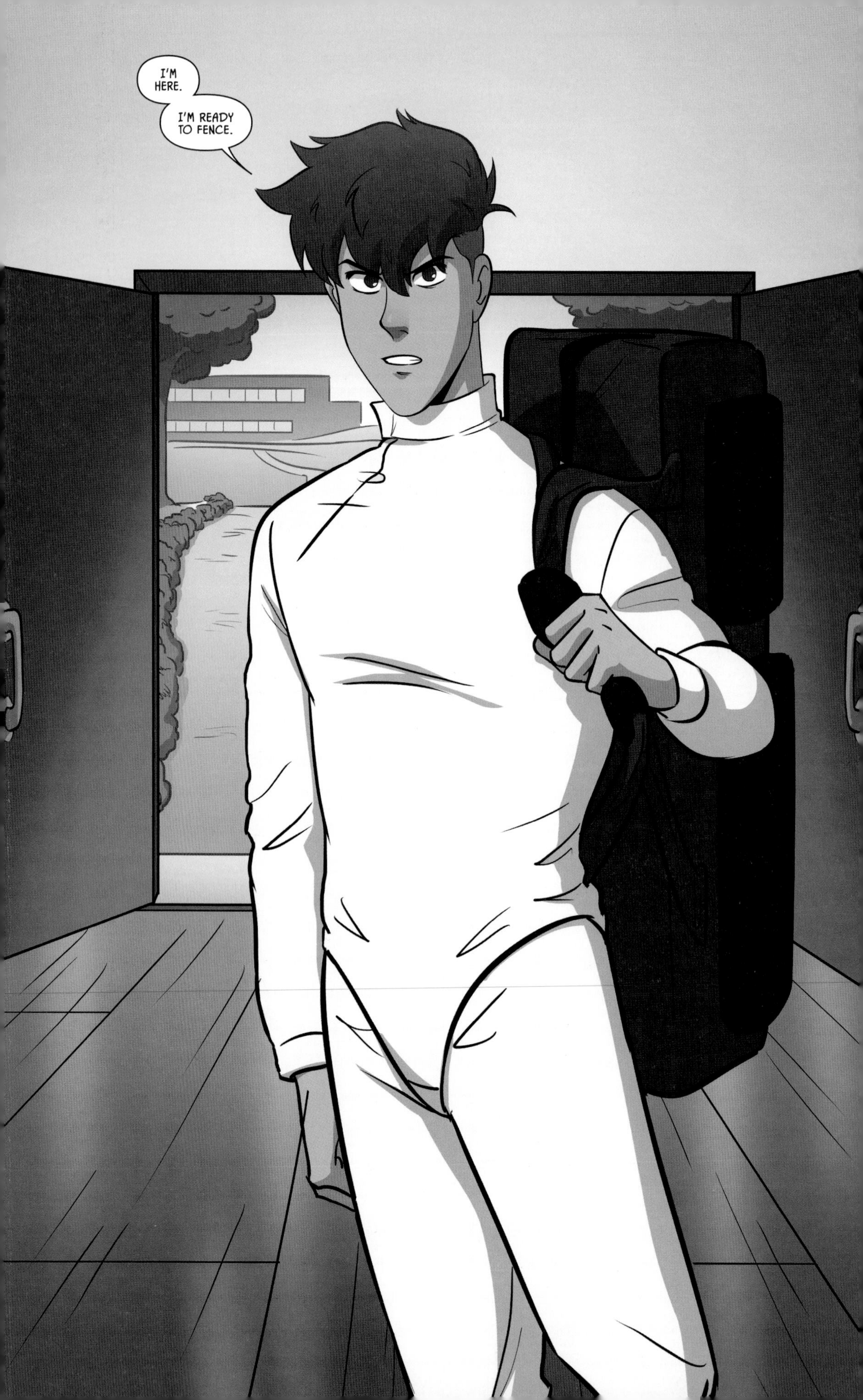
I'M HERE.
I'M READY TO FENCE.

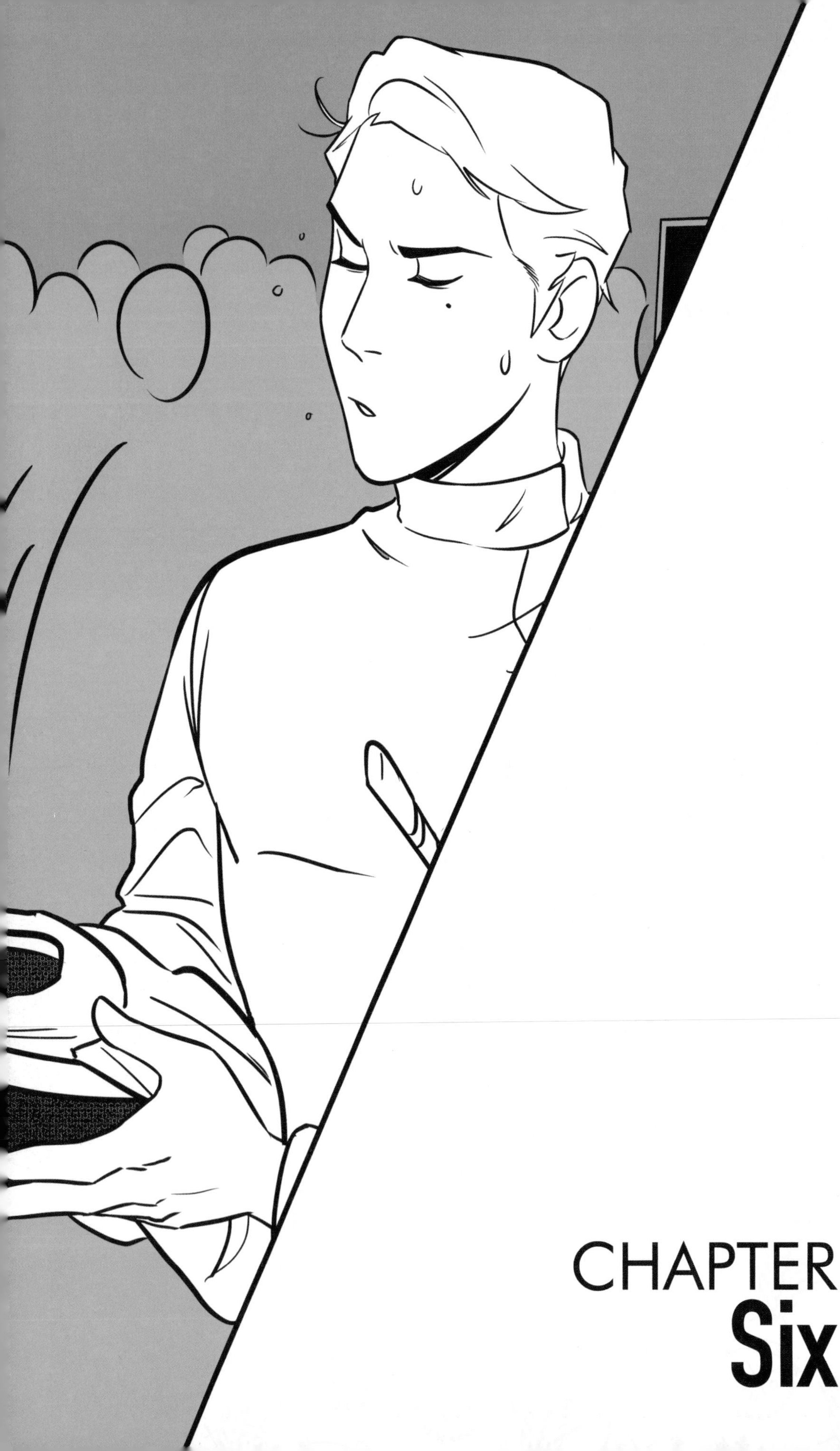

CHAPTER
Six

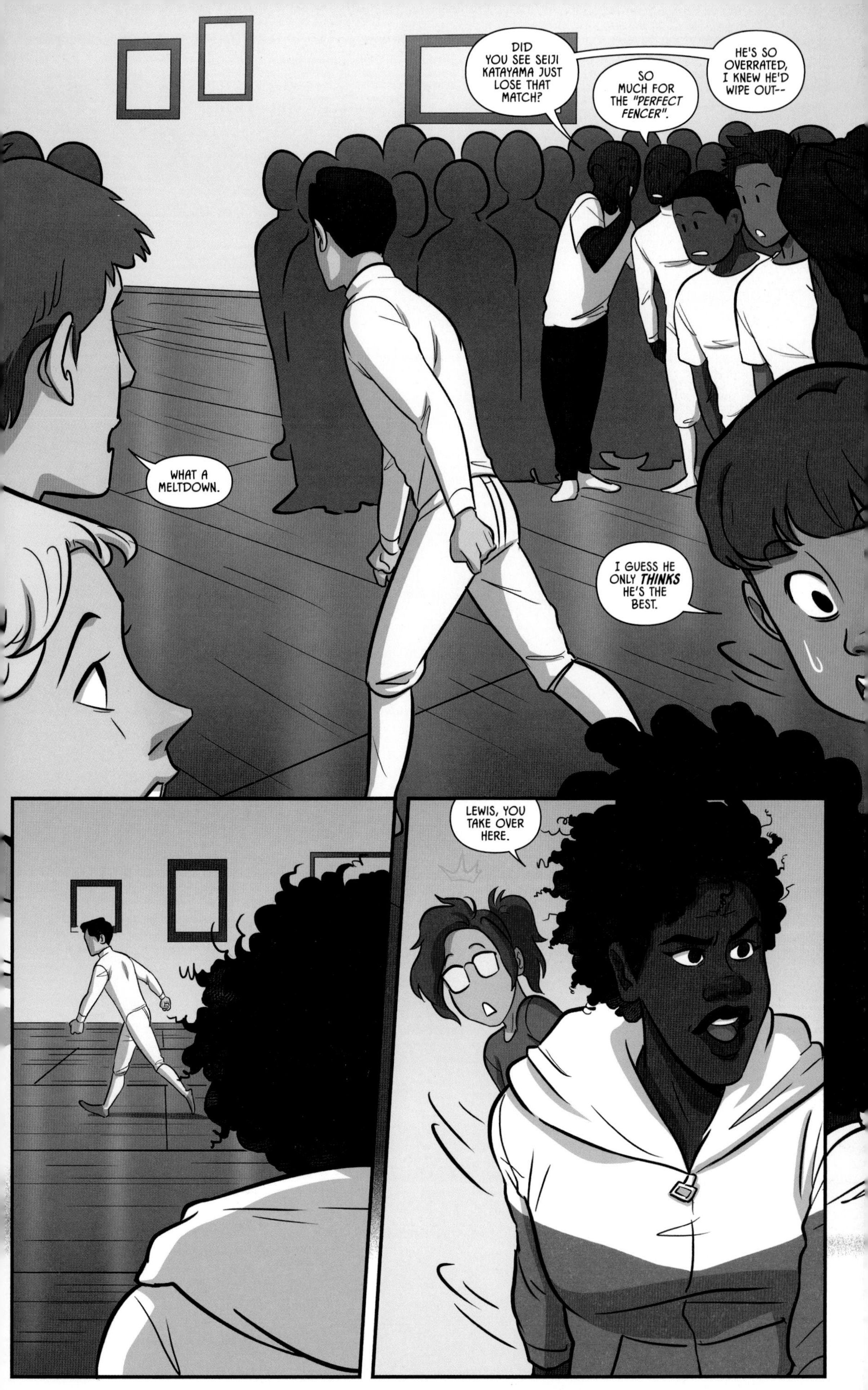
DID YOU SEE SEIJI KATAYAMA JUST LOSE THAT MATCH?
SO MUCH FOR THE "PERFECT FENCER".
HE'S SO OVERRATED, I KNEW HE'D WIPE OUT--
WHAT A MELTDOWN.
I GUESS HE ONLY THINKS HE'S THE BEST.
LEWIS, YOU TAKE OVER HERE.

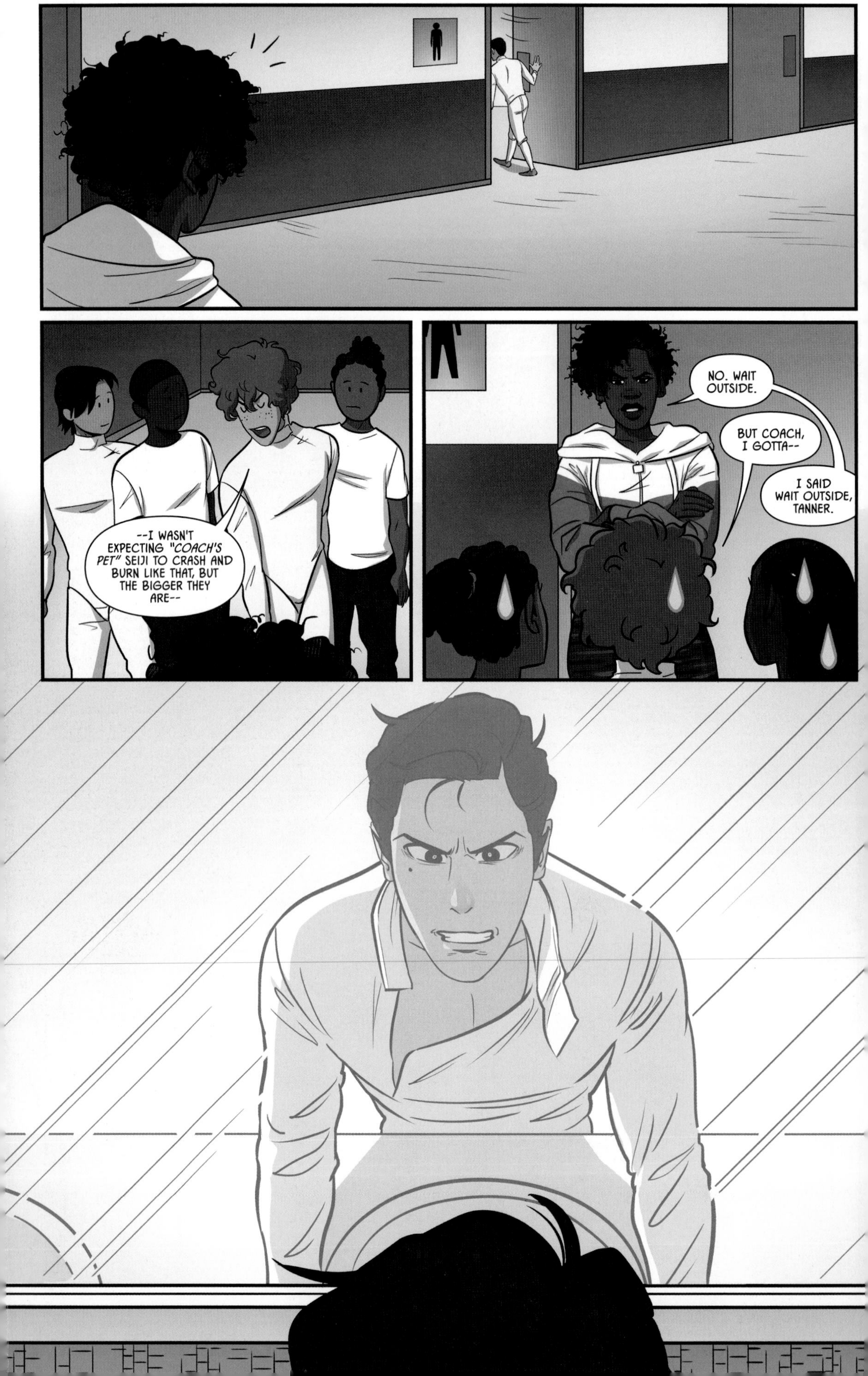
--I WASN'T EXPECTING "COACH'S PET" SEIJI TO CRASH AND BURN LIKE THAT, BUT THE BIGGER THEY ARE--
NO. WAIT OUTSIDE.
BUT COACH, I GOTTA--
I SAID WAIT OUTSIDE, TANNER.

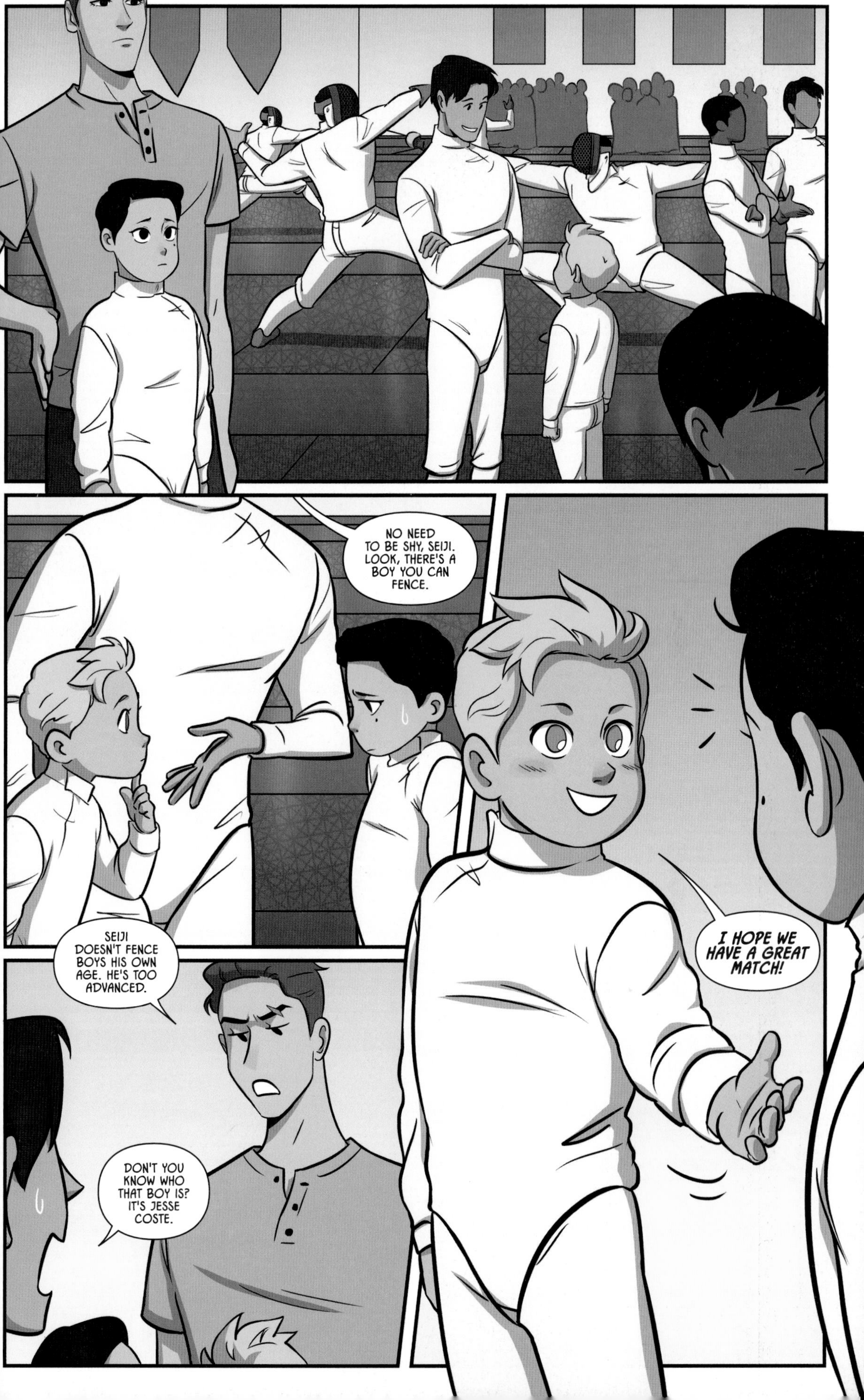
NO NEED TO BE SHY, SEIJI. LOOK, THERE'S A BOY YOU CAN FENCE.
SEIJI DOESN'T FENCE BOYS HIS OWN AGE. HE'S TOO ADVANCED.
DON'T YOU KNOW WHO THAT BOY IS? IT'S JESSE COSTE.
I HOPE WE HAVE A GREAT MATCH!

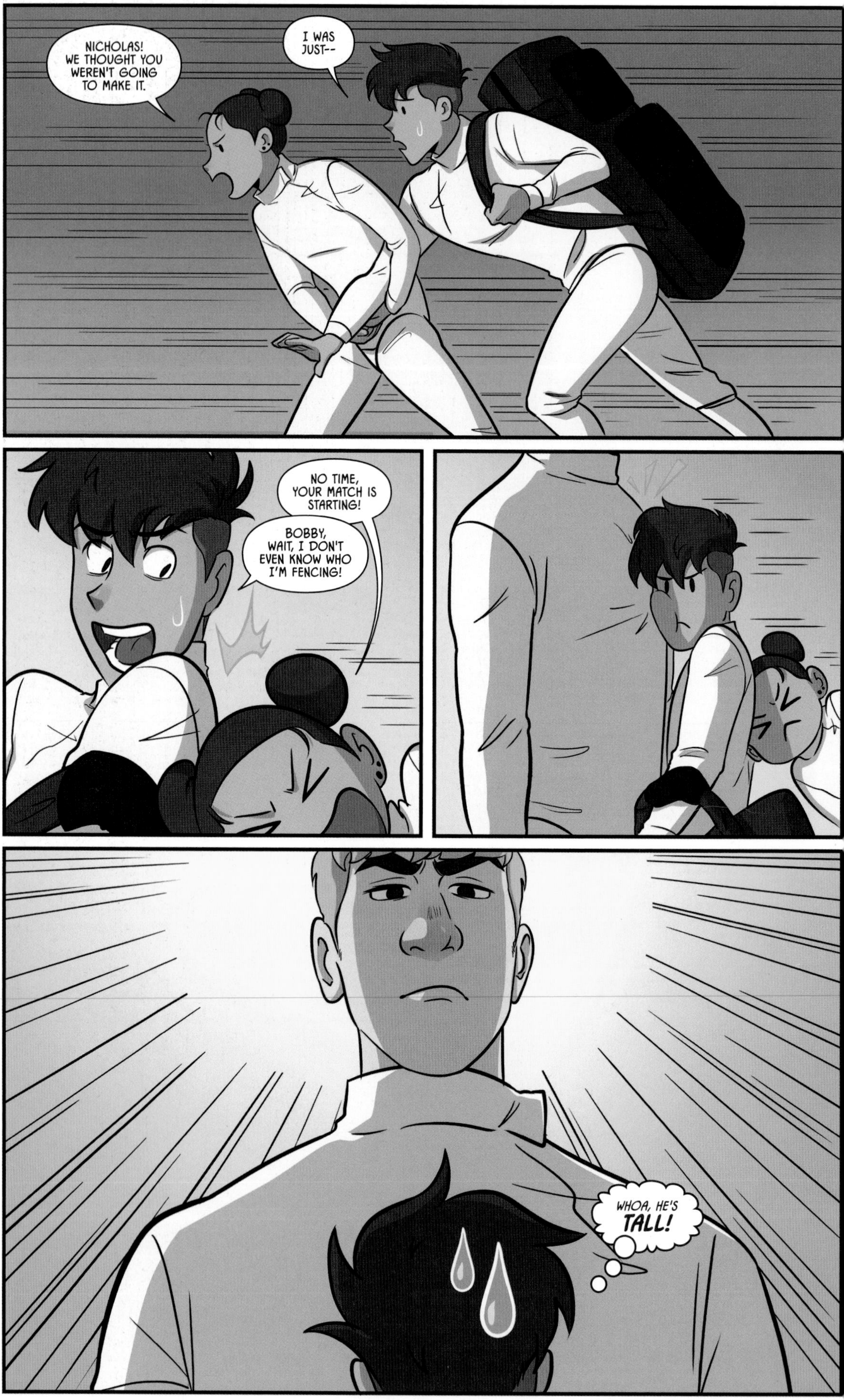
NICHOLAS! WE THOUGHT YOU WEREN'T GOING TO MAKE IT.
I WAS JUST--
NO TIME, YOUR MATCH IS STARTING!
BOBBY, WAIT, I DON'T EVEN KNOW WHO I'M FENCING!
WHOA, HE'S TALL!

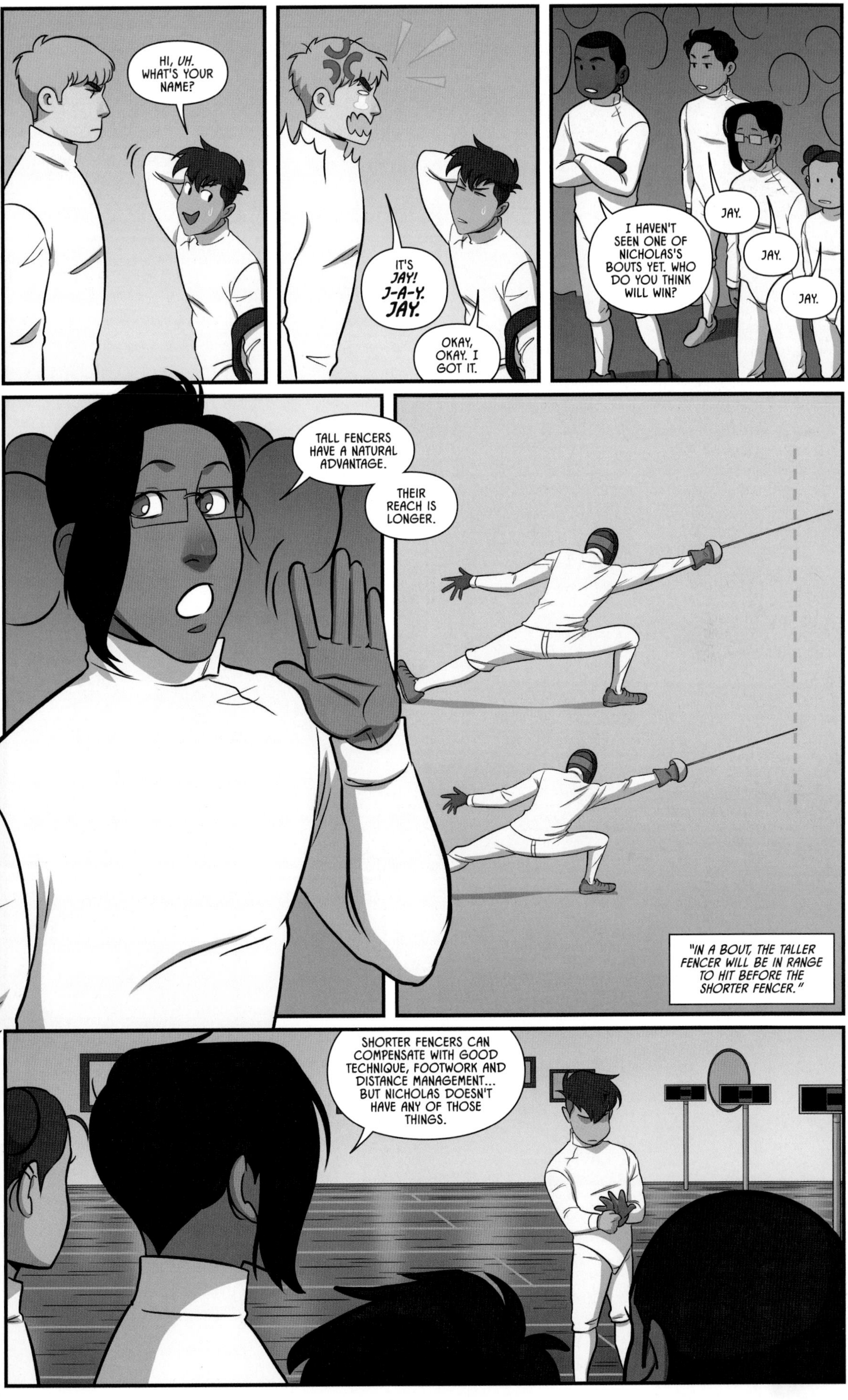
HI, UH. WHAT'S YOUR NAME?
IT'S JAY! J-A-Y. JAY.
OKAY, OKAY. I GOT IT.
I HAVEN'T SEEN ONE OF NICHOLAS'S BOUTS YET. WHO DO YOU THINK WILL WIN?
JAY.
JAY.
JAY.
TALL FENCERS HAVE A NATURAL ADVANTAGE.
THEIR REACH IS LONGER.
"IN A BOUT, THE TALLER FENCER WILL BE IN RANGE TO HIT BEFORE THE SHORTER FENCER."
SHORTER FENCERS CAN COMPENSATE WITH GOOD TECHNIQUE, FOOTWORK AND DISTANCE MANAGEMENT... BUT NICHOLAS DOESN'T HAVE ANY OF THOSE THINGS.

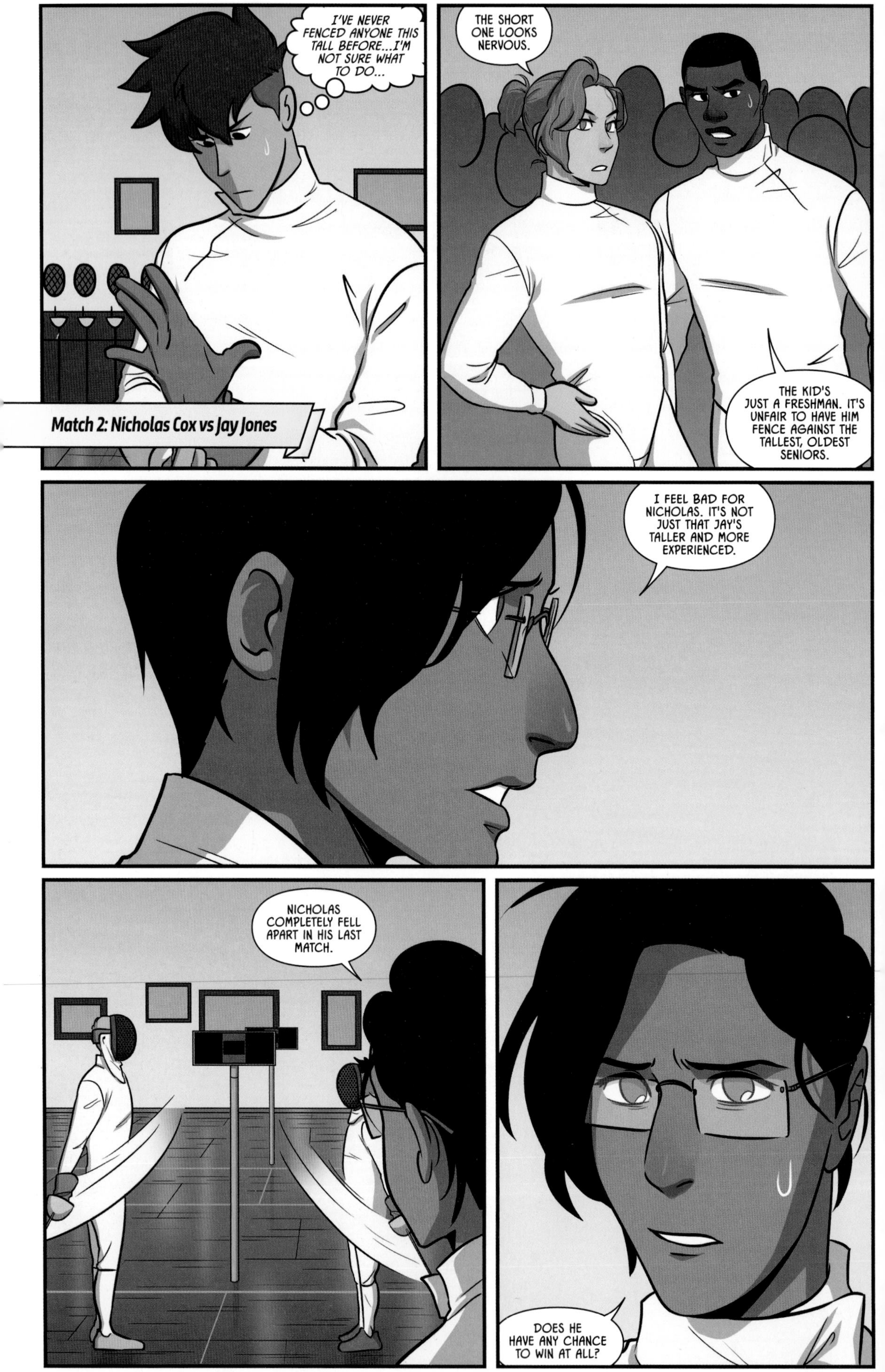
I'VE NEVER FENCED ANYONE THIS TALL BEFORE...I'M NOT SURE WHAT TO DO...
Match 2: Nicholas Cox vs Jay Jones
THE SHORT ONE LOOKS NERVOUS.
THE KID'S JUST A FRESHMAN. IT'S UNFAIR TO HAVE HIM FENCE AGAINST THE TALLEST, OLDEST SENIORS.
I FEEL BAD FOR NICHOLAS. IT'S NOT JUST THAT JAY'S TALLER AND MORE EXPERIENCED.
NICHOLAS COMPLETELY FELL APART IN HIS LAST MATCH.
DOES HE HAVE ANY CHANCE TO WIN AT ALL?

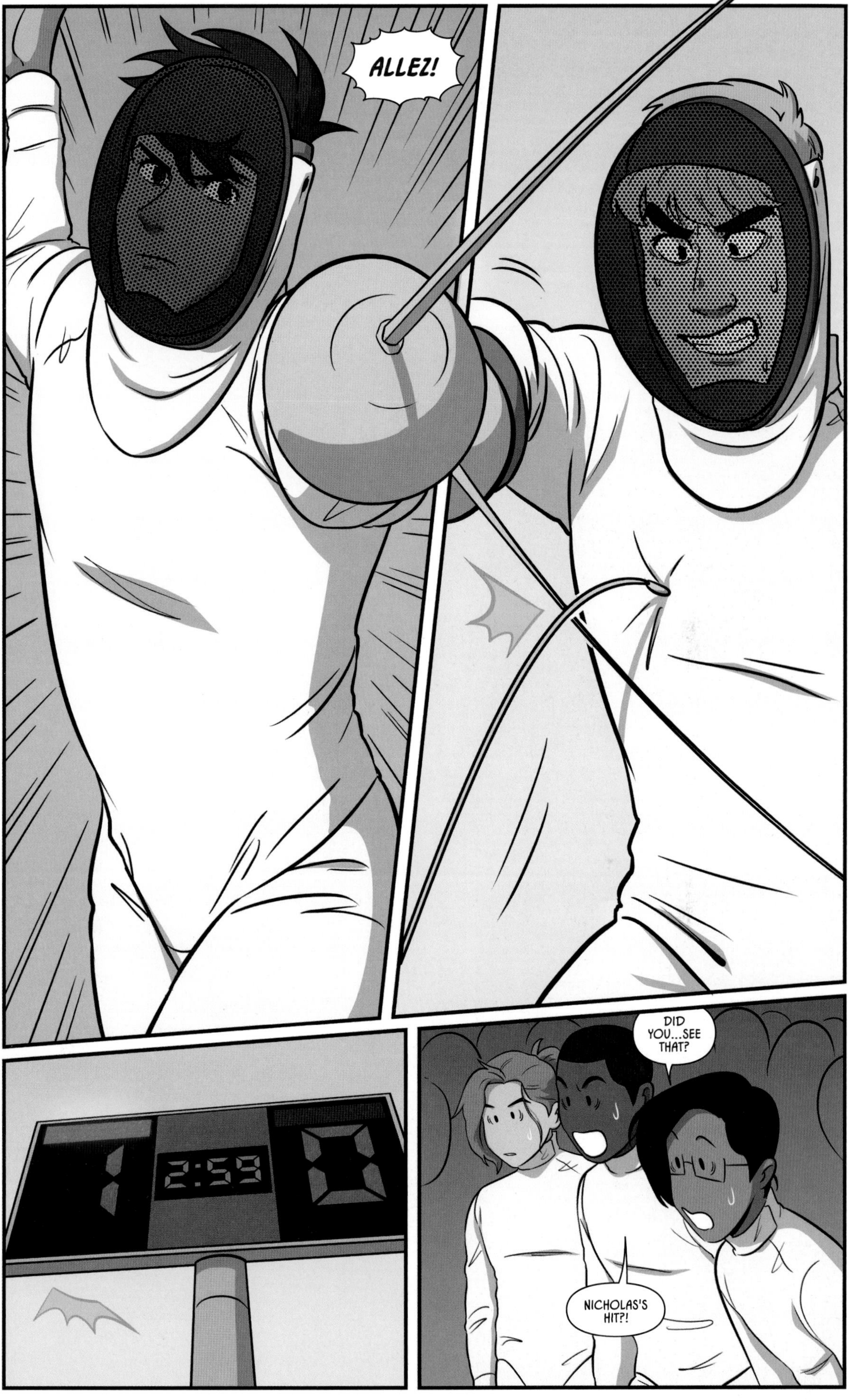
ALLEZ!
DID YOU...SEE THAT?
NICHOLAS'S HIT?!

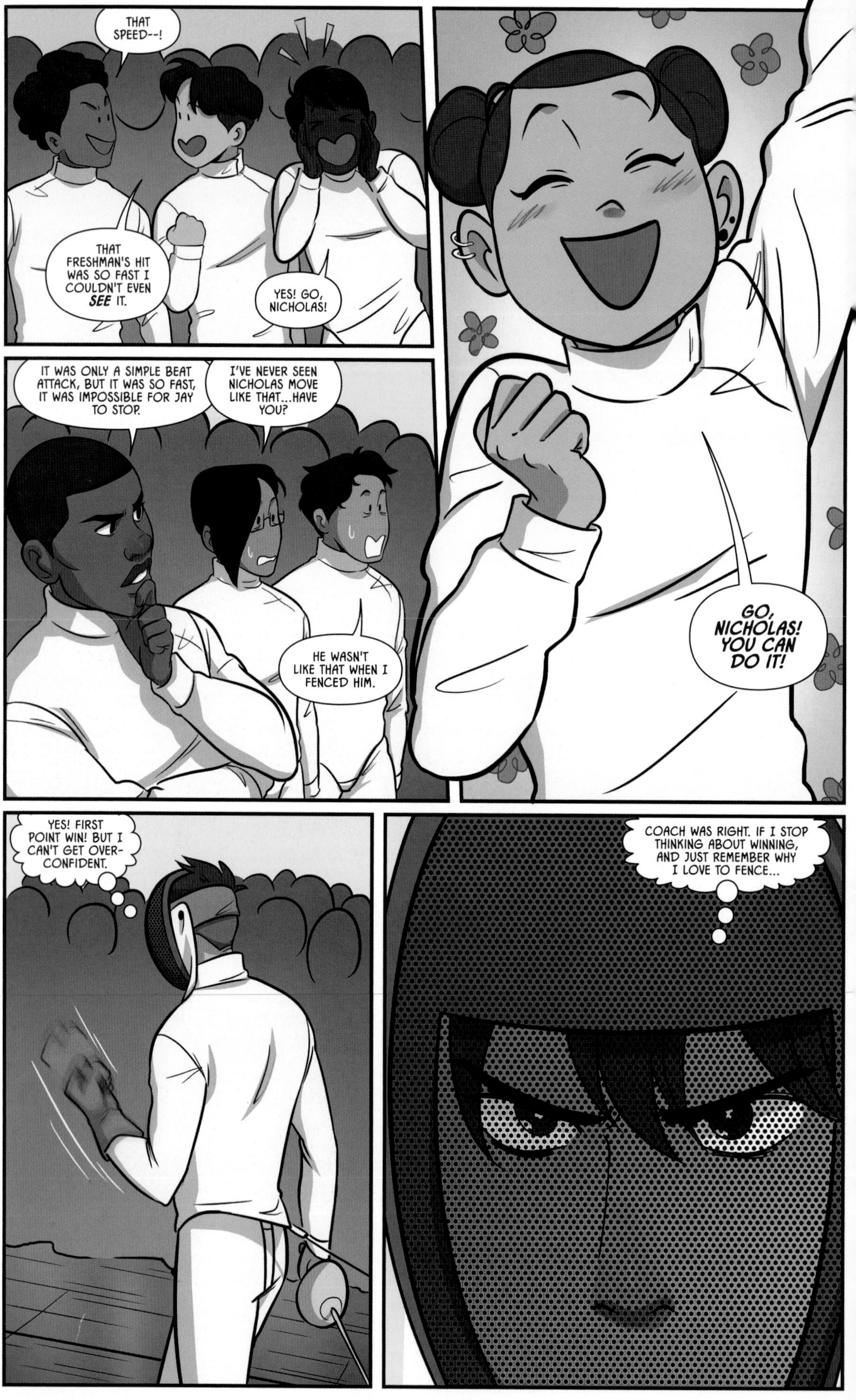
THAT SPEED--!
THAT FRESHMAN'S HIT WAS SO FAST I COULDN'T EVEN SEE IT.
YES! GO, NICHOLAS!
IT WAS ONLY A SIMPLE BEAT ATTACK, BUT IT WAS SO FAST, IT WAS IMPOSSIBLE FOR JAY TO STOP.
I'VE NEVER SEEN NICHOLAS MOVE LIKE THAT...HAVE YOU?
HE WASN'T LIKE THAT WHEN I FENCED HIM.
GO, NICHOLAS! YOU CAN DO IT!
YES! FIRST POINT WIN! BUT I CAN'T GET OVER-CONFIDENT.
COACH WAS RIGHT. IF I STOP THINKING ABOUT WINNING, AND JUST REMEMBER WHY I LOVE TO FENCE...

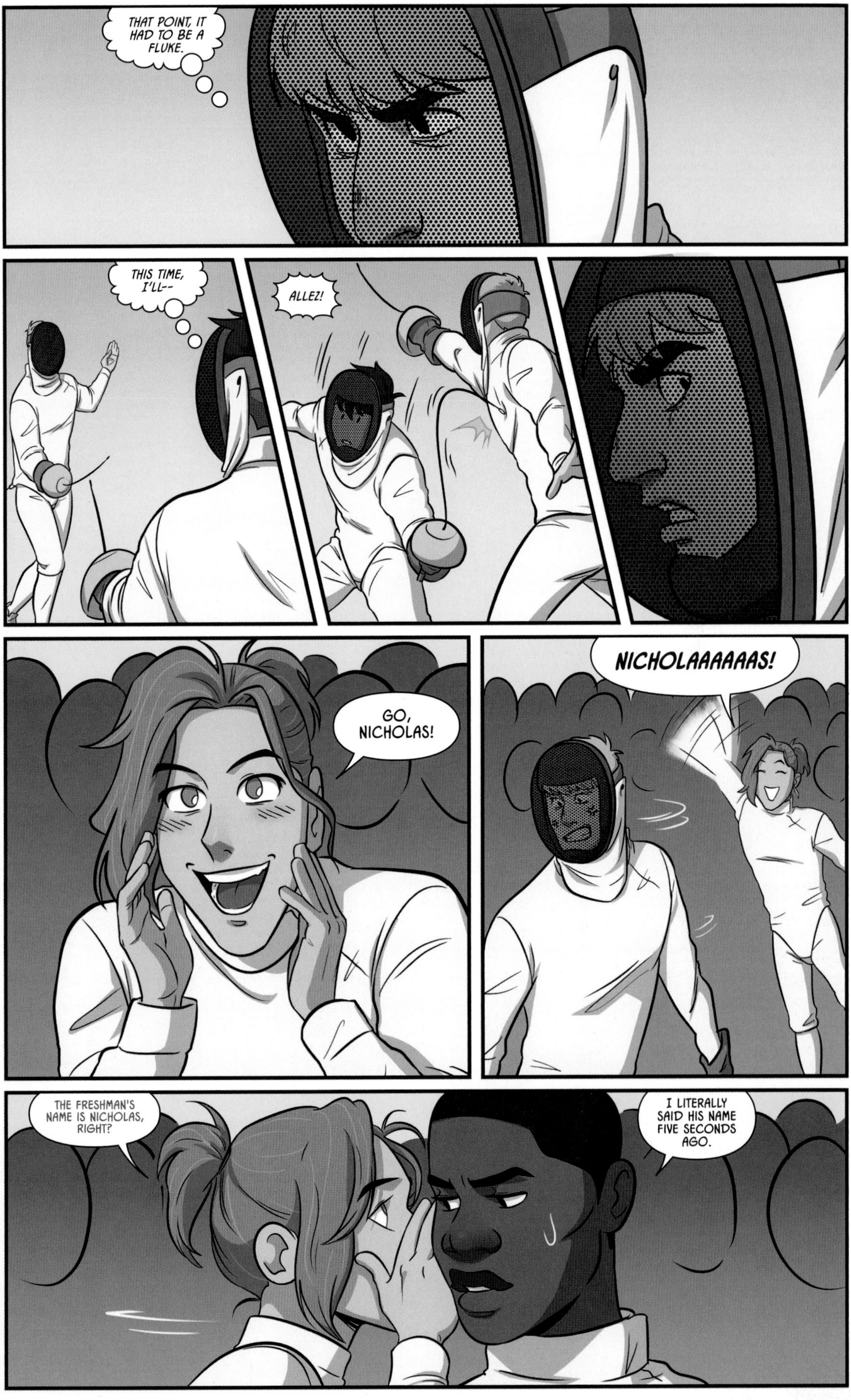
THAT POINT, IT HAD TO BE A FLUKE.
THIS TIME, I'LL--
ALLEZ!
GO, NICHOLAS!
NICHOLAAAAAAS!
THE FRESHMAN'S NAME IS NICHOLAS, RIGHT?
I LITERALLY SAID HIS NAME FIVE SECONDS AGO.

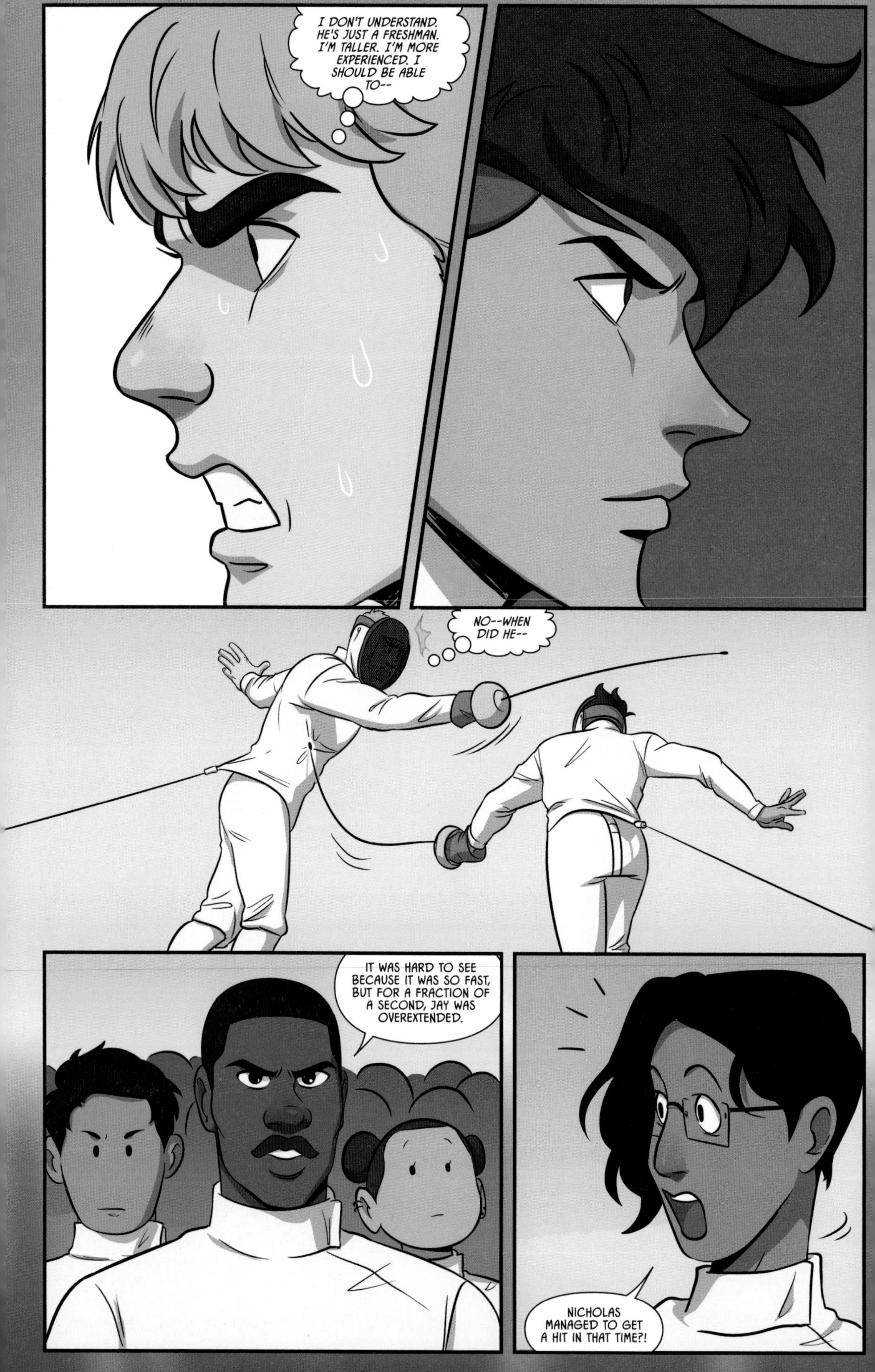
I DON'T UNDERSTAND. HE'S JUST A FRESHMAN. I'M TALLER. I'M MORE EXPERIENCED. I SHOULD BE ABLE TO--
NO--WHEN DID HE--
IT WAS HARD TO SEE BECAUSE IT WAS SO FAST, BUT FOR A FRACTION OF A SECOND, JAY WAS OVEREXTENDED.
NICHOLAS MANAGED TO GET A HIT IN THAT TIME?!

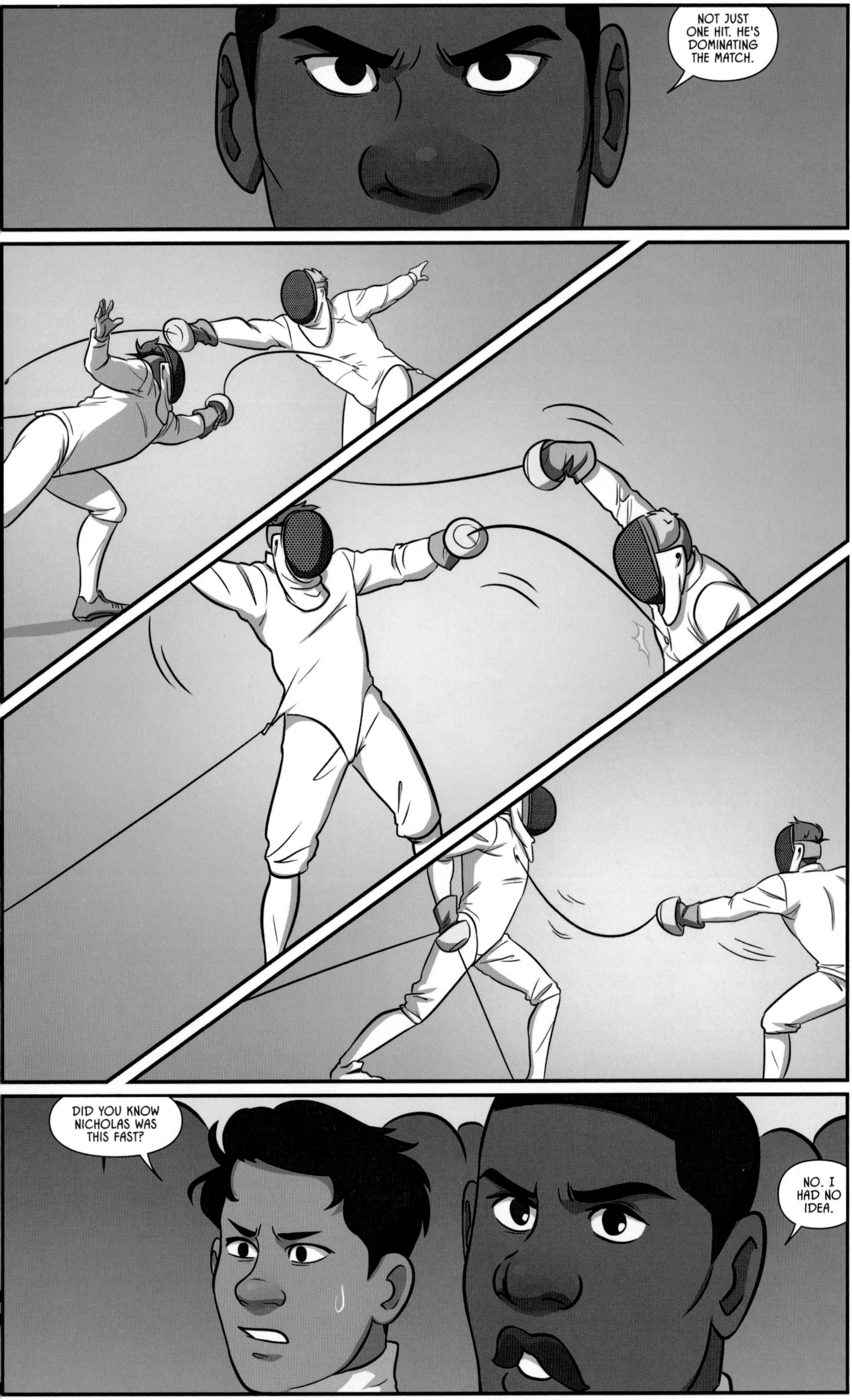
NOT JUST ONE HIT. HE'S DOMINATING THE MATCH.
DID YOU KNOW NICHOLAS WAS THIS FAST?
NO. I HAD NO IDEA.

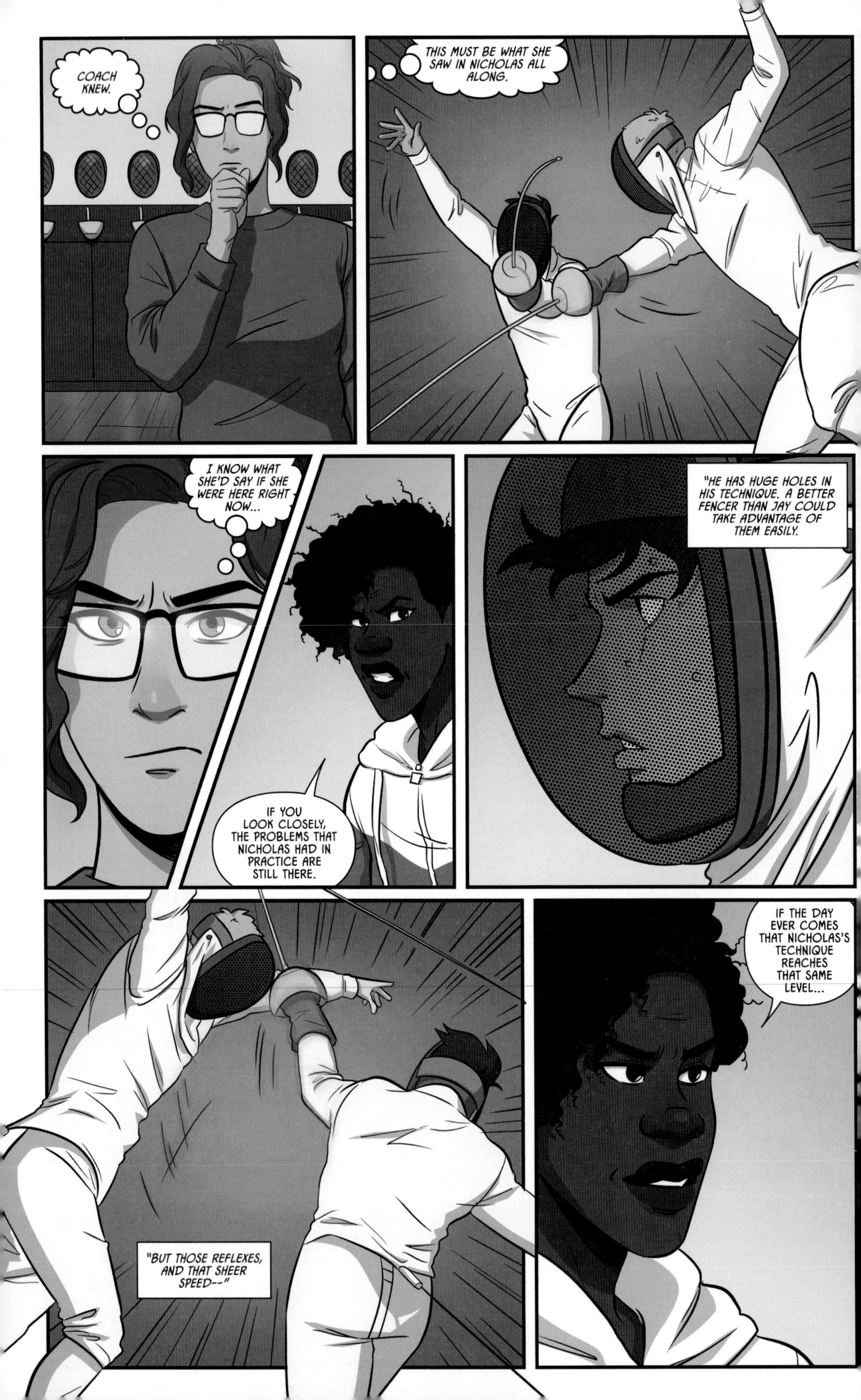
COACH KNEW.
THIS MUST BE WHAT SHE SAW IN NICHOLAS ALL ALONG.
I KNOW WHAT SHE'D SAY IF SHE WERE HERE RIGHT NOW...
IF YOU LOOK CLOSELY, THE PROBLEMS THAT NICHOLAS HAD IN PRACTICE ARE STILL THERE.
"HE HAS HUGE HOLES IN HIS TECHNIQUE. A BETTER FENCER THAN JAY COULD TAKE ADVANTAGE OF THEM EASILY.
"BUT THOSE REFLEXES, AND THAT SHEER SPEED--"
IF THE DAY EVER COMES THAT NICHOLAS'S TECHNIQUE REACHES THAT SAME LEVEL...

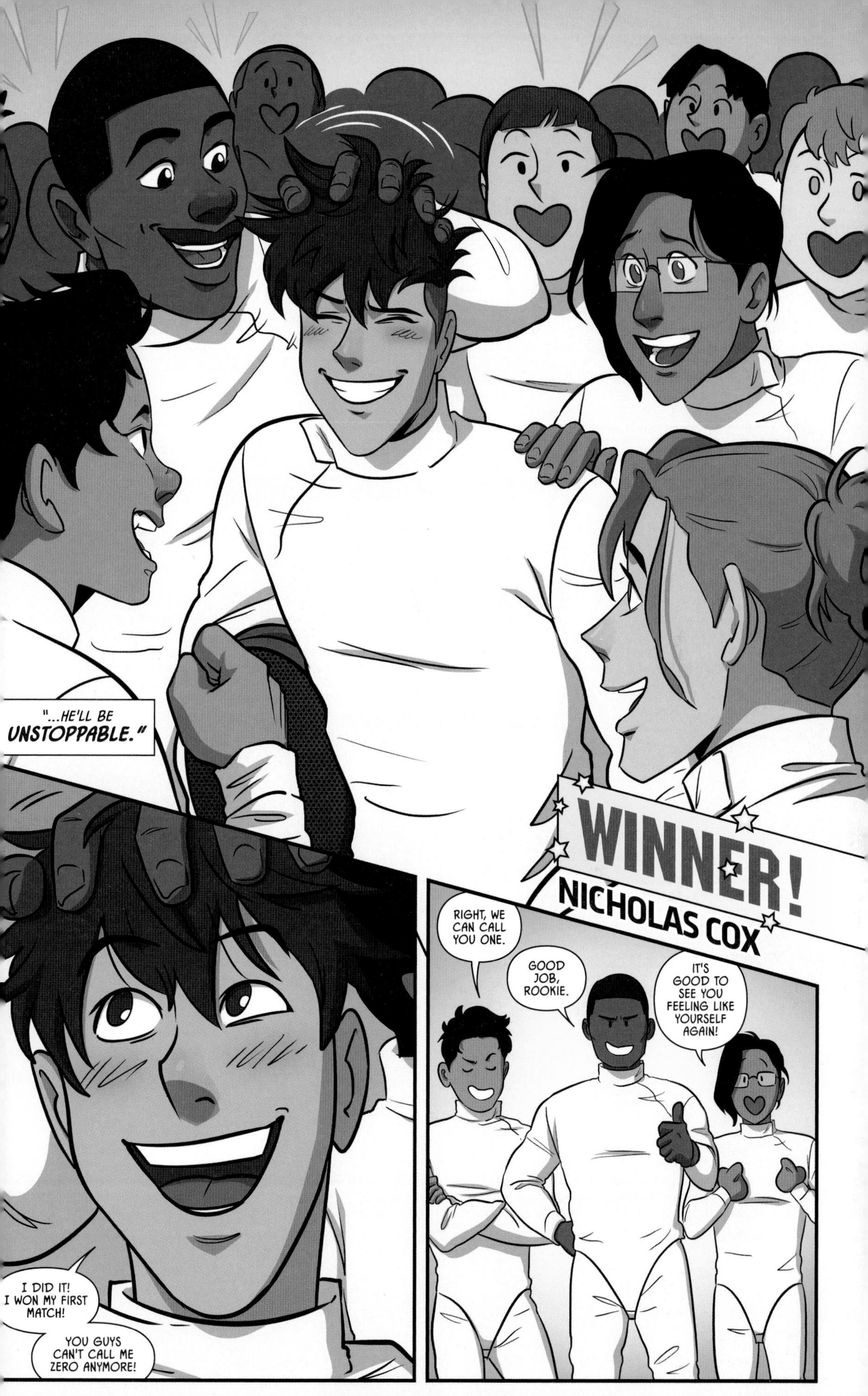
"...HE'LL BE UNSTOPPABLE."
WINNER!
NICHOLAS COX
I DID IT! I WON MY FIRST MATCH!
YOU GUYS CAN'T CALL ME ZERO ANYMORE!
RIGHT, WE CAN CALL YOU ONE.
GOOD JOB, ROOKIE.
IT'S GOOD TO SEE YOU FEELING LIKE YOURSELF AGAIN!

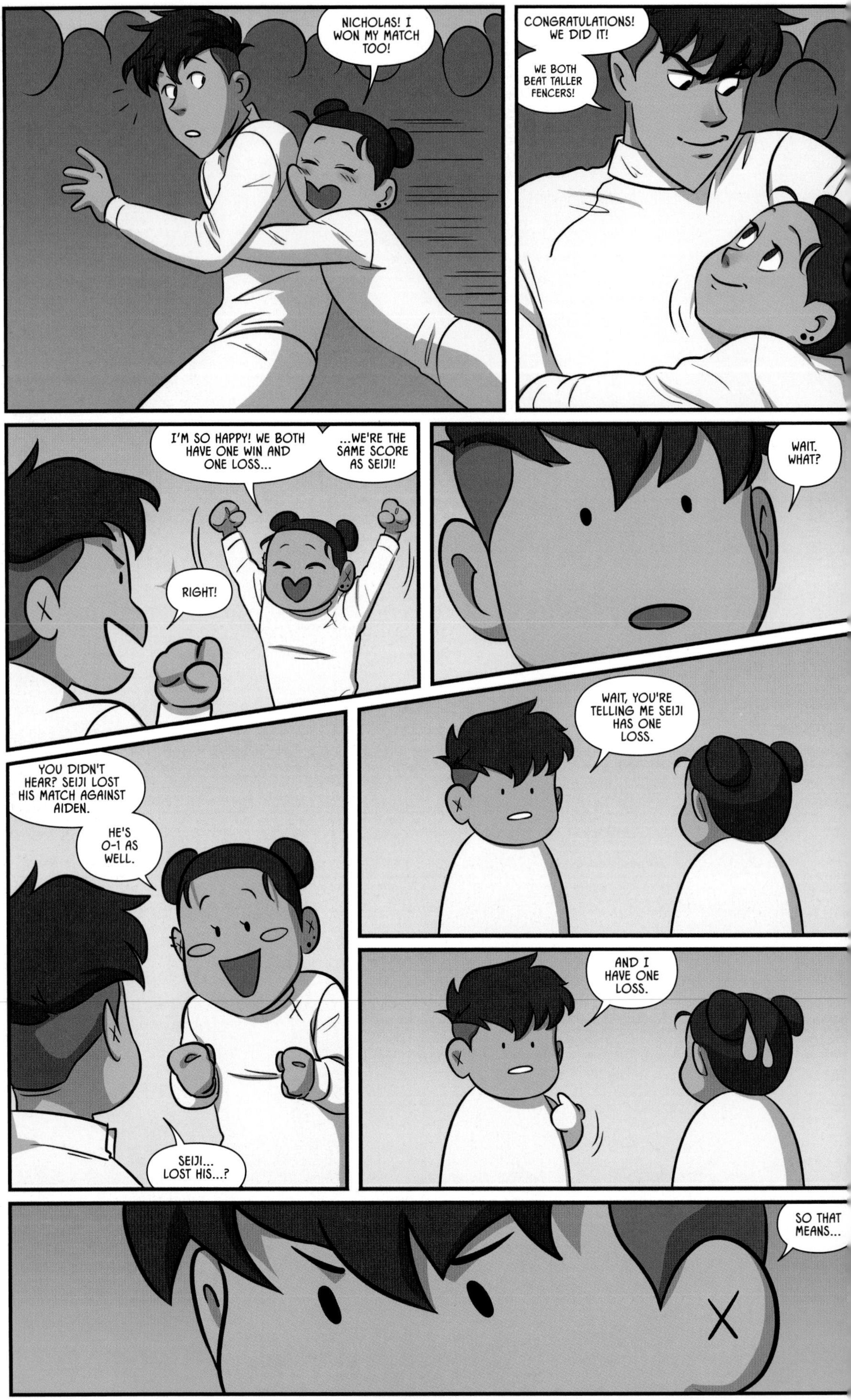
NICHOLAS! I WON MY MATCH TOO!
CONGRATULATIONS! WE DID IT!
WE BOTH BEAT TALLER FENCERS!
I'M SO HAPPY! WE BOTH HAVE ONE WIN AND ONE LOSS...
...WE'RE THE SAME SCORE AS SEIJI!
RIGHT!
WAIT. WHAT?
WAIT, YOU'RE TELLING ME SEIJI HAS ONE LOSS.
YOU DIDN'T HEAR? SEIJI LOST HIS MATCH AGAINST AIDEN.
HE'S 0-1 AS WELL.
SEIJI... LOST HIS...?
AND I HAVE ONE LOSS.
SO THAT MEANS...

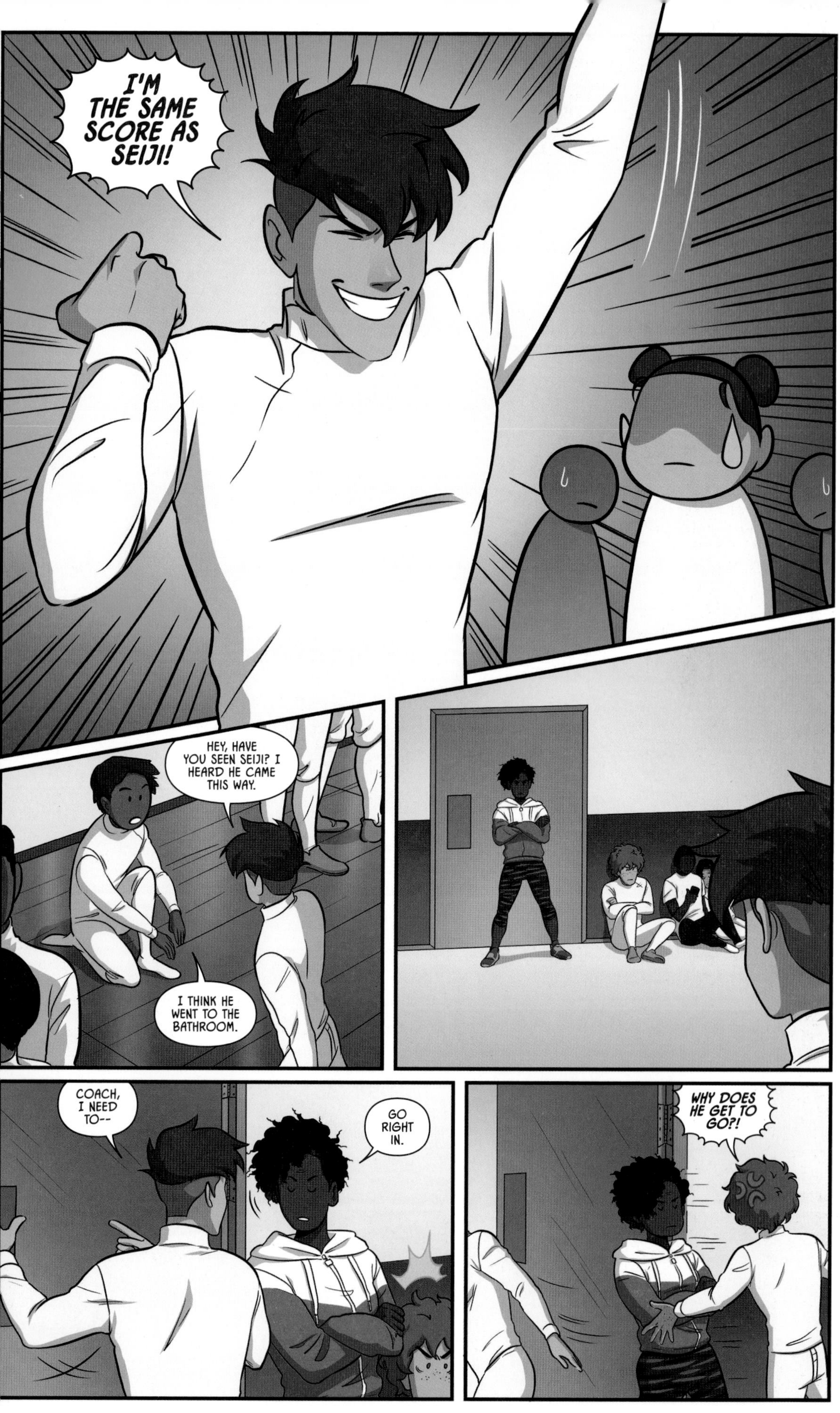
I'M THE SAME SCORE AS SEIJI!
HEY, HAVE YOU SEEN SEIJI? I HEARD HE CAME THIS WAY.
I THINK HE WENT TO THE BATHROOM.
COACH, I NEED TO--
GO RIGHT IN.
WHY DOES HE GET TO GO?!

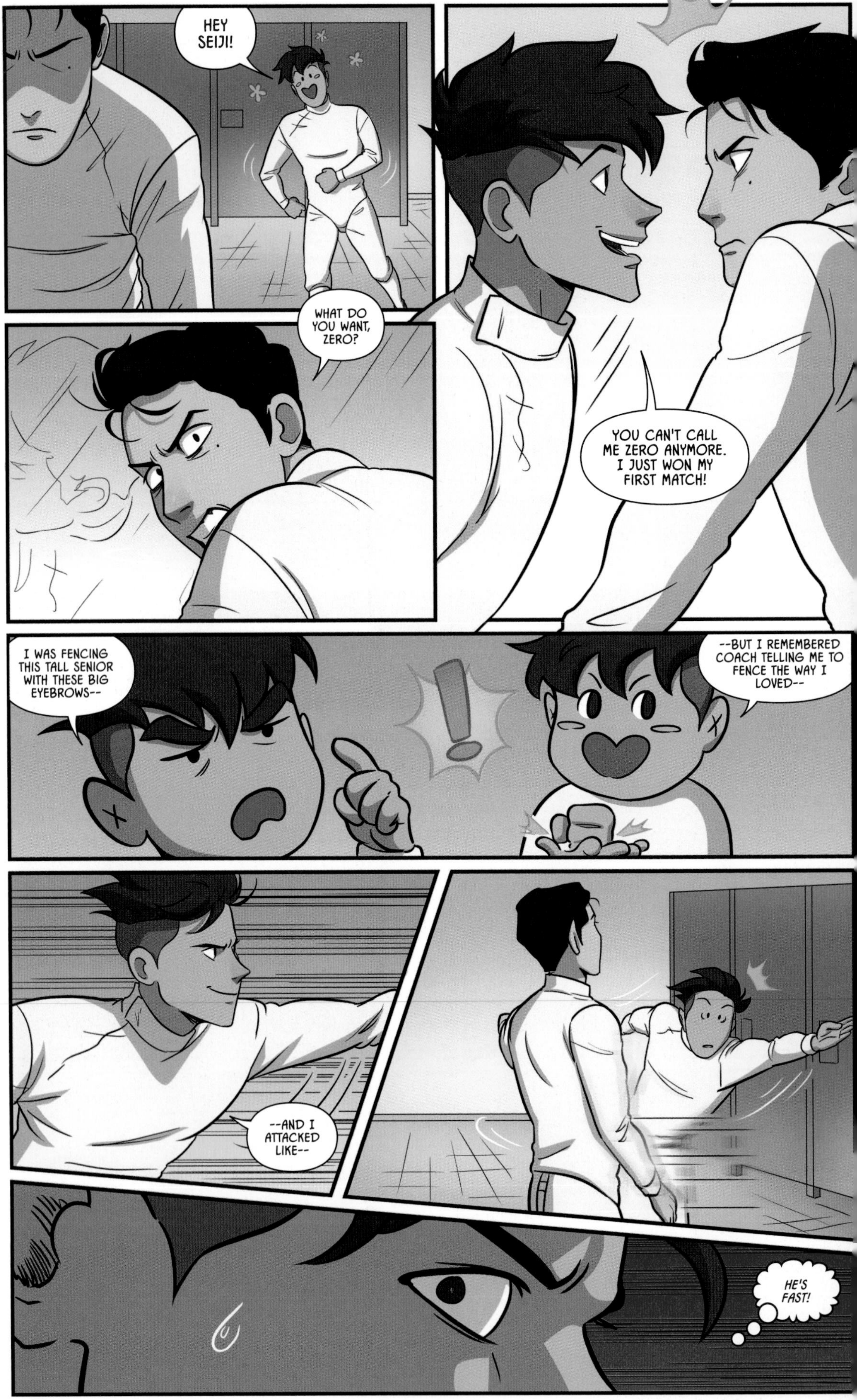
HEY SEIJI!
WHAT DO YOU WANT, ZERO?
YOU CAN'T CALL ME ZERO ANYMORE. I JUST WON MY FIRST MATCH!
I WAS FENCING THIS TALL SENIOR WITH THESE BIG EYEBROWS--
--BUT I REMEMBERED COACH TELLING ME TO FENCE THE WAY I LOVED--
--AND I ATTACKED LIKE--
HE'S FAST!

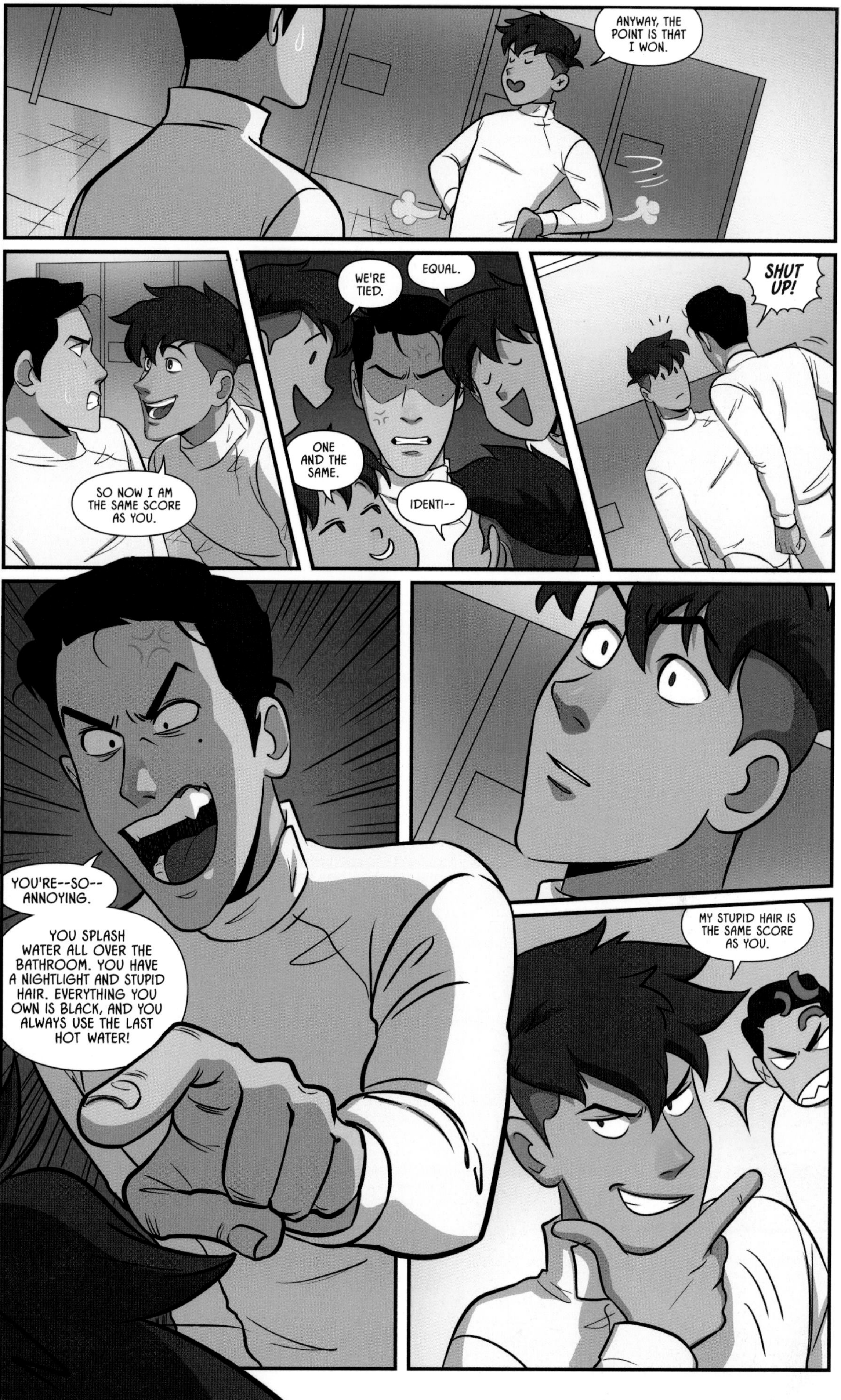
ANYWAY, THE POINT IS THAT I WON.
SO NOW I AM THE SAME SCORE AS YOU.
WE'RE TIED.
EQUAL.
ONE AND THE SAME.
IDENTI--
SHUT UP!
YOU'RE--SO--ANNOYING.
YOU SPLASH WATER ALL OVER THE BATHROOM. YOU HAVE A NIGHTLIGHT AND STUPID HAIR. EVERYTHING YOU OWN IS BLACK, AND YOU ALWAYS USE THE LAST HOT WATER!
MY STUPID HAIR IS THE SAME SCORE AS YOU.

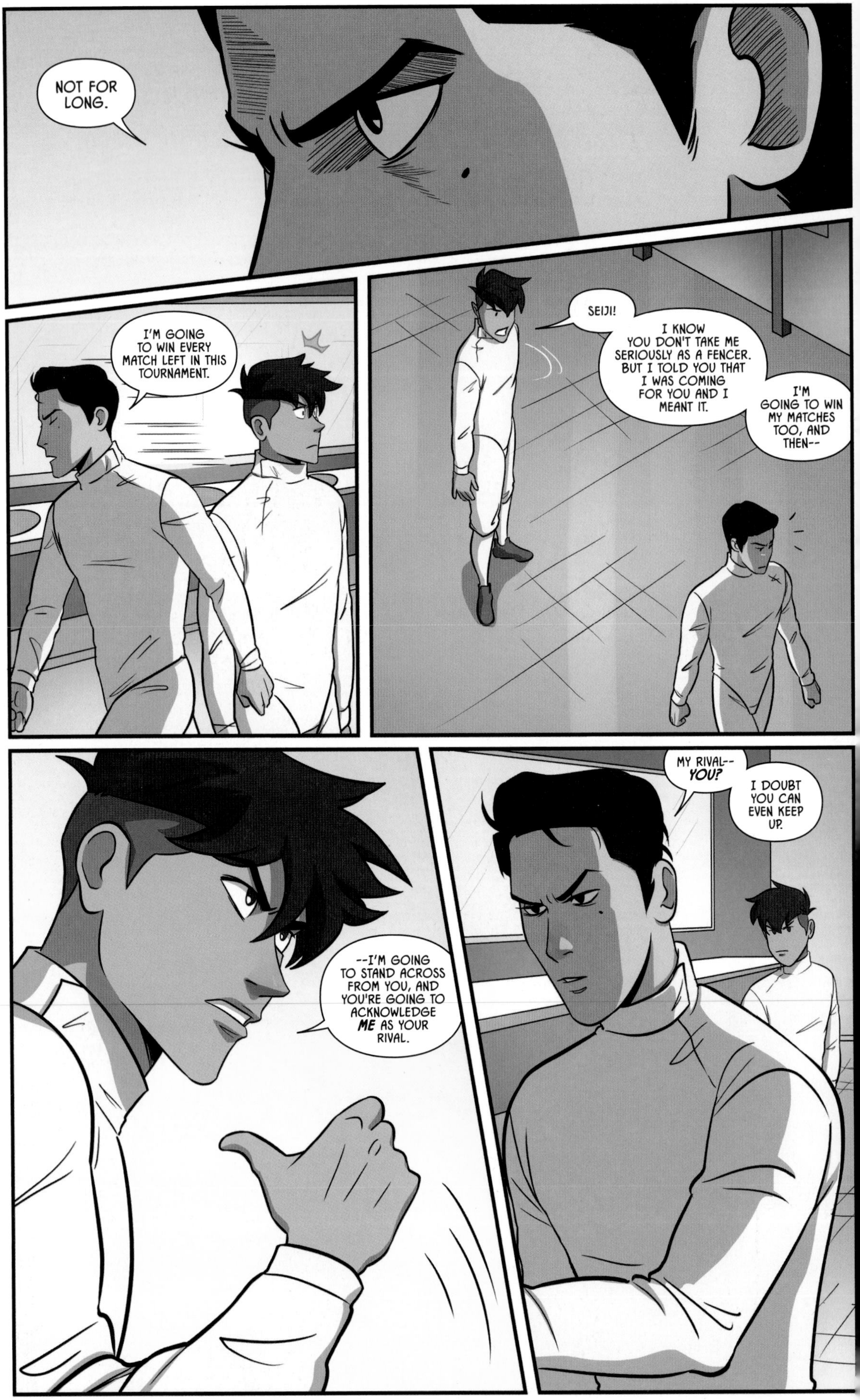
NOT FOR LONG.
I'M GOING TO WIN EVERY MATCH LEFT IN THIS TOURNAMENT.
SEIJI!
I KNOW YOU DON'T TAKE ME SERIOUSLY AS A FENCER. BUT I TOLD YOU THAT I WAS COMING FOR YOU AND I MEANT IT.
I'M GOING TO WIN MY MATCHES TOO, AND THEN--
--I'M GOING TO STAND ACROSS FROM YOU, AND YOU'RE GOING TO ACKNOWLEDGE *ME* AS YOUR RIVAL.
MY RIVAL-- *YOU?*
I DOUBT YOU CAN EVEN KEEP UP.

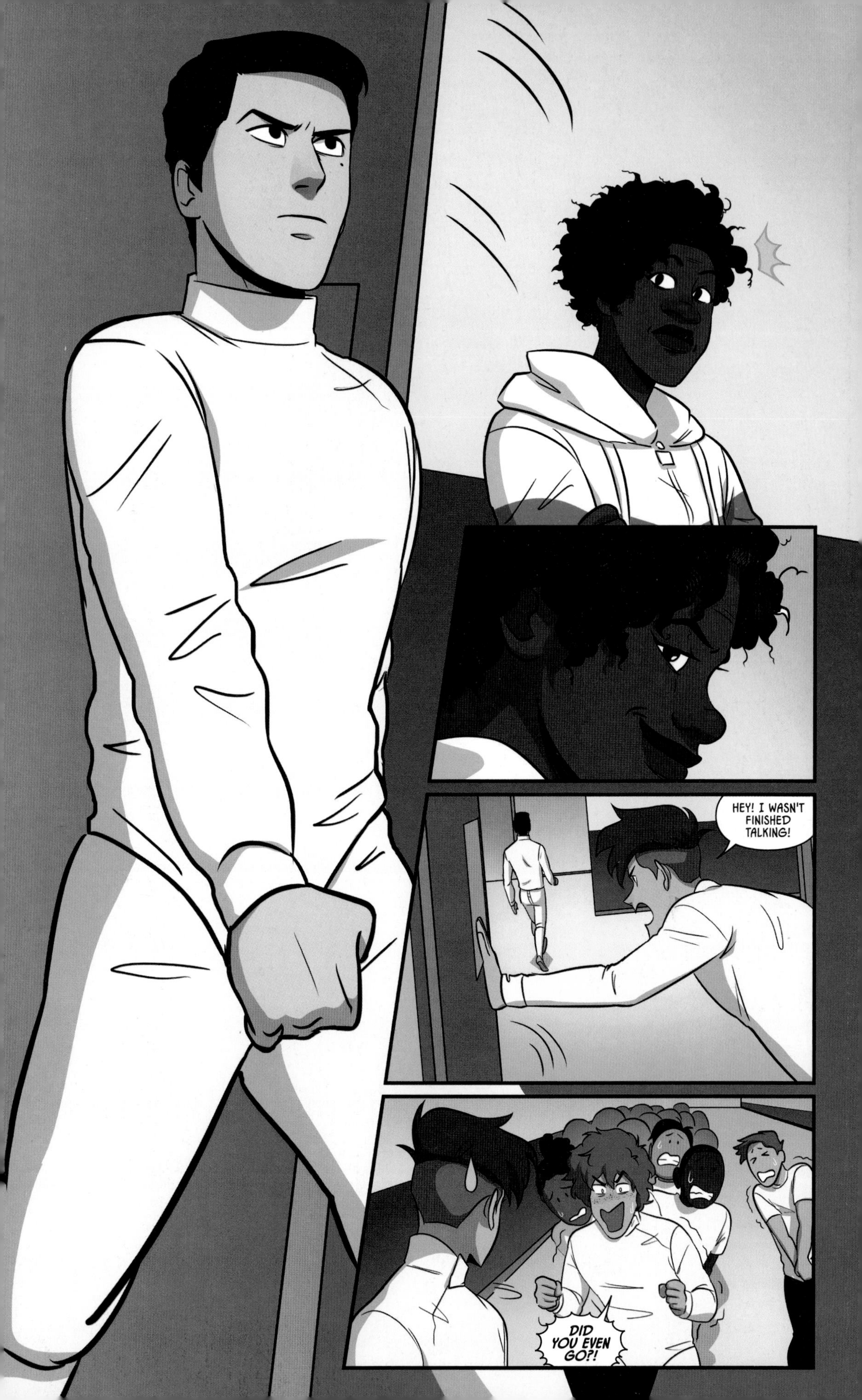
HEY! I WASN'T FINISHED TALKING!
DID YOU EVEN GO?!

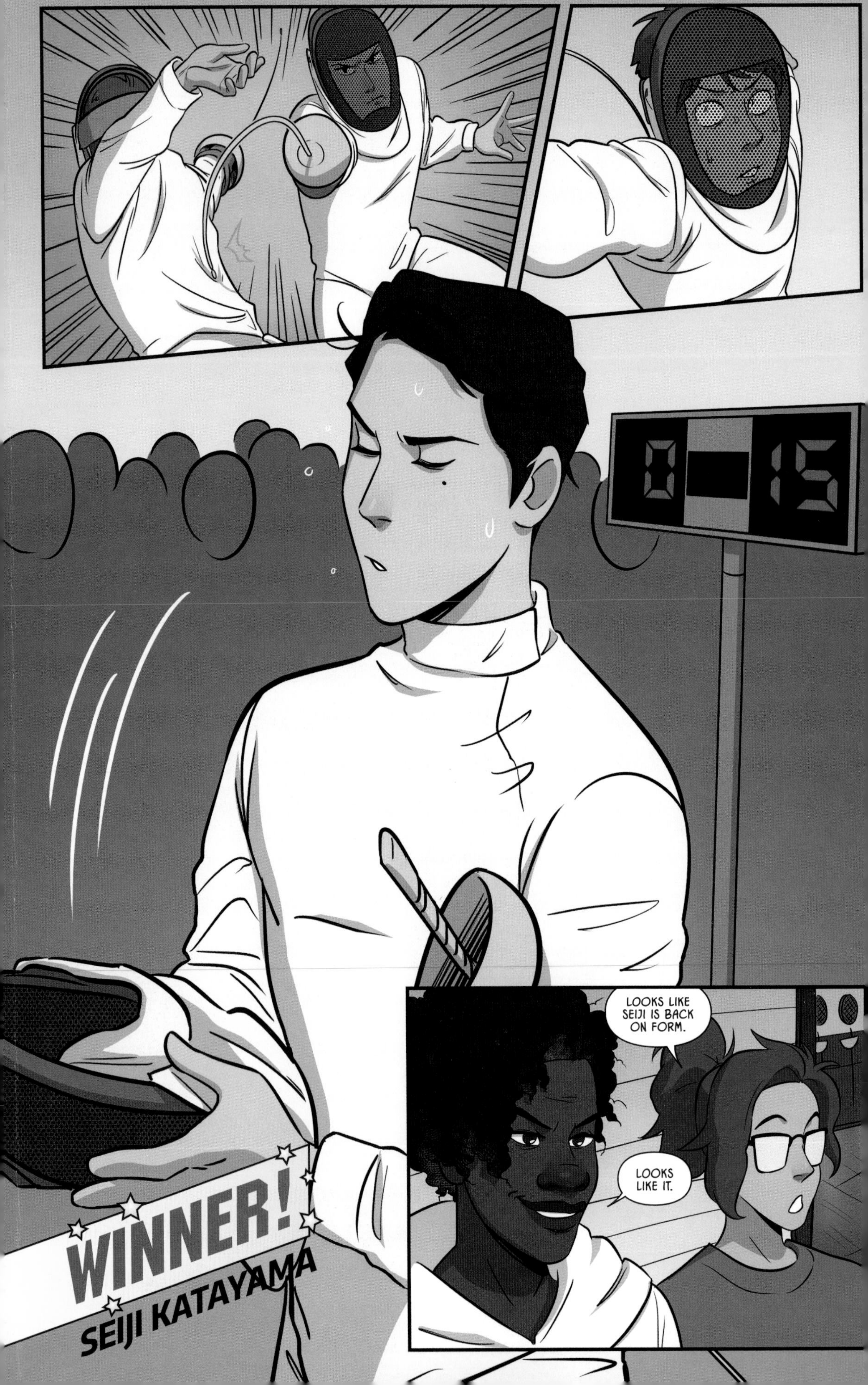
0 15
WINNER!
SEIJI KATAYAMA
LOOKS LIKE SEIJI IS BACK ON FORM.
LOOKS LIKE IT.

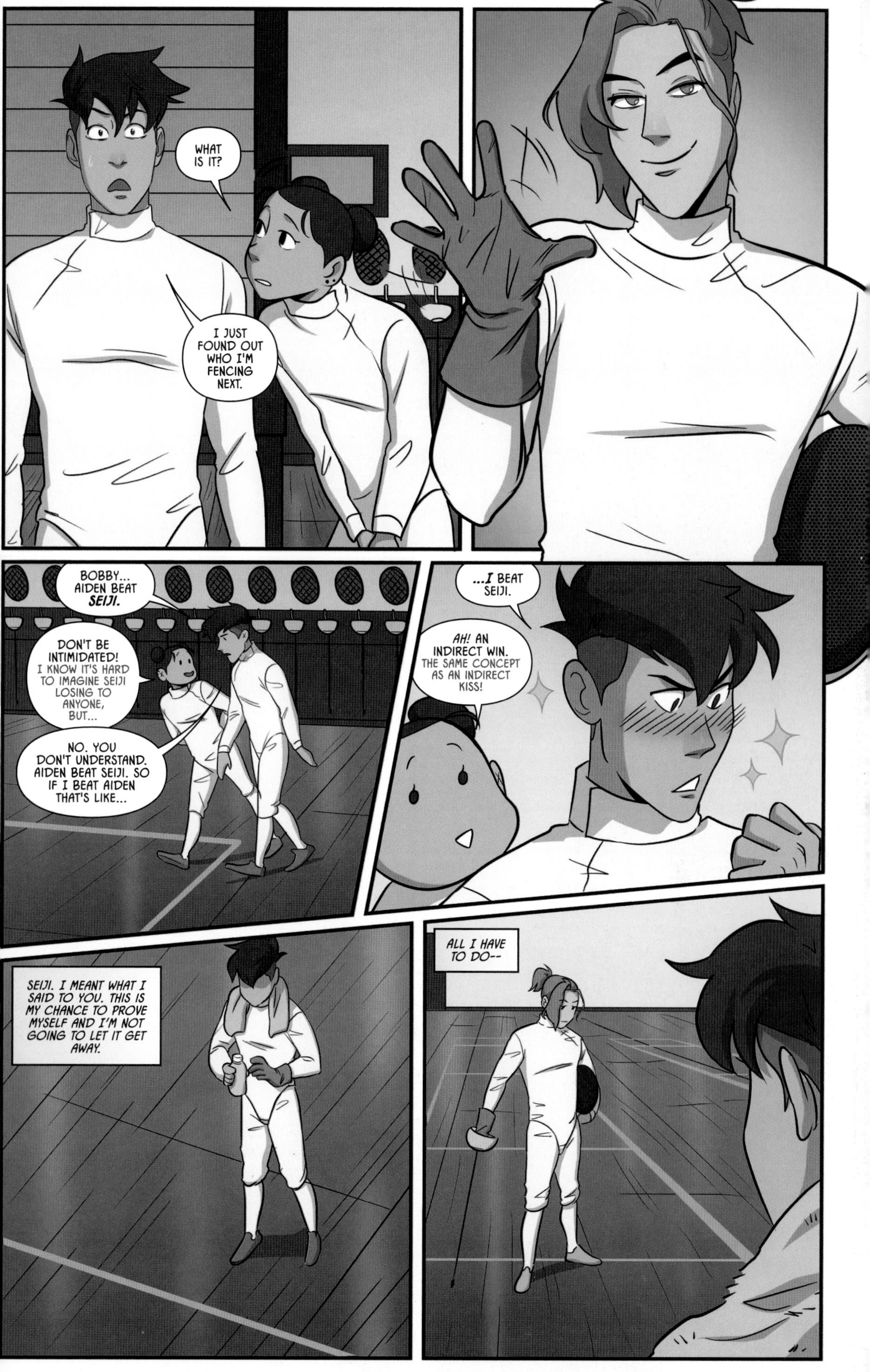
WHAT IS IT?
I JUST FOUND OUT WHO I'M FENCING NEXT.
BOBBY... AIDEN BEAT *SEIJI.*
DON'T BE INTIMIDATED! I KNOW IT'S HARD TO IMAGINE SEIJI LOSING TO ANYONE, BUT...
NO. YOU DON'T UNDERSTAND. AIDEN BEAT SEIJI. SO IF I BEAT AIDEN THAT'S LIKE...
...*I* BEAT SEIJI.
AH! AN INDIRECT WIN. THE SAME CONCEPT AS AN INDIRECT KISS!
SEIJI. I MEANT WHAT I SAID TO YOU. THIS IS MY CHANCE TO PROVE MYSELF AND I'M NOT GOING TO LET IT GET AWAY.
ALL I HAVE TO DO--

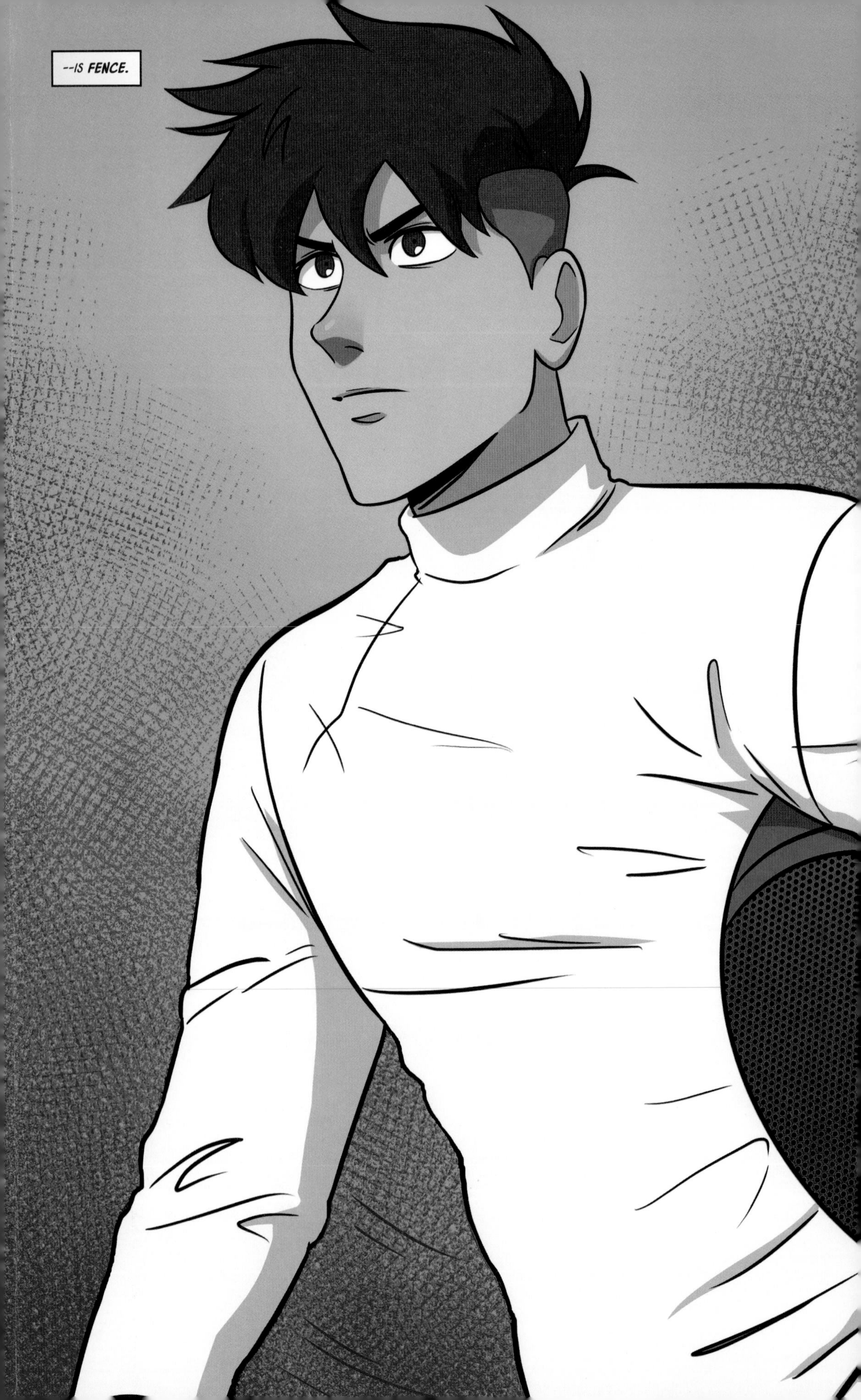
--IS FENCE.

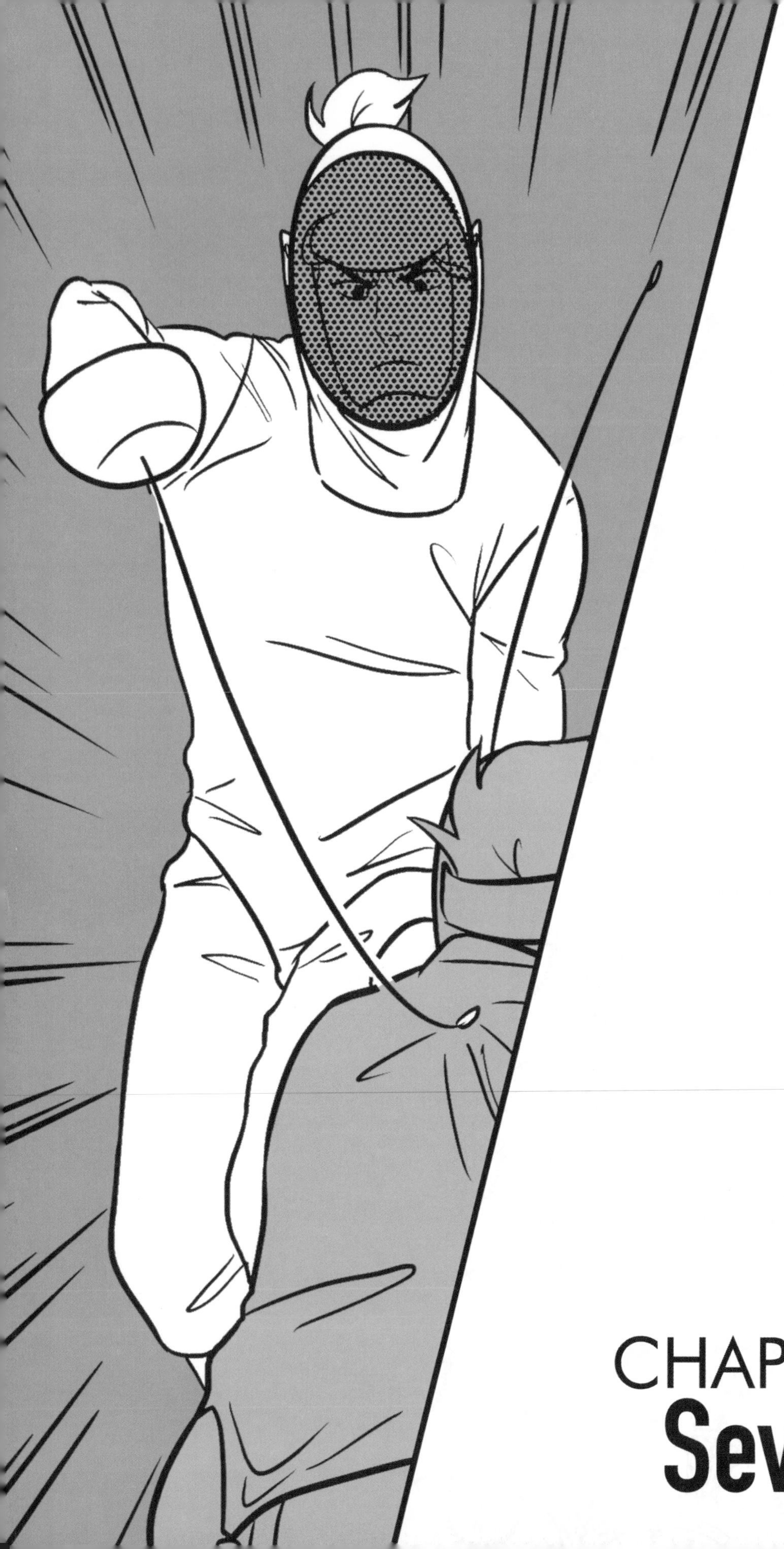

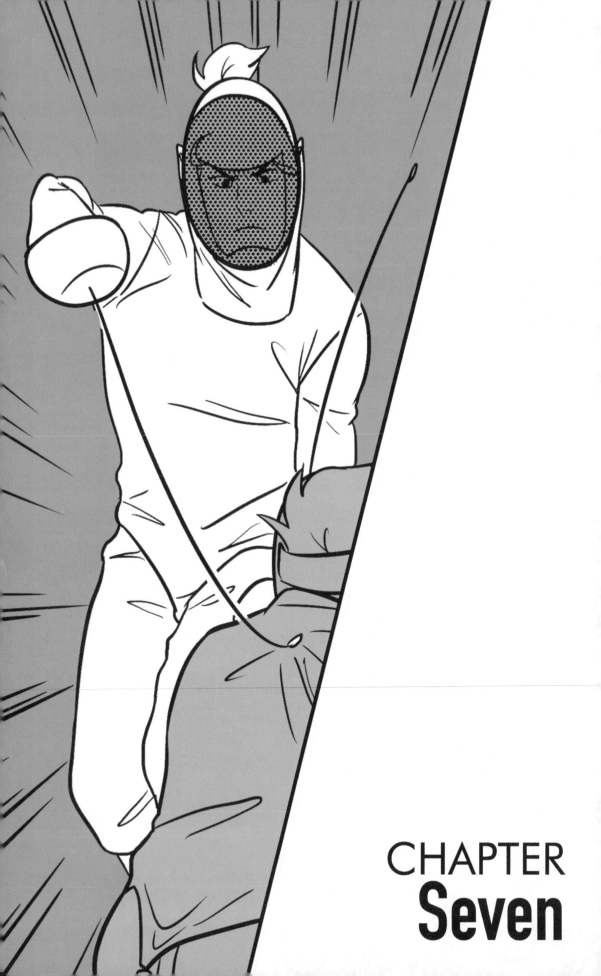

CHAPTER **Seven**

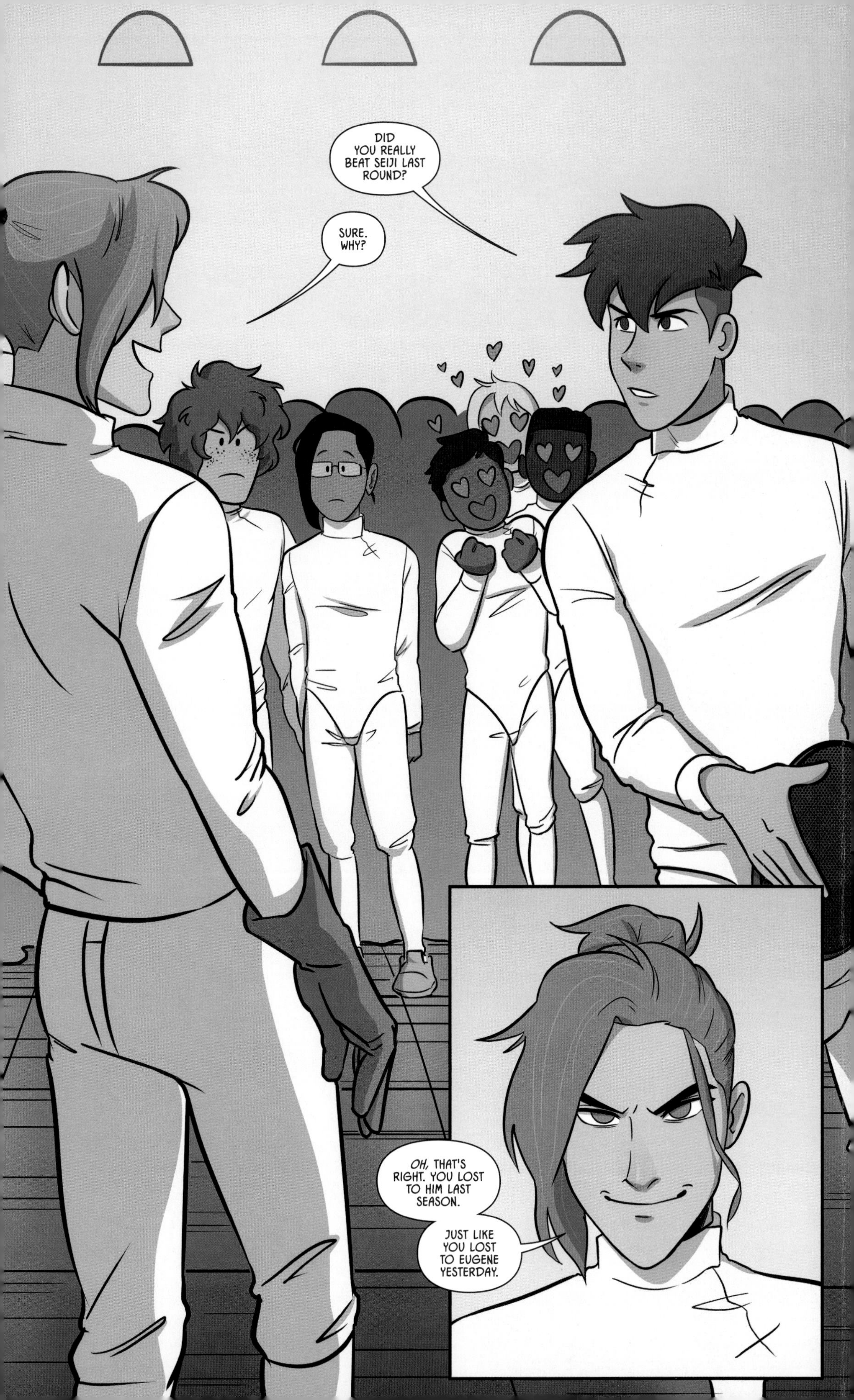
DID YOU REALLY BEAT SEIJI LAST ROUND?
SURE. WHY?
OH, THAT'S RIGHT. YOU LOST TO HIM LAST SEASON.
JUST LIKE YOU LOST TO EUGENE YESTERDAY.

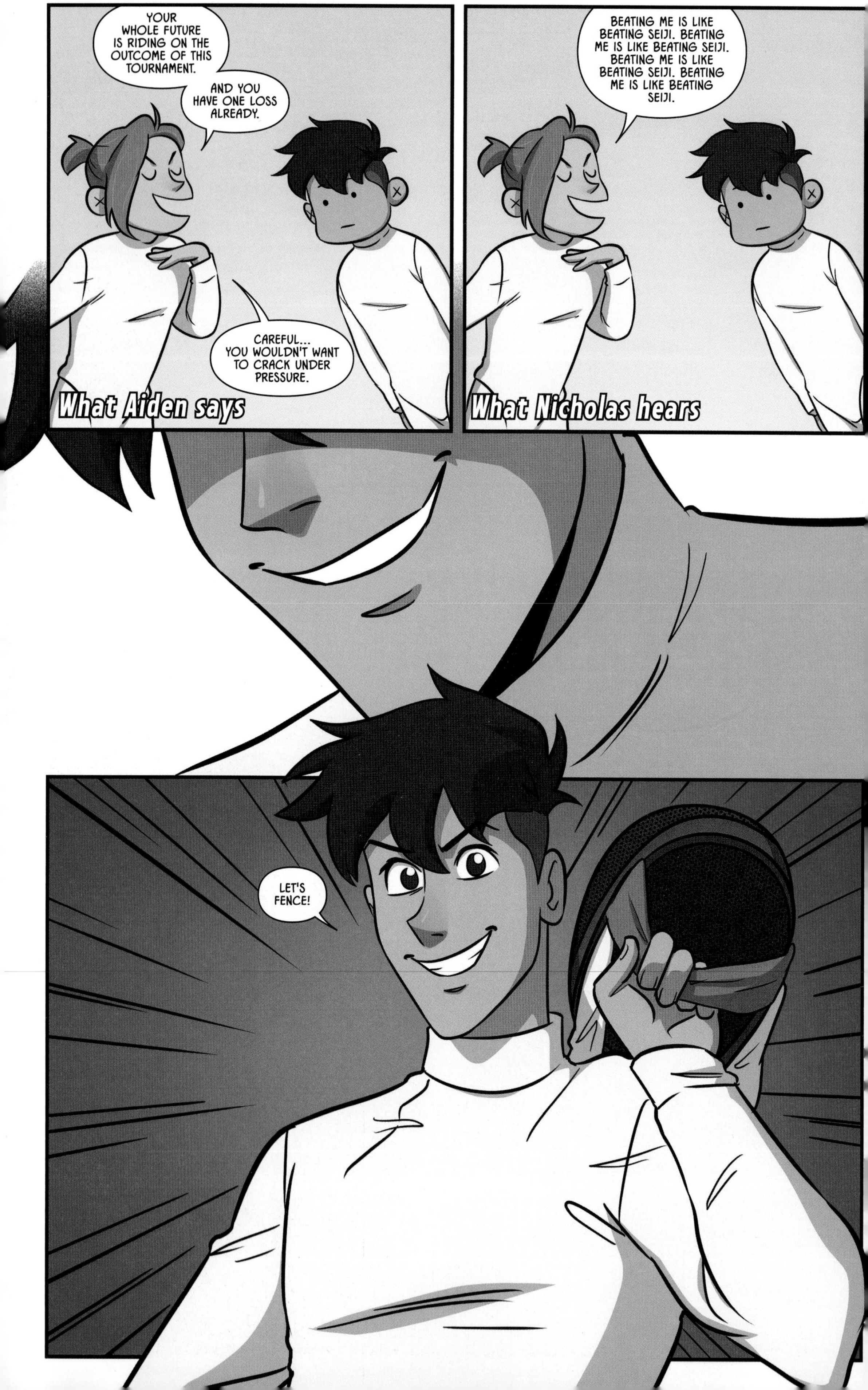
YOUR WHOLE FUTURE IS RIDING ON THE OUTCOME OF THIS TOURNAMENT.
AND YOU HAVE ONE LOSS ALREADY.
CAREFUL... YOU WOULDN'T WANT TO CRACK UNDER PRESSURE.
What Aiden says
BEATING ME IS LIKE BEATING SEIJI. BEATING ME IS LIKE BEATING SEIJI. BEATING ME IS LIKE BEATING SEIJI. BEATING ME IS LIKE BEATING SEIJI.
What Nicholas hears
LET'S FENCE!

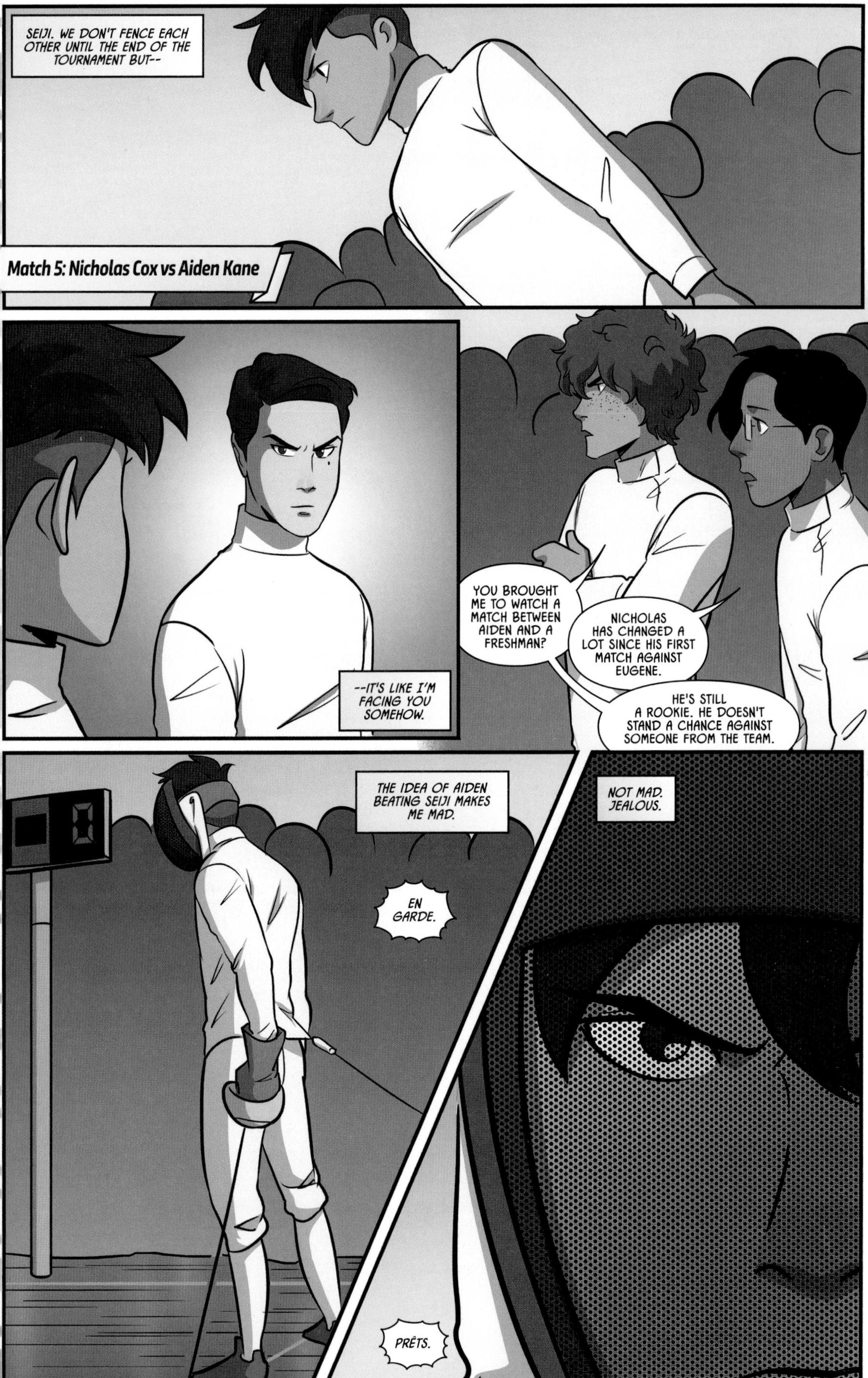
SEIJI. WE DON'T FENCE EACH OTHER UNTIL THE END OF THE TOURNAMENT BUT--
Match 5: Nicholas Cox vs Aiden Kane
--IT'S LIKE I'M FACING YOU SOMEHOW.
YOU BROUGHT ME TO WATCH A MATCH BETWEEN AIDEN AND A FRESHMAN?
NICHOLAS HAS CHANGED A LOT SINCE HIS FIRST MATCH AGAINST EUGENE.
HE'S STILL A ROOKIE. HE DOESN'T STAND A CHANCE AGAINST SOMEONE FROM THE TEAM.
THE IDEA OF AIDEN BEATING SEIJI MAKES ME MAD.
EN GARDE.
PRÊTS.
NOT MAD. JEALOUS.

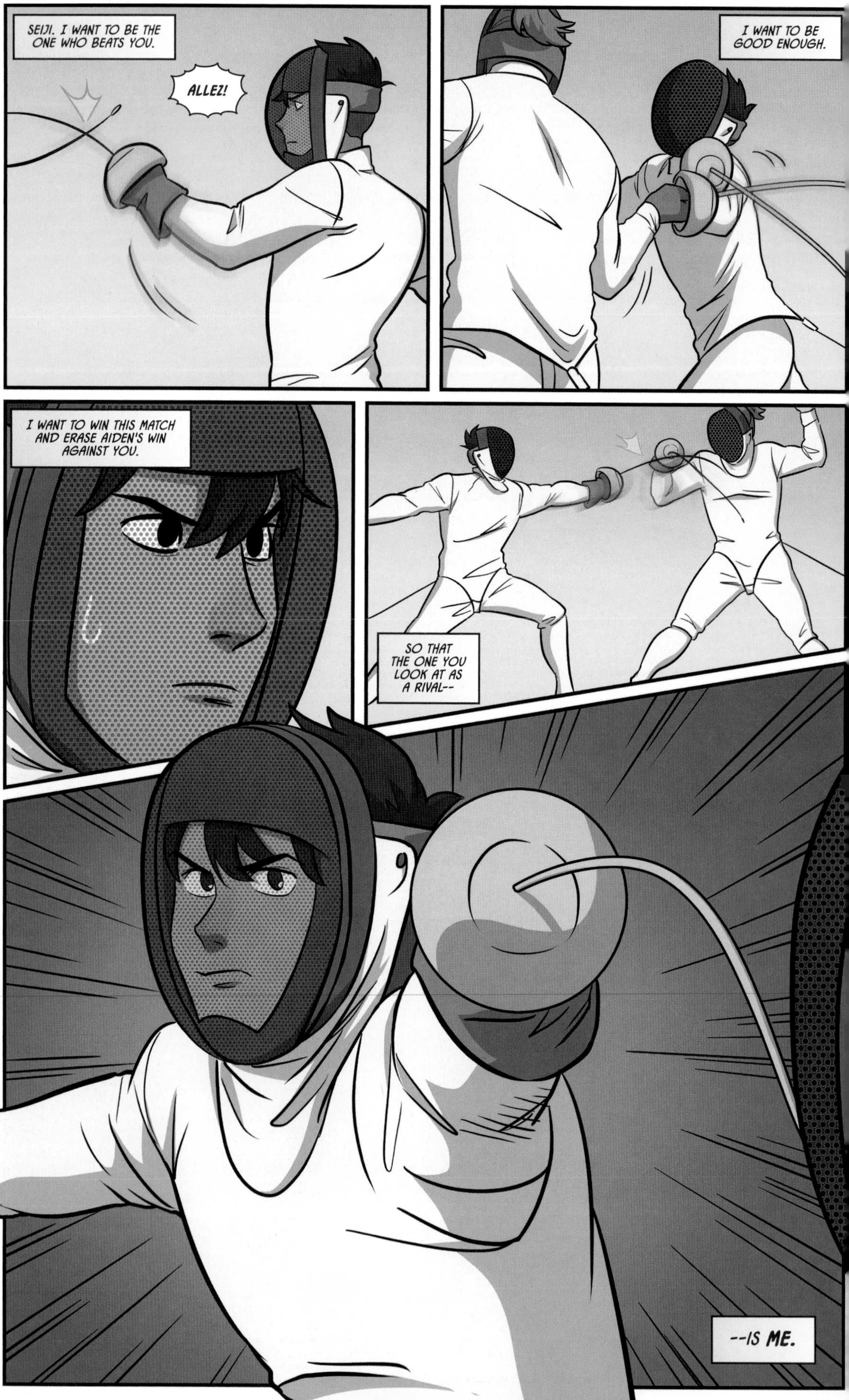
SEIJI. I WANT TO BE THE ONE WHO BEATS YOU.
ALLEZ!
I WANT TO BE GOOD ENOUGH.
I WANT TO WIN THIS MATCH AND ERASE AIDEN'S WIN AGAINST YOU.
SO THAT THE ONE YOU LOOK AT AS A RIVAL--
--IS ME.

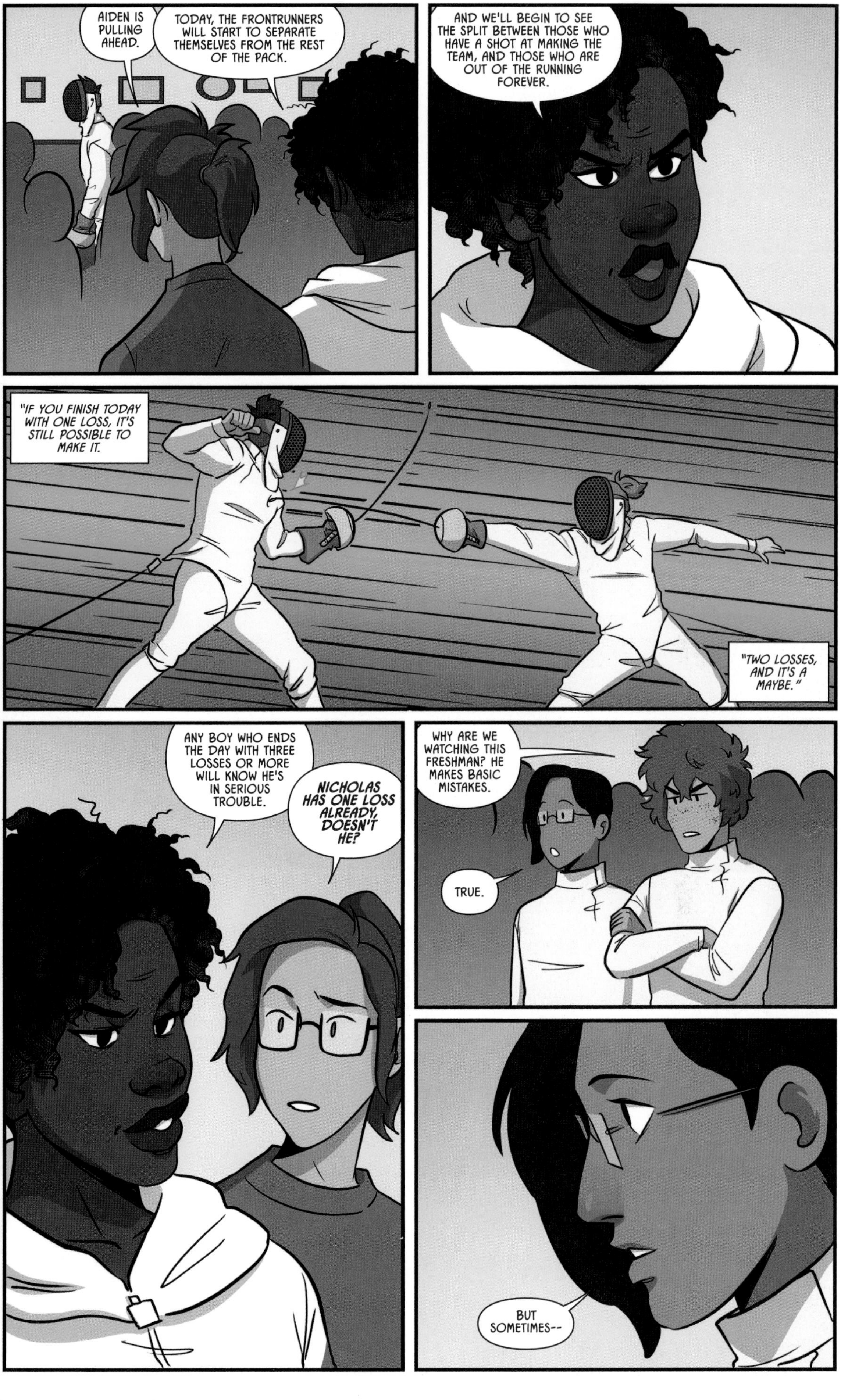
AIDEN IS PULLING AHEAD.
TODAY, THE FRONTRUNNERS WILL START TO SEPARATE THEMSELVES FROM THE REST OF THE PACK.
AND WE'LL BEGIN TO SEE THE SPLIT BETWEEN THOSE WHO HAVE A SHOT AT MAKING THE TEAM, AND THOSE WHO ARE OUT OF THE RUNNING FOREVER.
"IF YOU FINISH TODAY WITH ONE LOSS, IT'S STILL POSSIBLE TO MAKE IT.
"TWO LOSSES, AND IT'S A MAYBE."
ANY BOY WHO ENDS THE DAY WITH THREE LOSSES OR MORE WILL KNOW HE'S IN SERIOUS TROUBLE.
NICHOLAS HAS ONE LOSS ALREADY, DOESN'T HE?
WHY ARE WE WATCHING THIS FRESHMAN? HE MAKES BASIC MISTAKES.
TRUE.
BUT SOMETIMES--

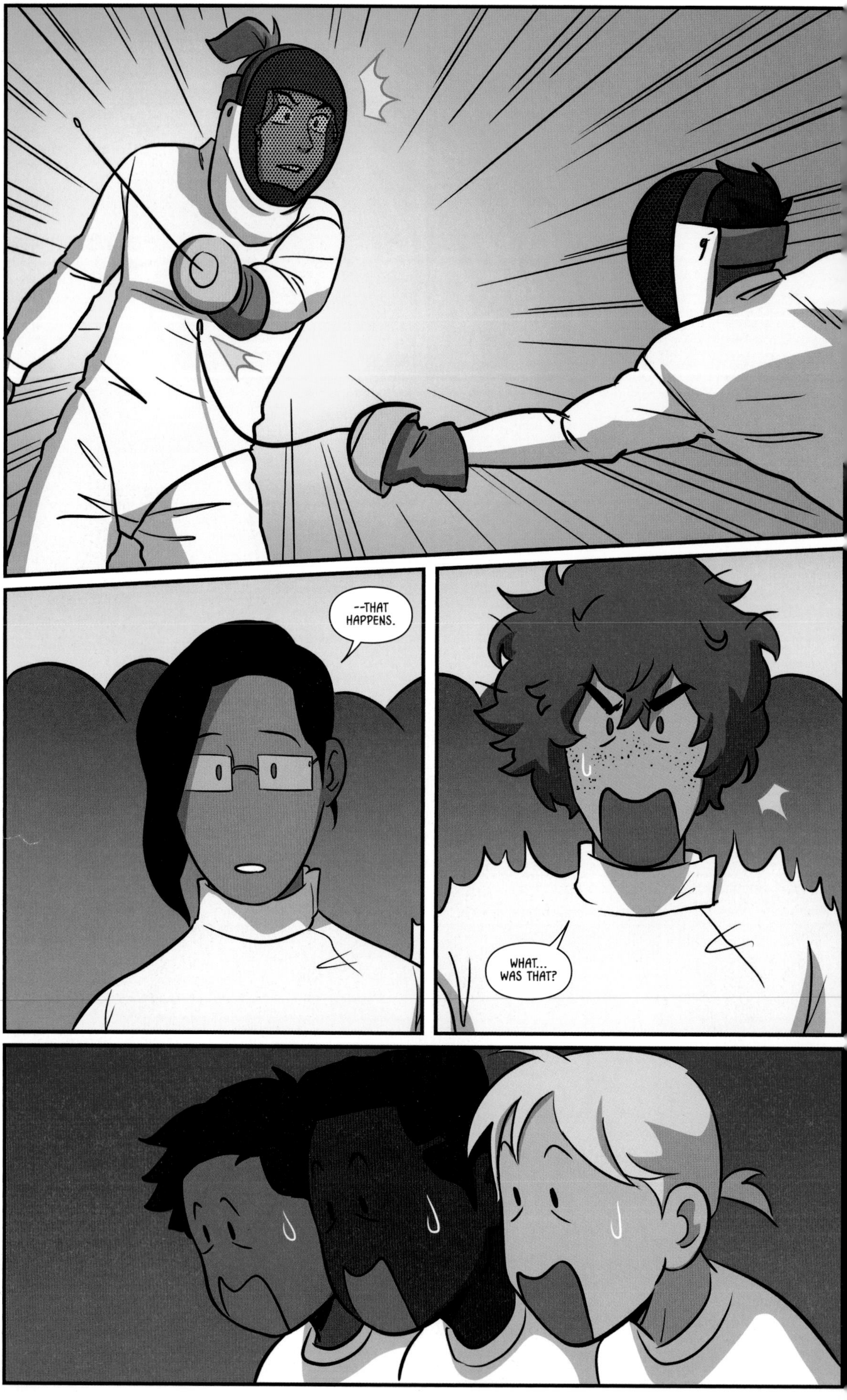
--THAT
HAPPENS.
WHAT...
WAS THAT?

WE CAN'T LET AIDEN DOWN!

LET'S CHEER OUR HARDEST!

WE'VE GOT THIS!

GO AIDEN!

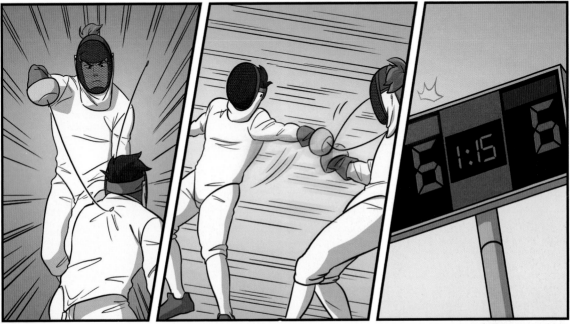

AIDEN GET YOUR HEAD IN THE GAME!

THE HONOR OF THE TEAM IS ON THE LINE!

ALL OF NICHOLAS'S MISTAKES ARE STILL THERE, BUT AIDEN'S HAVING TROUBLE TAKING ADVANTAGE OF THEM.

NOT TO MENTION--

"--EVERYTHING THAT WORKED ON SEIJI IS FAILING ON NICHOLAS."

BLAH BLAH BLAH BLAH...

THIS GUY TALKS A LOT.

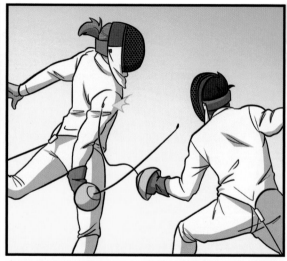

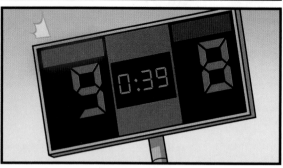

0:39

JUST A SLIP!

WHEN YOU THINK ABOUT IT, NICHOLAS IS AIDEN'S WORST OPPONENT.

mind games don't penetrate

bad at listening

oblivious

inconsistent style hard to plan against

AIDEN USED TO HAVE THE SAME TROUBLE FENCING ME, FOR SOME REASON.

MMM.

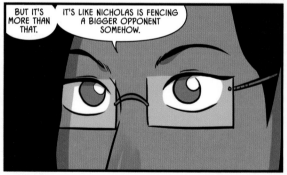

BUT IT'S MORE THAN THAT.

IT'S LIKE NICHOLAS IS FENCING A BIGGER OPPONENT SOMEHOW.

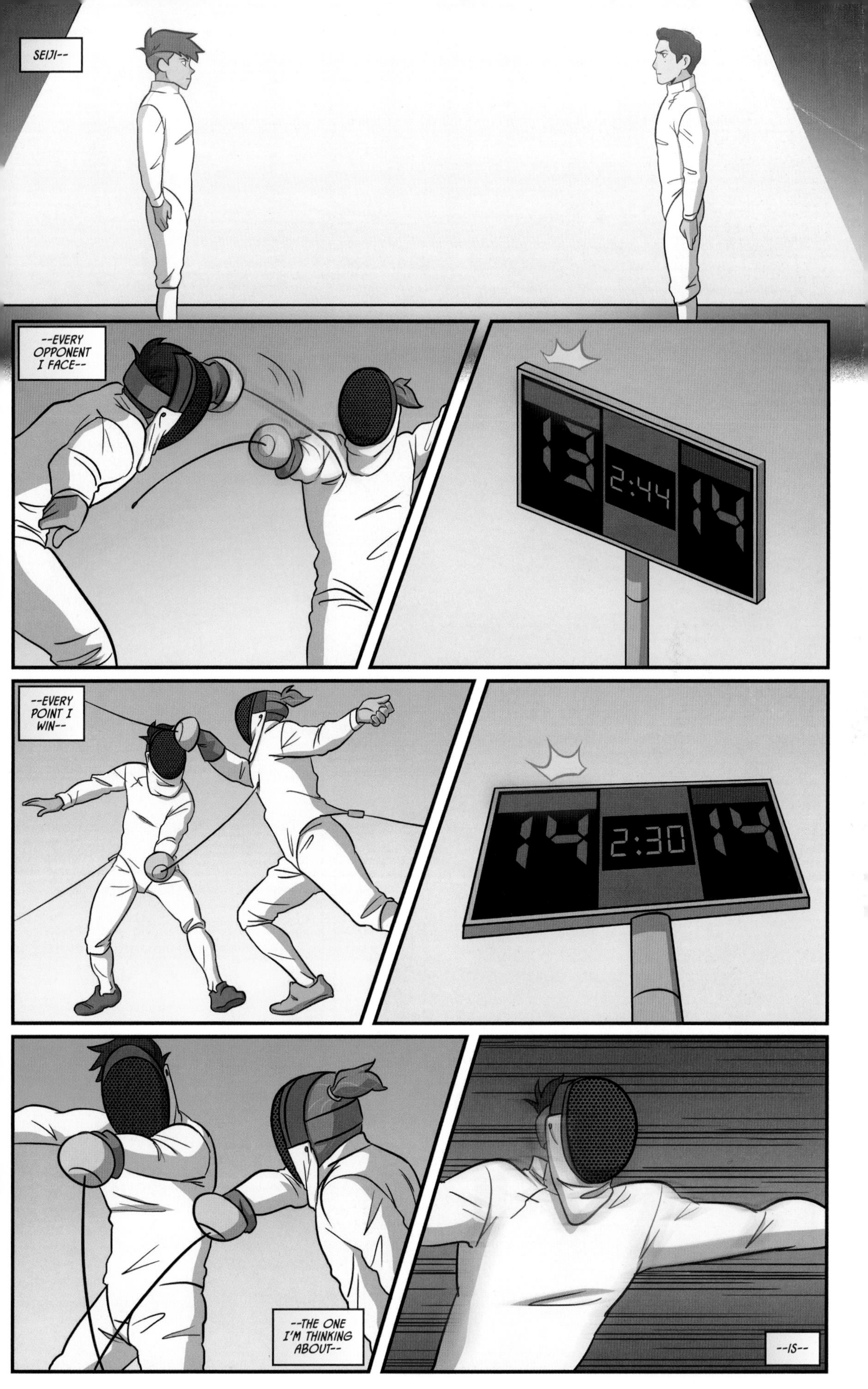
SEIJI--
--EVERY OPPONENT I FACE--
13 2:44 14
--EVERY POINT I WIN--
14 2:30 14
--THE ONE I'M THINKING ABOUT--
--IS--

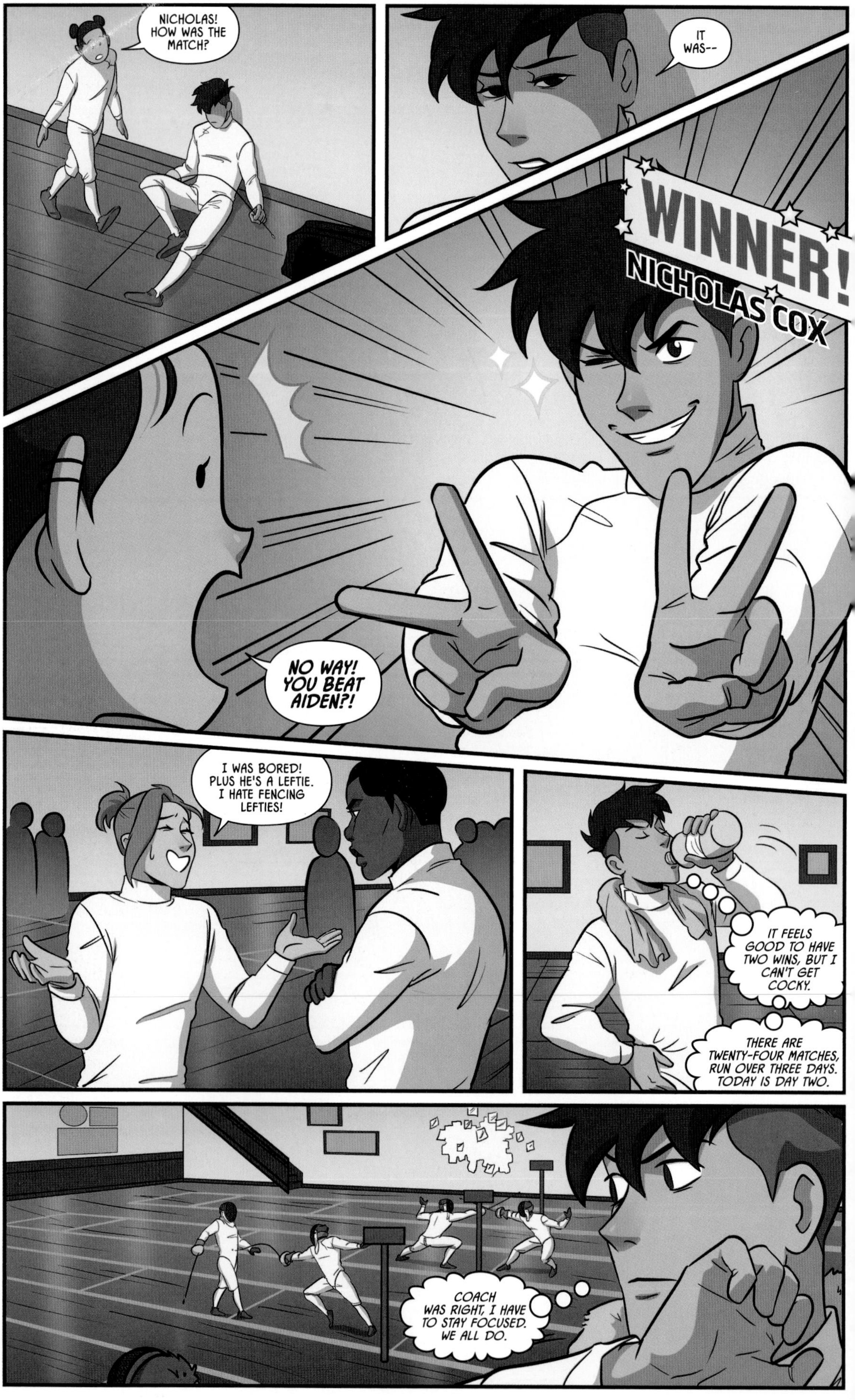
NICHOLAS! HOW WAS THE MATCH?
IT WAS--
WINNER!
NICHOLAS COX
NO WAY! YOU BEAT AIDEN?!
I WAS BORED! PLUS HE'S A LEFTIE. I HATE FENCING LEFTIES!
IT FEELS GOOD TO HAVE TWO WINS, BUT I CAN'T GET COCKY.
THERE ARE TWENTY-FOUR MATCHES, RUN OVER THREE DAYS. TODAY IS DAY TWO.
COACH WAS RIGHT, I HAVE TO STAY FOCUSED. WE ALL DO.

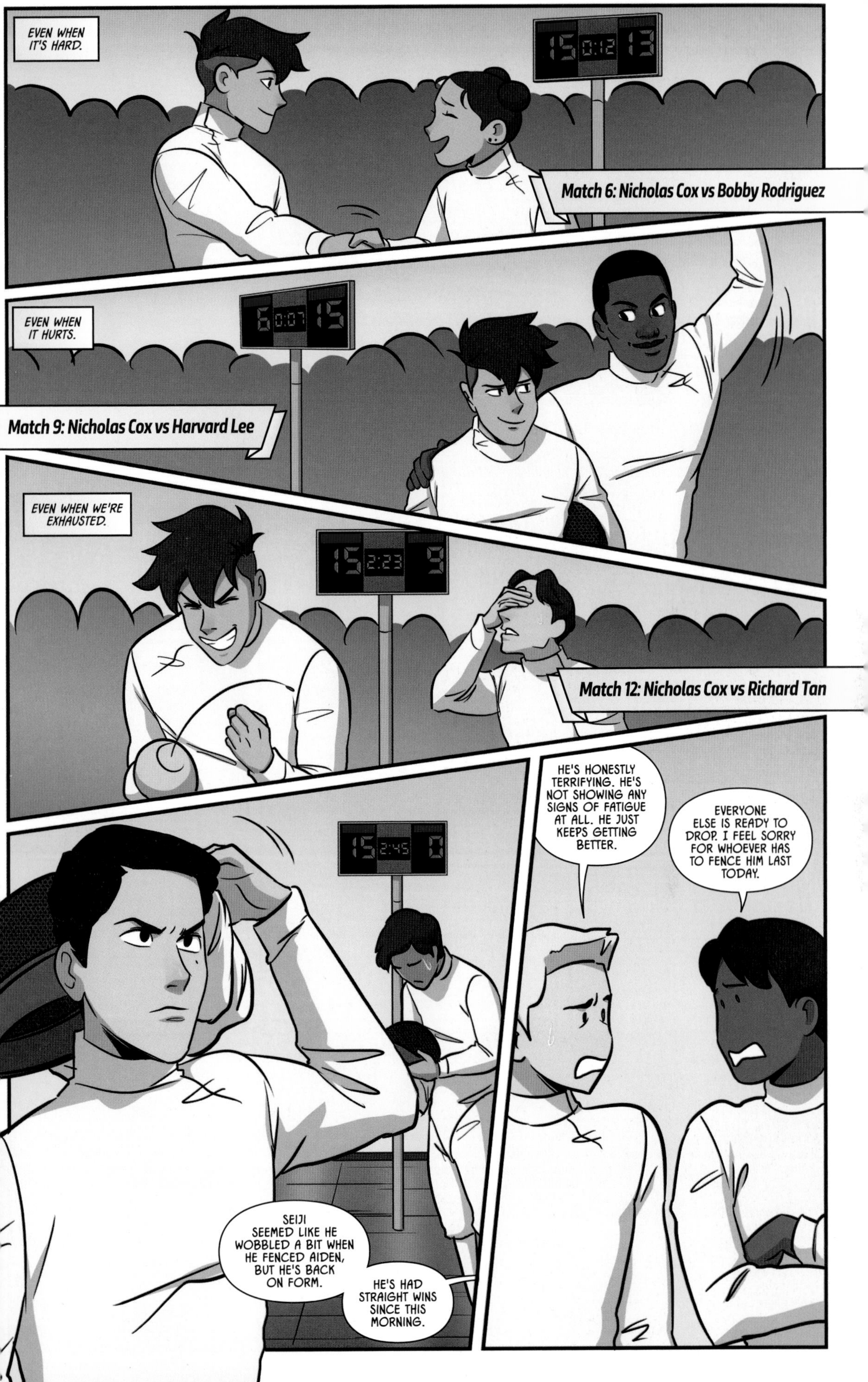
EVEN WHEN IT'S HARD.
Match 6: Nicholas Cox vs Bobby Rodriguez
EVEN WHEN IT HURTS.
Match 9: Nicholas Cox vs Harvard Lee
EVEN WHEN WE'RE EXHAUSTED.
Match 12: Nicholas Cox vs Richard Tan
SEIJI SEEMED LIKE HE WOBBLED A BIT WHEN HE FENCED AIDEN, BUT HE'S BACK ON FORM.
HE'S HAD STRAIGHT WINS SINCE THIS MORNING.
HE'S HONESTLY TERRIFYING. HE'S NOT SHOWING ANY SIGNS OF FATIGUE AT ALL. HE JUST KEEPS GETTING BETTER.
EVERYONE ELSE IS READY TO DROP. I FEEL SORRY FOR WHOEVER HAS TO FENCE HIM LAST TODAY.

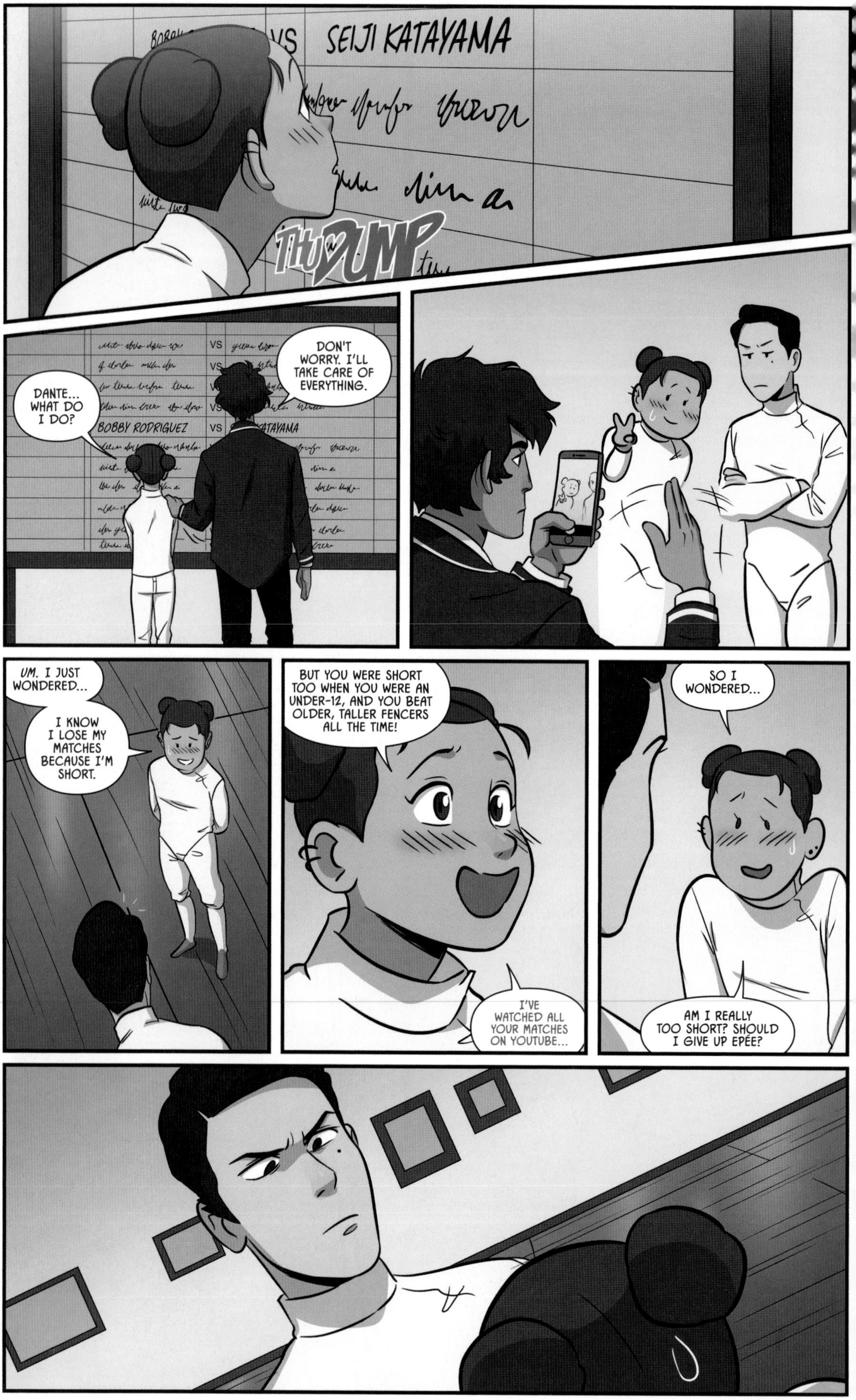

SEIJI KATAYAMA
VS
THUDUMP
DANTE... WHAT DO I DO?
DON'T WORRY. I'LL TAKE CARE OF EVERYTHING.
BOBBY RODRIGUEZ
VS
UM. I JUST WONDERED...
I KNOW I LOSE MY MATCHES BECAUSE I'M SHORT.
BUT YOU WERE SHORT TOO WHEN YOU WERE AN UNDER-12, AND YOU BEAT OLDER, TALLER FENCERS ALL THE TIME!
I'VE WATCHED ALL YOUR MATCHES ON YOUTUBE...
SO I WONDERED...
AM I REALLY TOO SHORT? SHOULD I GIVE UP EPÉE?

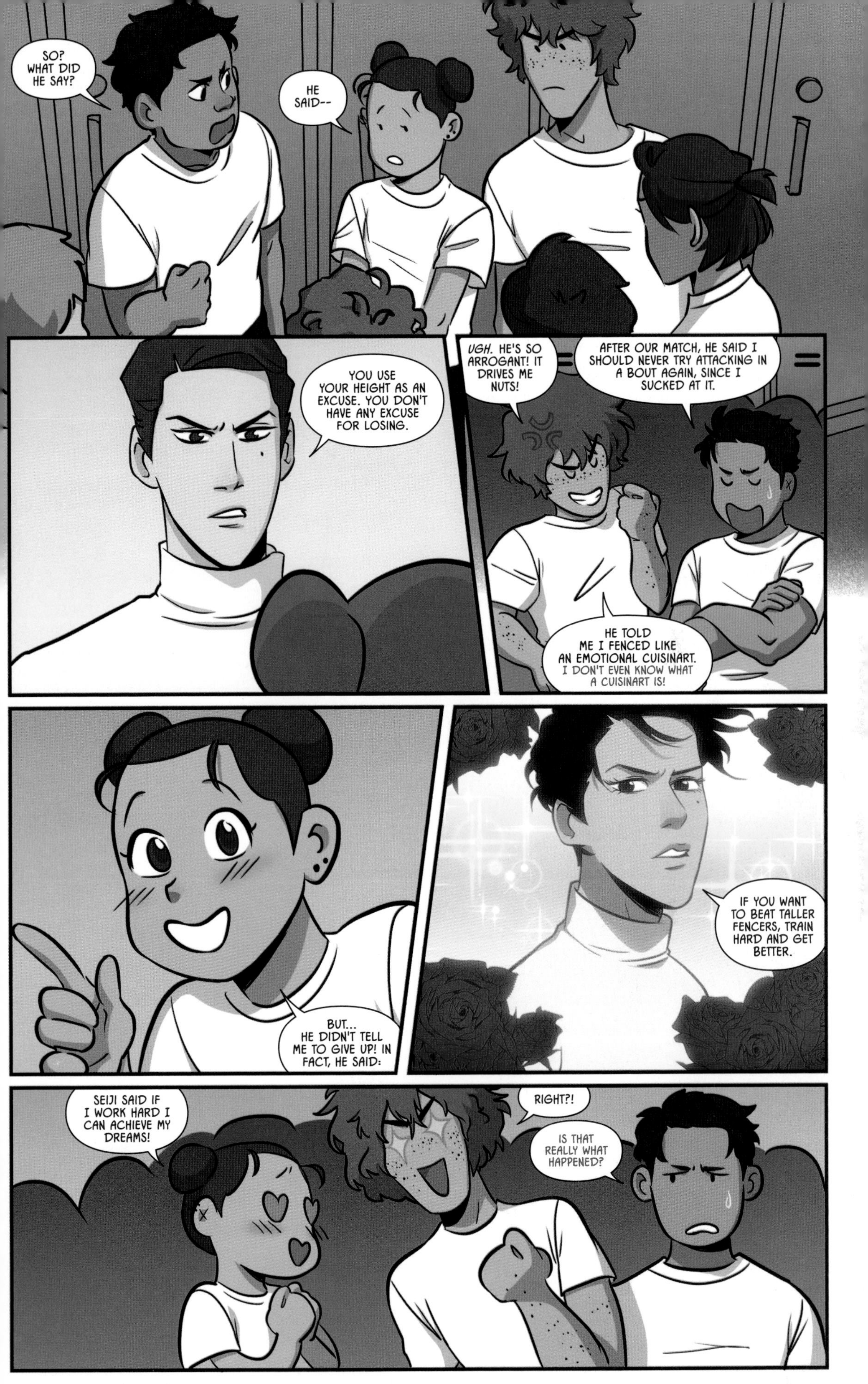
SO? WHAT DID HE SAY?
HE SAID--
YOU USE YOUR HEIGHT AS AN EXCUSE. YOU DON'T HAVE ANY EXCUSE FOR LOSING.
UGH. HE'S SO ARROGANT! IT DRIVES ME NUTS!
AFTER OUR MATCH, HE SAID I SHOULD NEVER TRY ATTACKING IN A BOUT AGAIN, SINCE I SUCKED AT IT.
HE TOLD ME I FENCED LIKE AN EMOTIONAL CUISINART. I DON'T EVEN KNOW WHAT A CUISINART IS!
BUT... HE DIDN'T TELL ME TO GIVE UP! IN FACT, HE SAID:
IF YOU WANT TO BEAT TALLER FENCERS, TRAIN HARD AND GET BETTER.
SEIJI SAID IF I WORK HARD I CAN ACHIEVE MY DREAMS!
RIGHT?!
IS THAT REALLY WHAT HAPPENED?

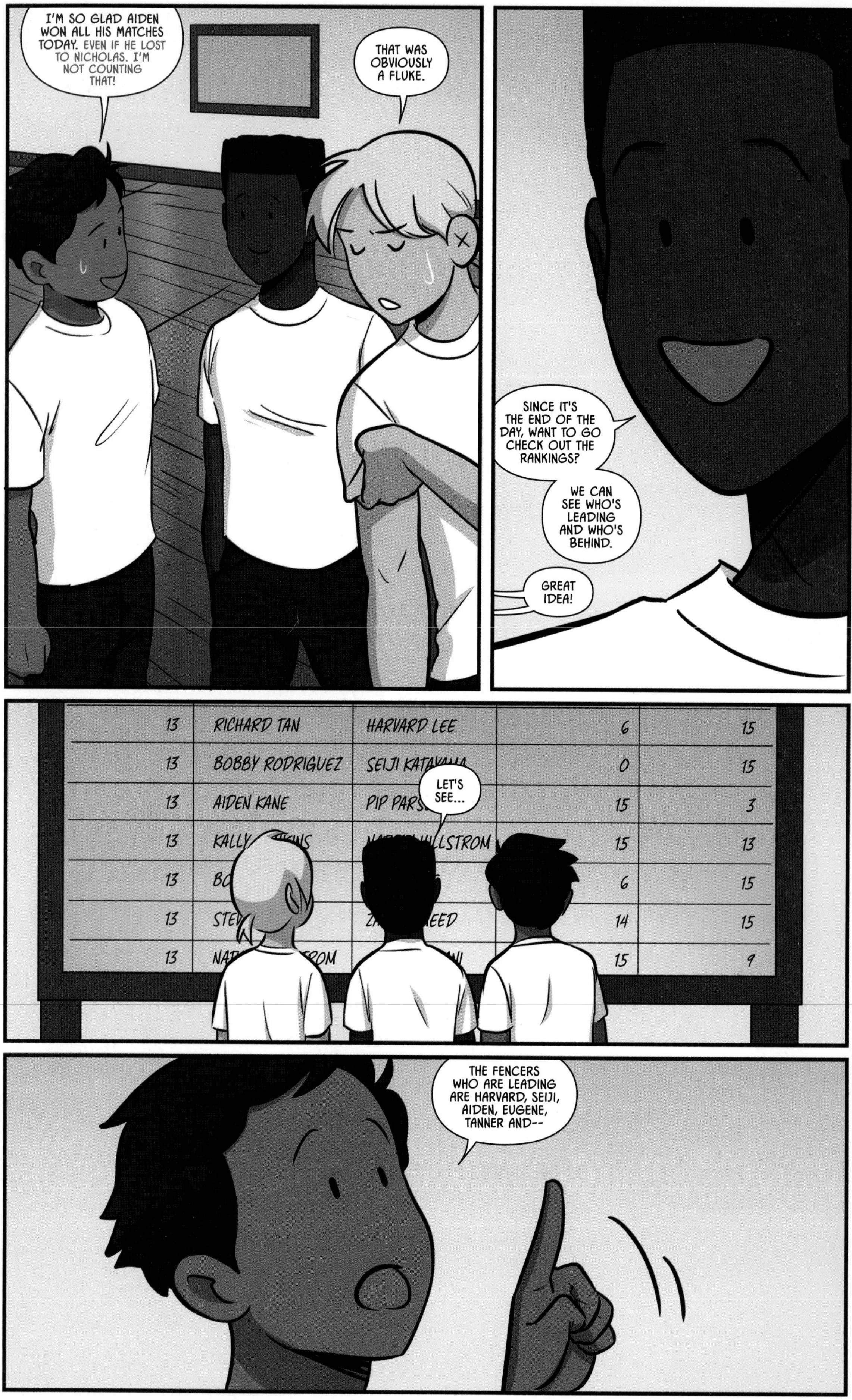
I'M SO GLAD AIDEN WON ALL HIS MATCHES TODAY. EVEN IF HE LOST TO NICHOLAS. I'M NOT COUNTING THAT!
THAT WAS OBVIOUSLY A FLUKE.
SINCE IT'S THE END OF THE DAY, WANT TO GO CHECK OUT THE RANKINGS?
WE CAN SEE WHO'S LEADING AND WHO'S BEHIND.
GREAT IDEA!
13 RICHARD TAN HARVARD LEE 6 15
LET'S SEE...
THE FENCERS WHO ARE LEADING ARE HARVARD, SEIJI, AIDEN, EUGENE, TANNER AND--

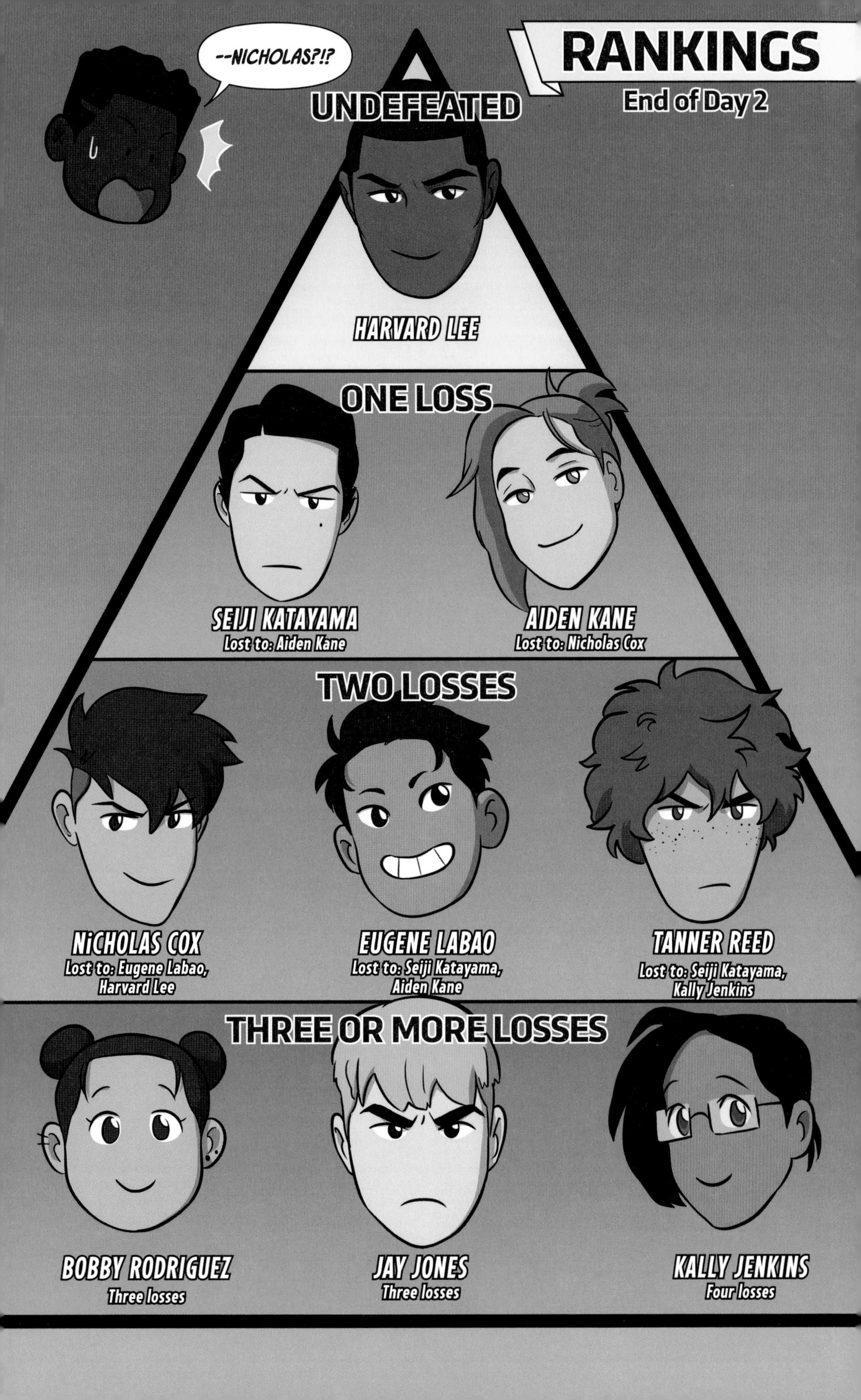
--NICHOLAS?!?
RANKINGS
End of Day 2
UNDEFEATED
HARVARD LEE
ONE LOSS
SEIJI KATAYAMA
Lost to: Aiden Kane
AIDEN KANE
Lost to: Nicholas Cox
TWO LOSSES
NiCHOLAS COX
Lost to: Eugene Labao, Harvard Lee
EUGENE LABAO
Lost to: Seiji Katayama, Aiden Kane
TANNER REED
Lost to: Seiji Katayama, Kally Jenkins
THREE OR MORE LOSSES
BOBBY RODRIGUEZ
Three losses
JAY JONES
Three losses
KALLY JENKINS
Four losses

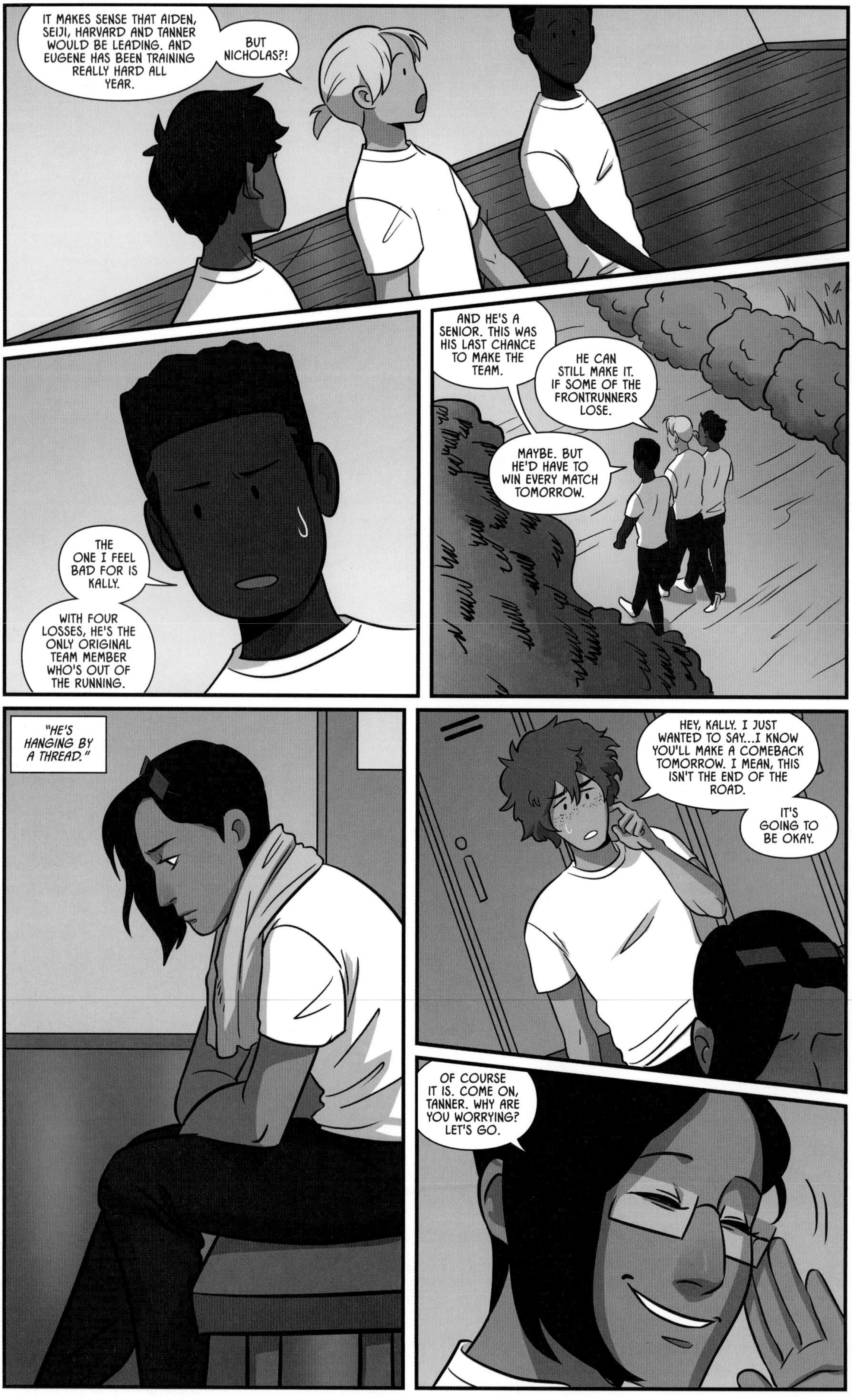
IT MAKES SENSE THAT AIDEN, SEIJI, HARVARD AND TANNER WOULD BE LEADING. AND EUGENE HAS BEEN TRAINING REALLY HARD ALL YEAR.
BUT NICHOLAS?!
AND HE'S A SENIOR. THIS WAS HIS LAST CHANCE TO MAKE THE TEAM.
HE CAN STILL MAKE IT. IF SOME OF THE FRONTRUNNERS LOSE.
MAYBE. BUT HE'D HAVE TO WIN EVERY MATCH TOMORROW.
THE ONE I FEEL BAD FOR IS KALLY.
WITH FOUR LOSSES, HE'S THE ONLY ORIGINAL TEAM MEMBER WHO'S OUT OF THE RUNNING.
"HE'S HANGING BY A THREAD."
HEY, KALLY. I JUST WANTED TO SAY...I KNOW YOU'LL MAKE A COMEBACK TOMORROW. I MEAN, THIS ISN'T THE END OF THE ROAD.
IT'S GOING TO BE OKAY.
OF COURSE IT IS. COME ON, TANNER. WHY ARE YOU WORRYING? LET'S GO.

TONIGHT IS A HARD NIGHT FOR EVERYONE.

"AND THE PRESSURE WILL ONLY INCREASE TOMORROW."

I'M ALREADY AT FIVE LOSSES. I FEEL LIKE IT'S OVER--

IT'S NOT OVER! EVERY ONE OF US HAS A CHANCE TO BEAT A FRONTRUNNER AND CAUSE AN UPSET TOMORROW.

"THE LEADERS KNOW THEY CAN'T LOSE A MATCH, OR THEY'LL LOSE THEIR SPOT."

RIGHT?! ALL IT WILL TAKE IS ONE OR TWO WINS AGAINST THE GUYS AT THE TOP--

"WHILE OTHERS JUST NEED ONE WIN TO TAKE THAT SPOT FOR THEMSELVES."

--AND WE'RE ALL BACK IN WITH A SHOT!

"TONIGHT, THEY'LL EACH DEAL WITH IT IN THEIR OWN WAYS."

GONNA WARM DOWN THEN HIT A PROTEIN SHAKE.

liked by danterossi Best
byrodriquez Best day of my life!

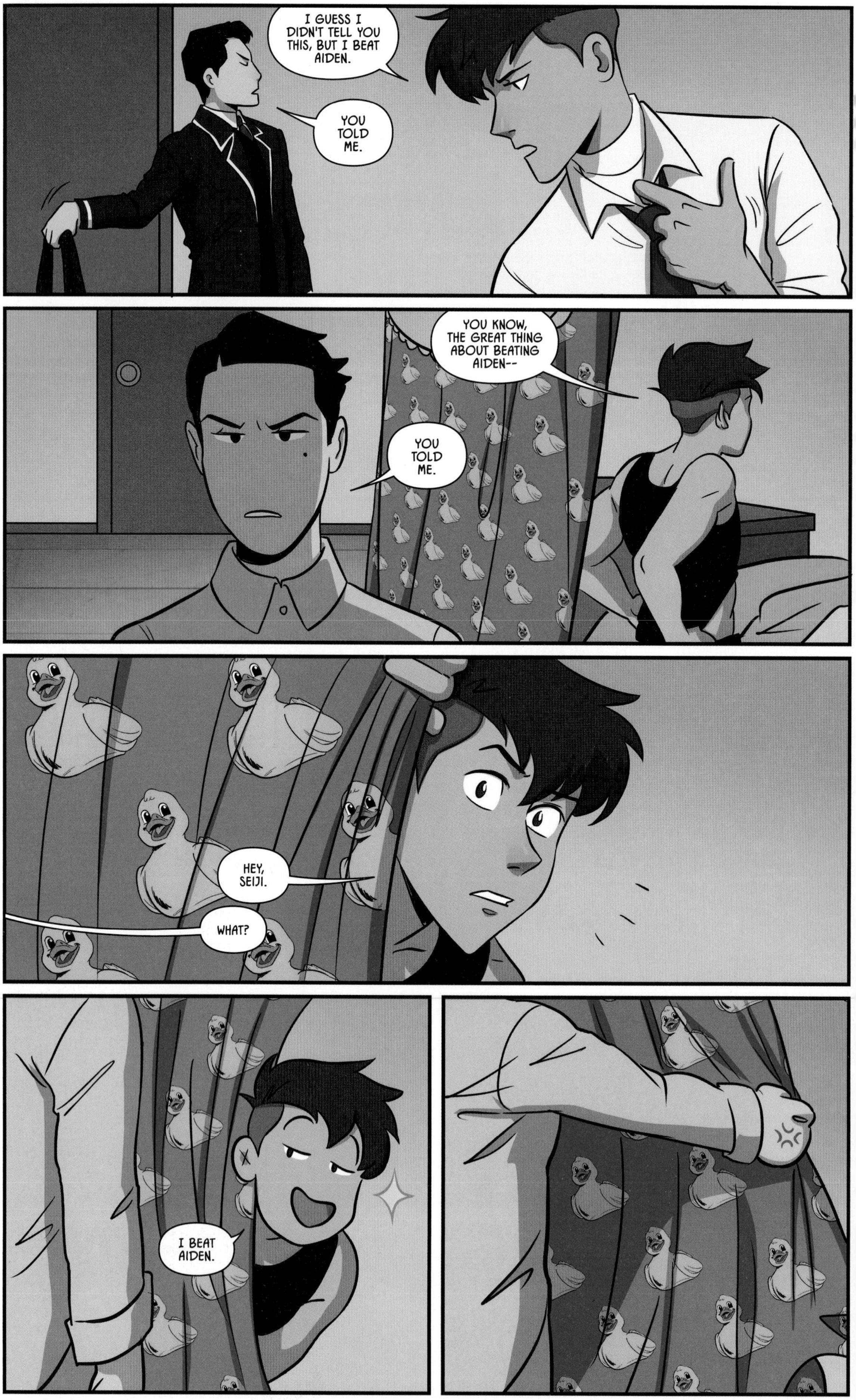
I GUESS I DIDN'T TELL YOU THIS, BUT I BEAT AIDEN.
YOU TOLD ME.
YOU KNOW, THE GREAT THING ABOUT BEATING AIDEN--
YOU TOLD ME.
HEY, SEIJI.
WHAT?
I BEAT AIDEN.

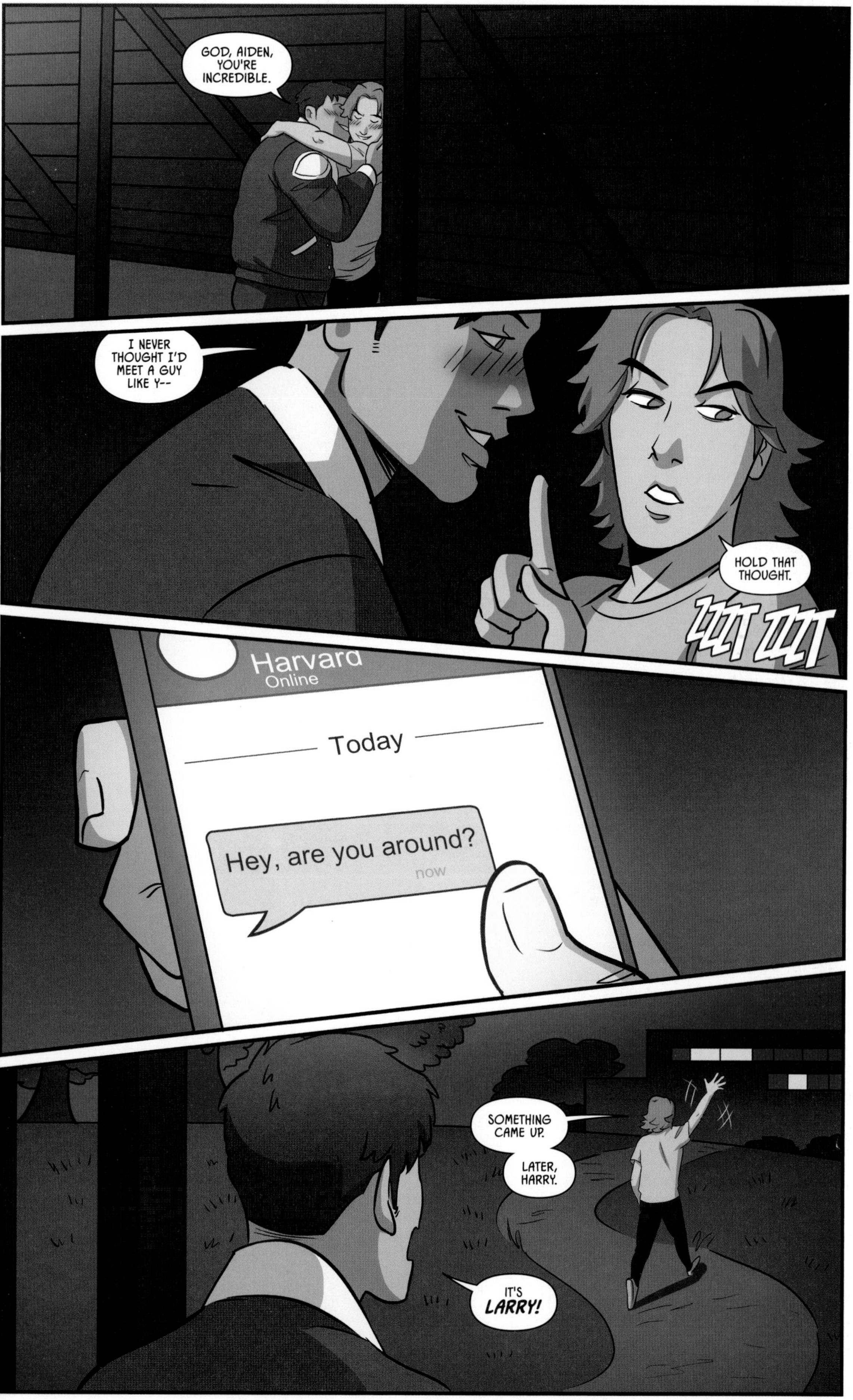
GOD, AIDEN, YOU'RE INCREDIBLE.
I NEVER THOUGHT I'D MEET A GUY LIKE Y--
HOLD THAT THOUGHT.
ZZZT ZZZT
Harvard
Online
Today
Hey, are you around?
now
SOMETHING CAME UP.
LATER, HARRY.
IT'S LARRY!

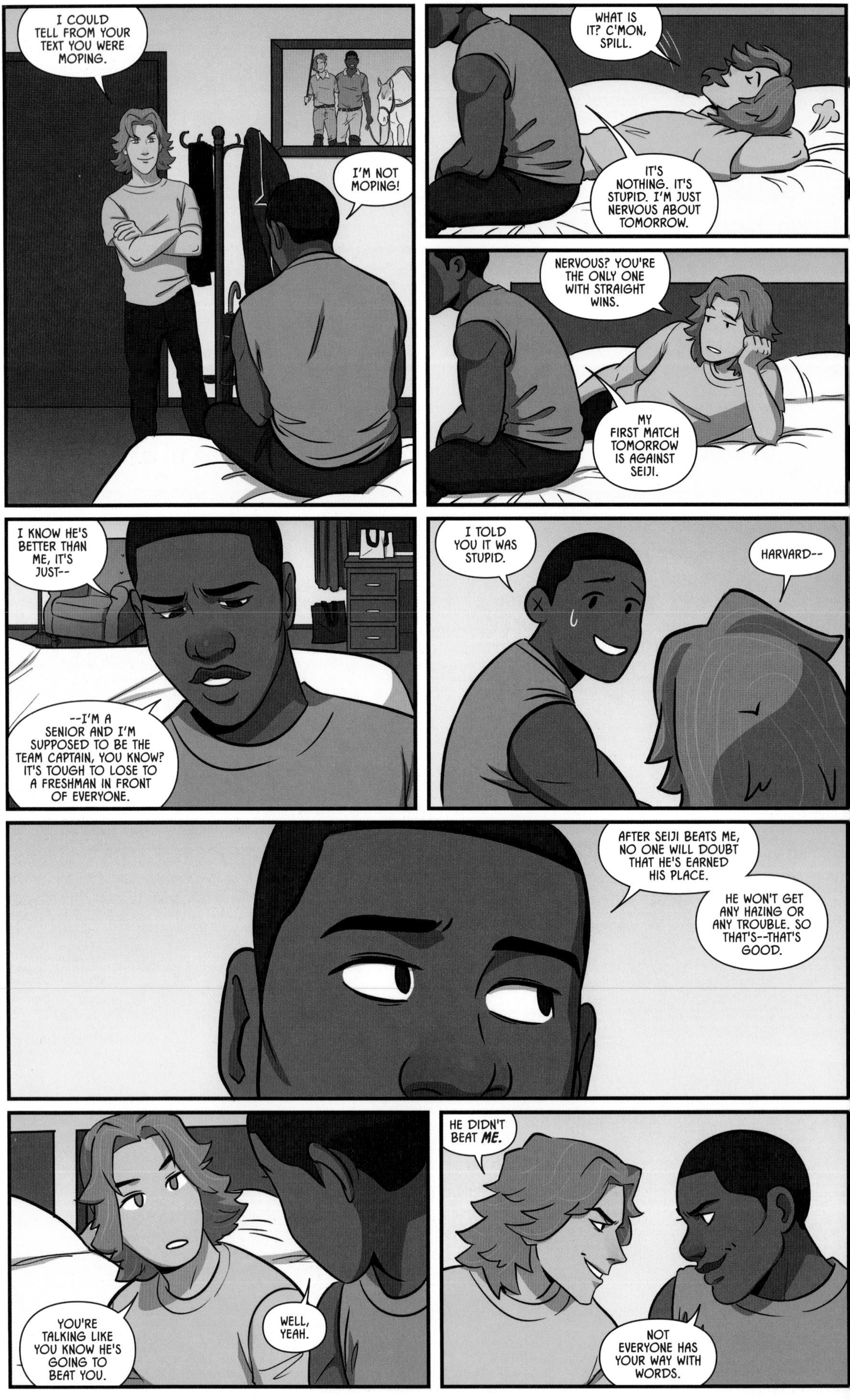

I COULD TELL FROM YOUR TEXT YOU WERE MOPING.
I'M NOT MOPING!
WHAT IS IT? C'MON, SPILL.
IT'S NOTHING. IT'S STUPID. I'M JUST NERVOUS ABOUT TOMORROW.
NERVOUS? YOU'RE THE ONLY ONE WITH STRAIGHT WINS.
MY FIRST MATCH TOMORROW IS AGAINST SEIJI.
I KNOW HE'S BETTER THAN ME, IT'S JUST--
--I'M A SENIOR AND I'M SUPPOSED TO BE THE TEAM CAPTAIN, YOU KNOW? IT'S TOUGH TO LOSE TO A FRESHMAN IN FRONT OF EVERYONE.
I TOLD YOU IT WAS STUPID.
HARVARD--
AFTER SEIJI BEATS ME, NO ONE WILL DOUBT THAT HE'S EARNED HIS PLACE.
HE WON'T GET ANY HAZING OR ANY TROUBLE. SO THAT'S--THAT'S GOOD.
YOU'RE TALKING LIKE YOU KNOW HE'S GOING TO BEAT YOU.
WELL, YEAH.
HE DIDN'T BEAT ***ME.***
NOT EVERYONE HAS YOUR WAY WITH WORDS.

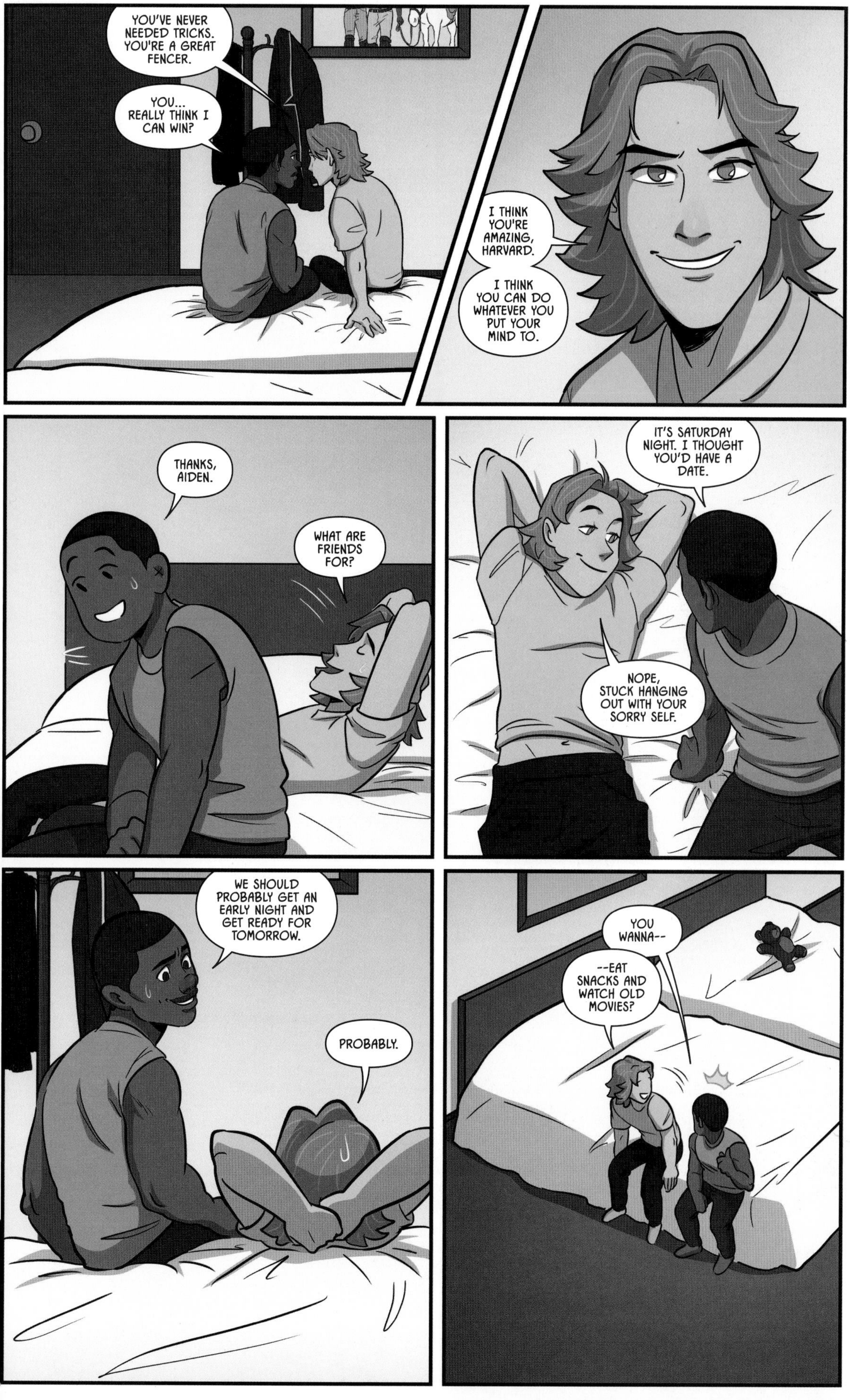
YOU'VE NEVER NEEDED TRICKS. YOU'RE A GREAT FENCER.
YOU... REALLY THINK I CAN WIN?
I THINK YOU'RE AMAZING, HARVARD.
I THINK YOU CAN DO WHATEVER YOU PUT YOUR MIND TO.
THANKS, AIDEN.
WHAT ARE FRIENDS FOR?
IT'S SATURDAY NIGHT. I THOUGHT YOU'D HAVE A DATE.
NOPE, STUCK HANGING OUT WITH YOUR SORRY SELF.
WE SHOULD PROBABLY GET AN EARLY NIGHT AND GET READY FOR TOMORROW.
PROBABLY.
YOU WANNA--
--EAT SNACKS AND WATCH OLD MOVIES?

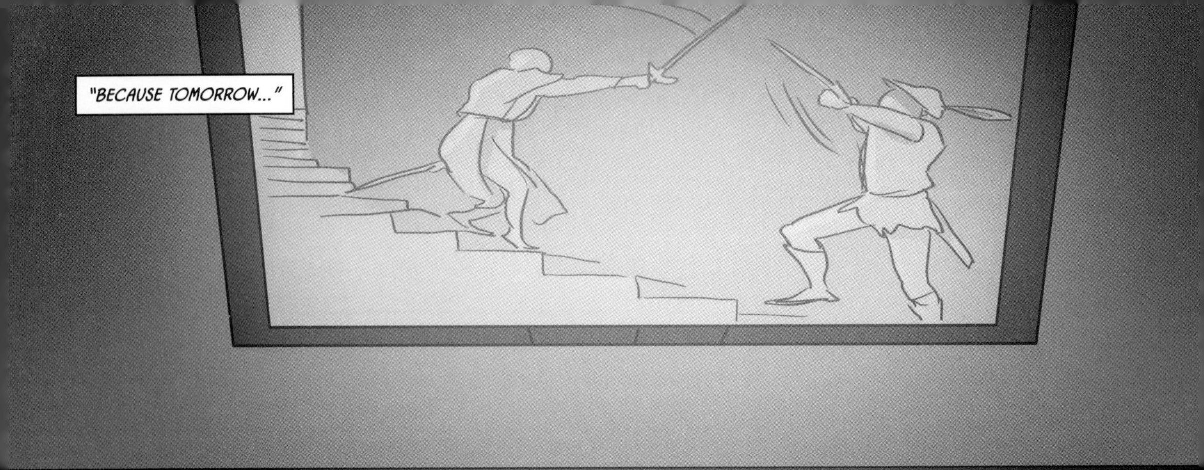
"BECAUSE TOMORROW..."

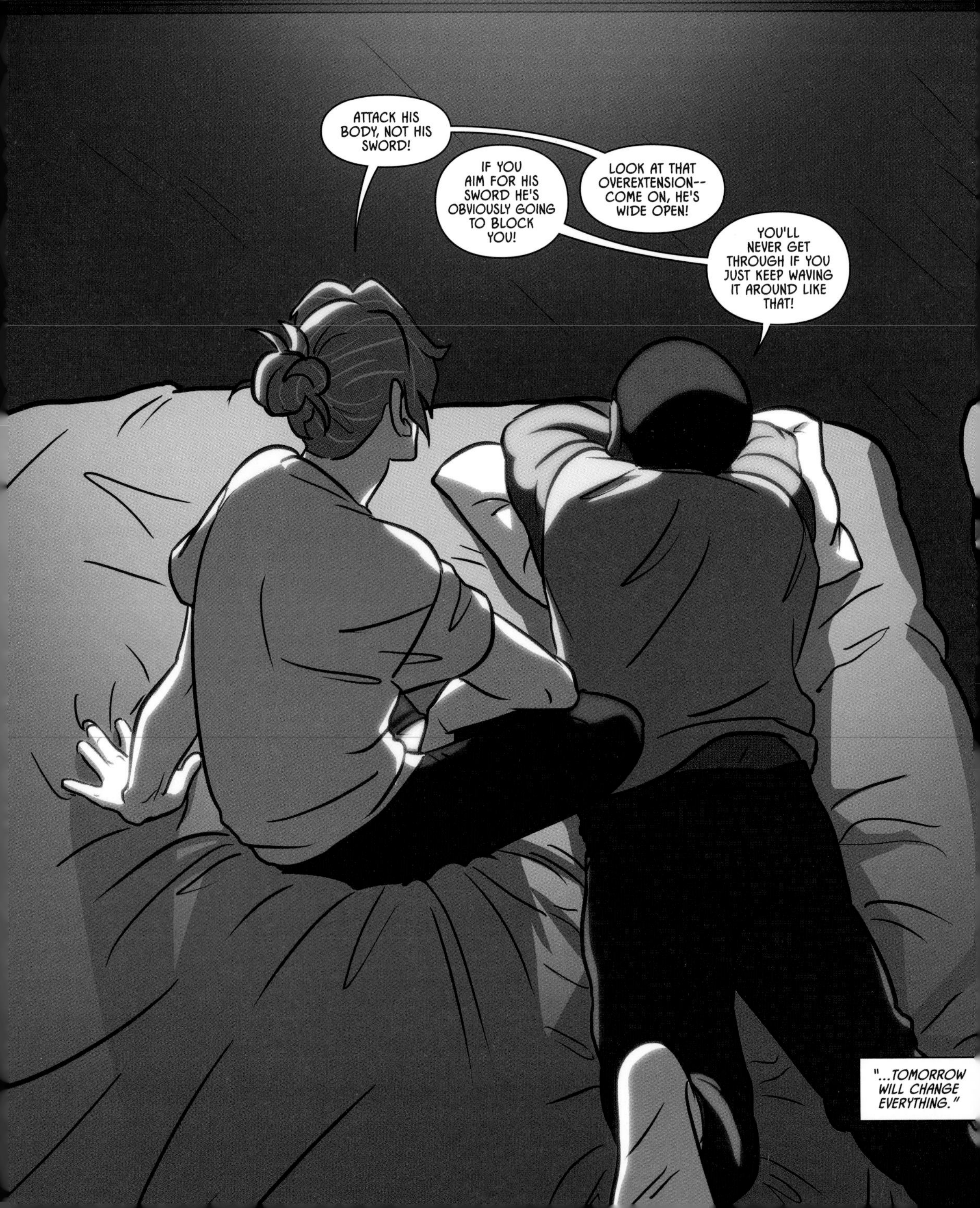
ATTACK HIS BODY, NOT HIS SWORD!
LOOK AT THAT OVEREXTENSION--COME ON, HE'S WIDE OPEN!
IF YOU AIM FOR HIS SWORD HE'S OBVIOUSLY GOING TO BLOCK YOU!
YOU'LL NEVER GET THROUGH IF YOU JUST KEEP WAVING IT AROUND LIKE THAT!
"...TOMORROW WILL CHANGE EVERYTHING."

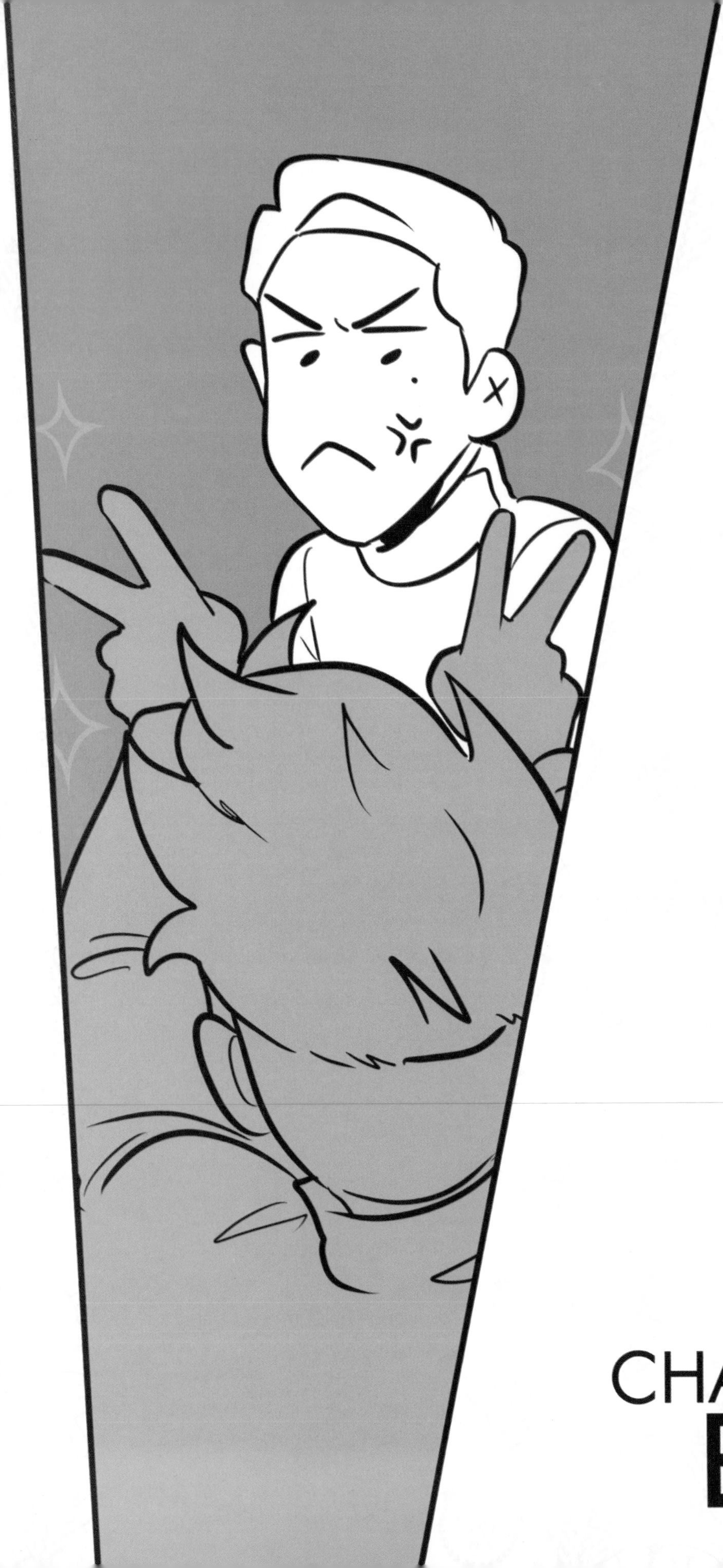

CHAPTER Eight

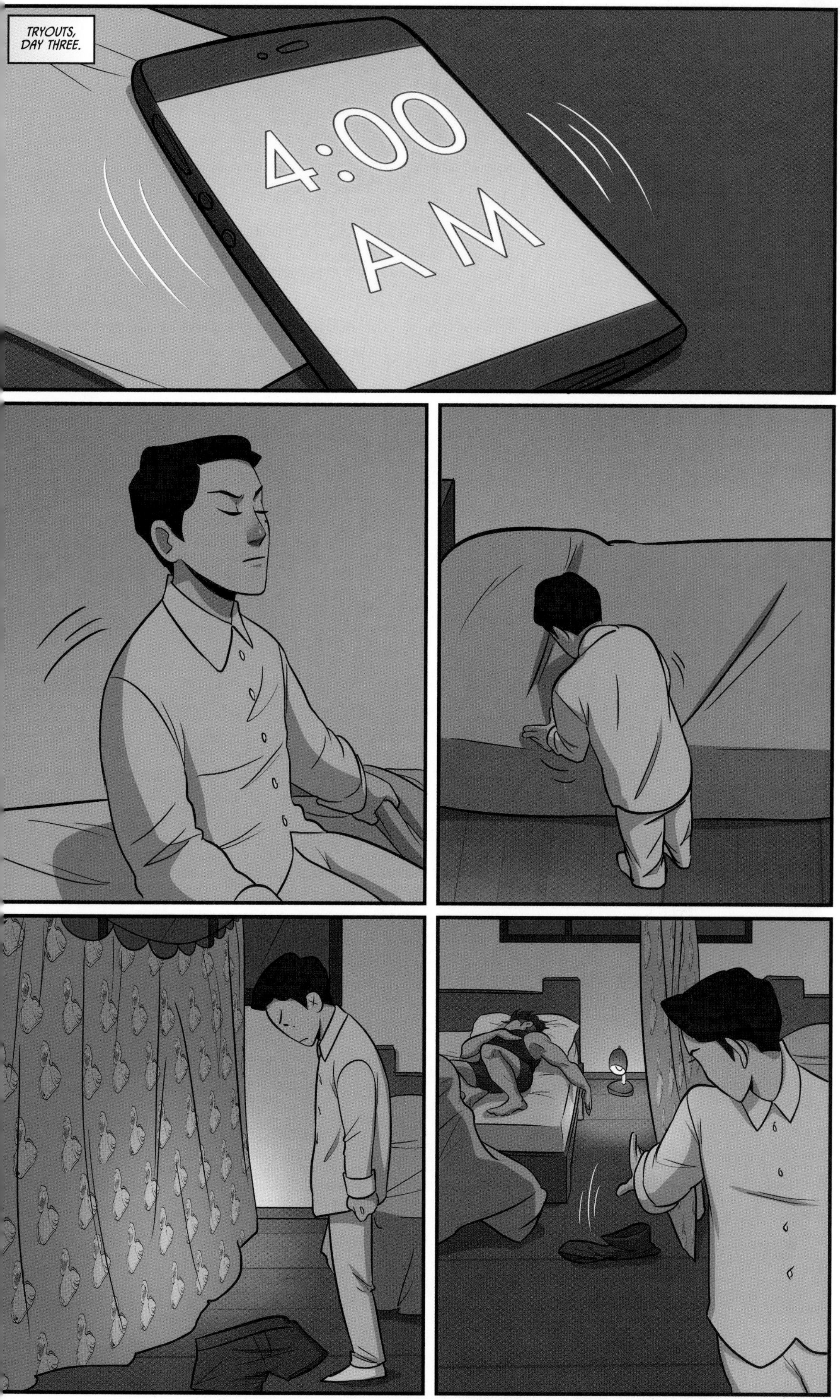
TRYOUTS, DAY THREE.
4:00 AM

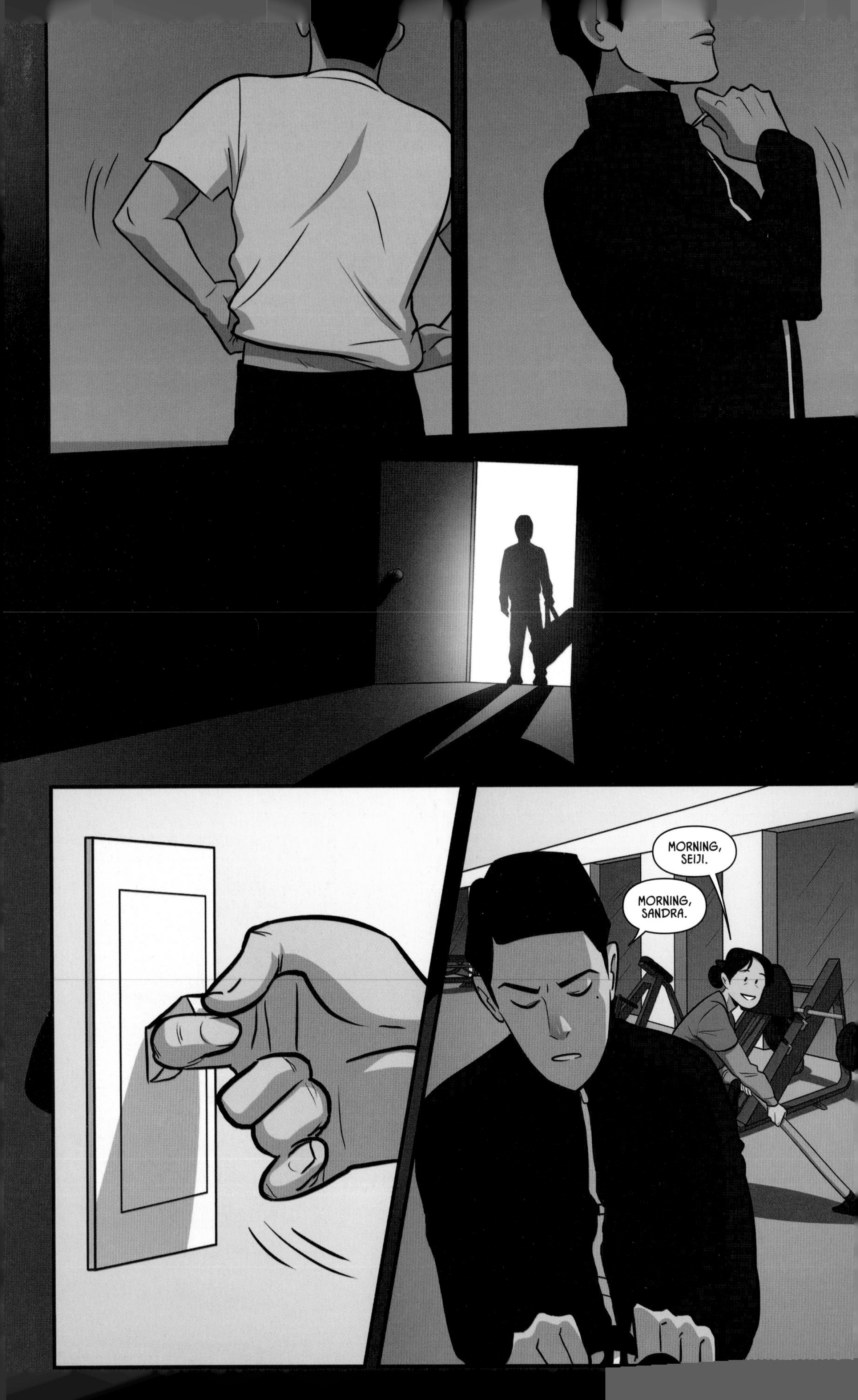
MORNING, SEIJI.
MORNING, SANDRA.

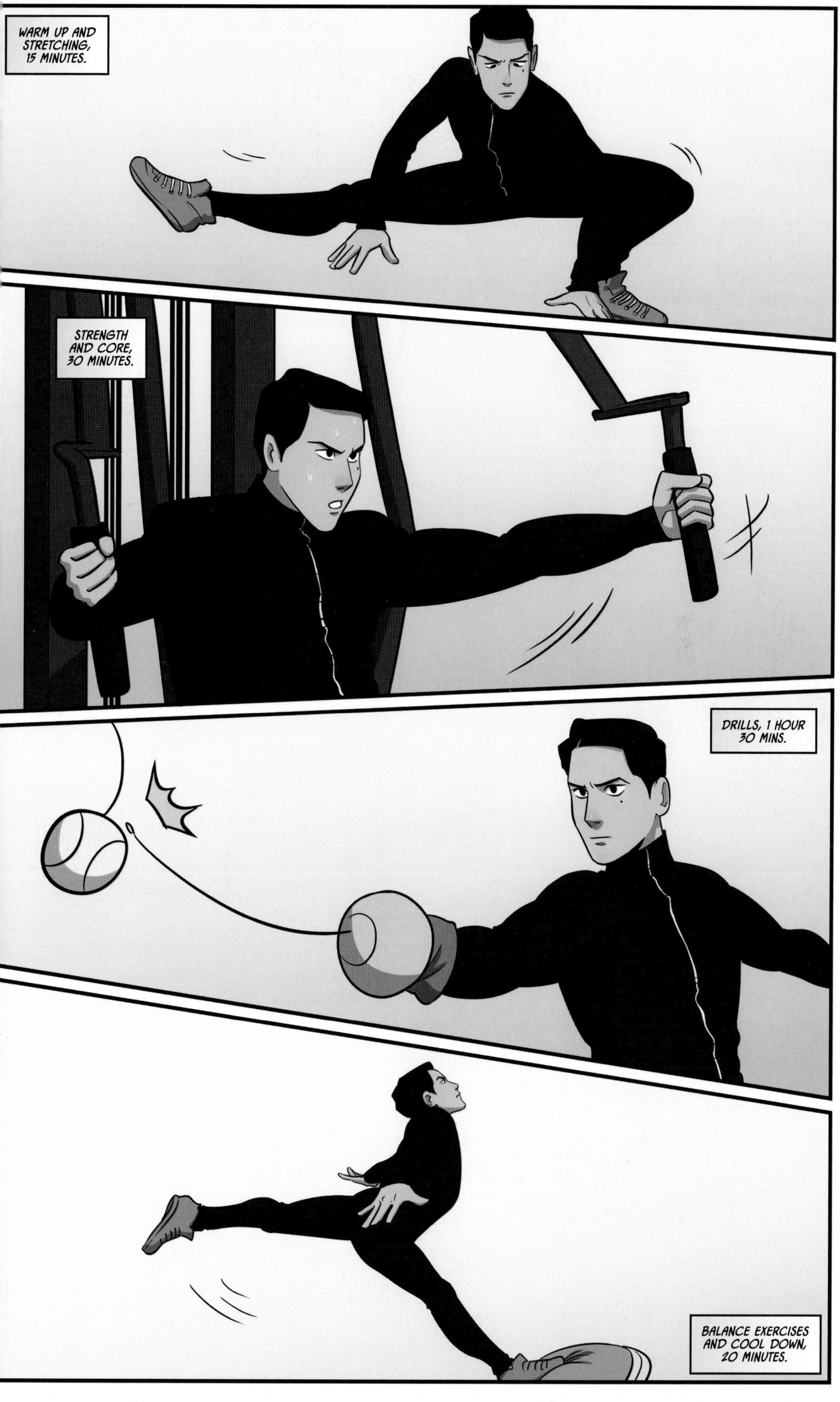
WARM UP AND STRETCHING, 15 MINUTES.
STRENGTH AND CORE, 30 MINUTES.
DRILLS, 1 HOUR 30 MINS.
BALANCE EXERCISES AND COOL DOWN, 20 MINUTES.

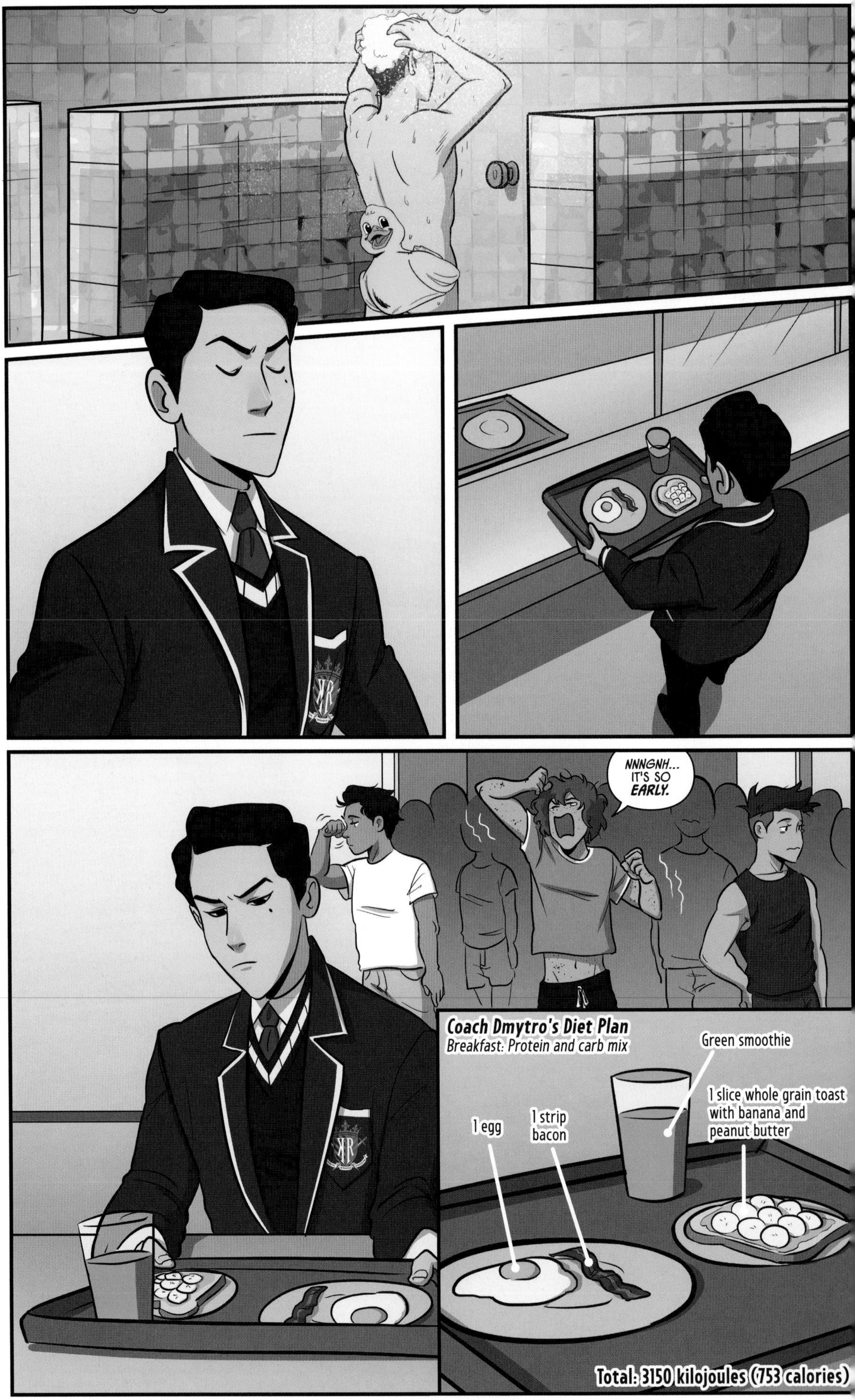
NNNGNH... IT'S SO EARLY.
Coach Dmytro's Diet Plan
Breakfast: Protein and carb mix
Green smoothie
1 slice whole grain toast with banana and peanut butter
1 egg
1 strip bacon
Total: 3150 kilojoules (753 calories)

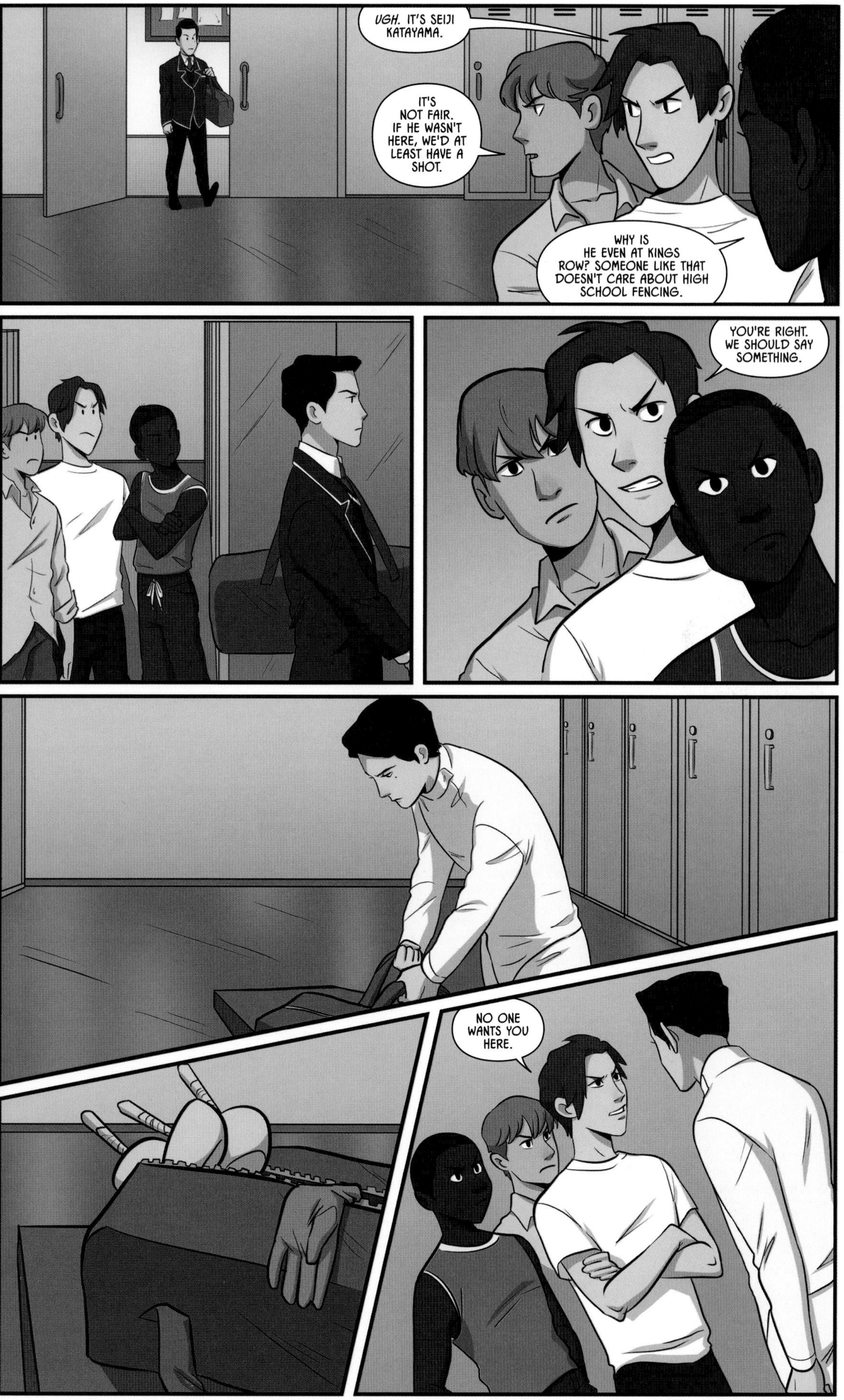
UGH. IT'S SEIJI KATAYAMA.
IT'S NOT FAIR. IF HE WASN'T HERE, WE'D AT LEAST HAVE A SHOT.
WHY IS HE EVEN AT KINGS ROW? SOMEONE LIKE THAT DOESN'T CARE ABOUT HIGH SCHOOL FENCING.
YOU'RE RIGHT. WE SHOULD SAY SOMETHING.
NO ONE WANTS YOU HERE.

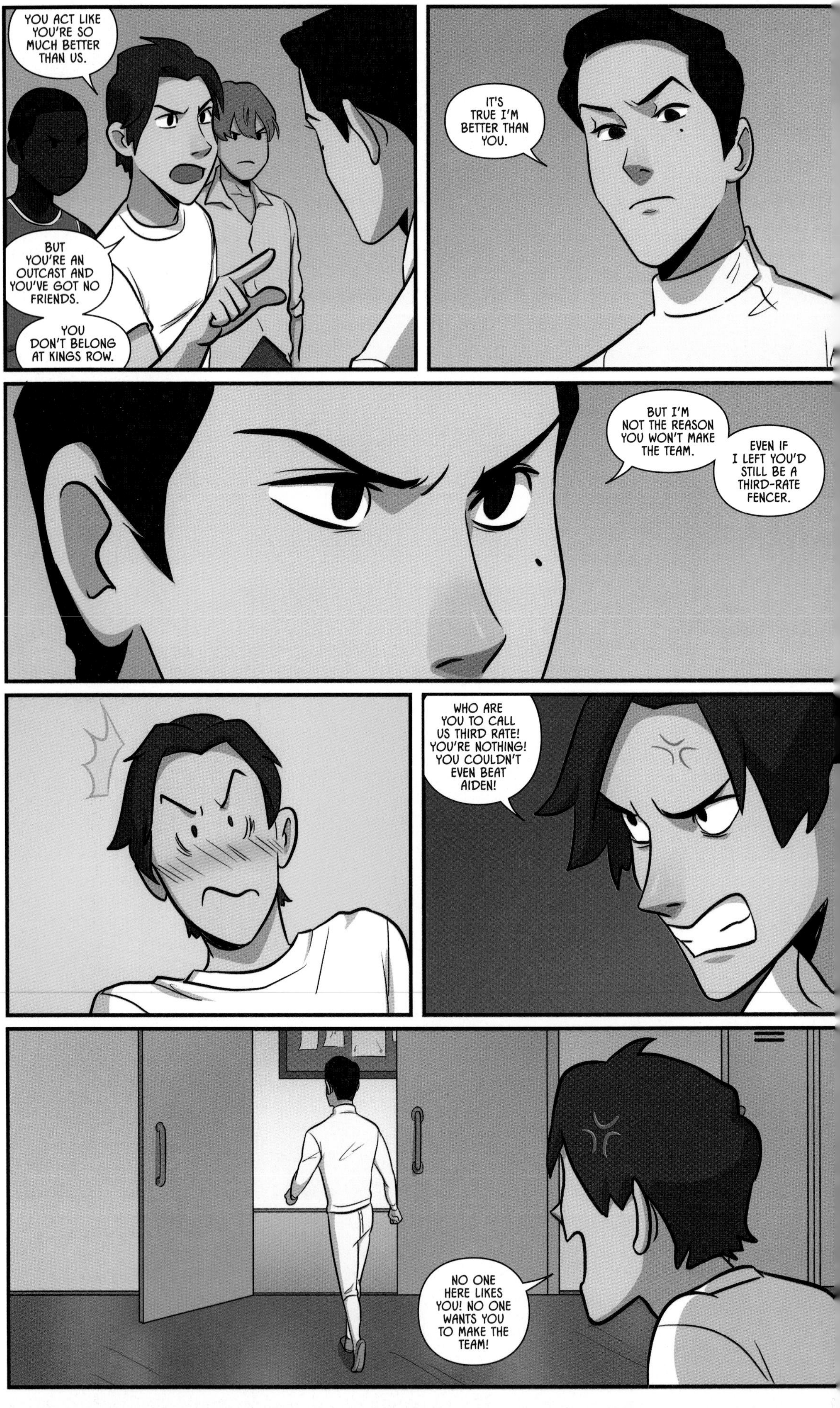
YOU ACT LIKE YOU'RE SO MUCH BETTER THAN US.
BUT YOU'RE AN OUTCAST AND YOU'VE GOT NO FRIENDS.
YOU DON'T BELONG AT KINGS ROW.
IT'S TRUE I'M BETTER THAN YOU.
BUT I'M NOT THE REASON YOU WON'T MAKE THE TEAM.
EVEN IF I LEFT YOU'D STILL BE A THIRD-RATE FENCER.
WHO ARE YOU TO CALL US THIRD RATE! YOU'RE NOTHING! YOU COULDN'T EVEN BEAT AIDEN!
NO ONE HERE LIKES YOU! NO ONE WANTS YOU TO MAKE THE TEAM!

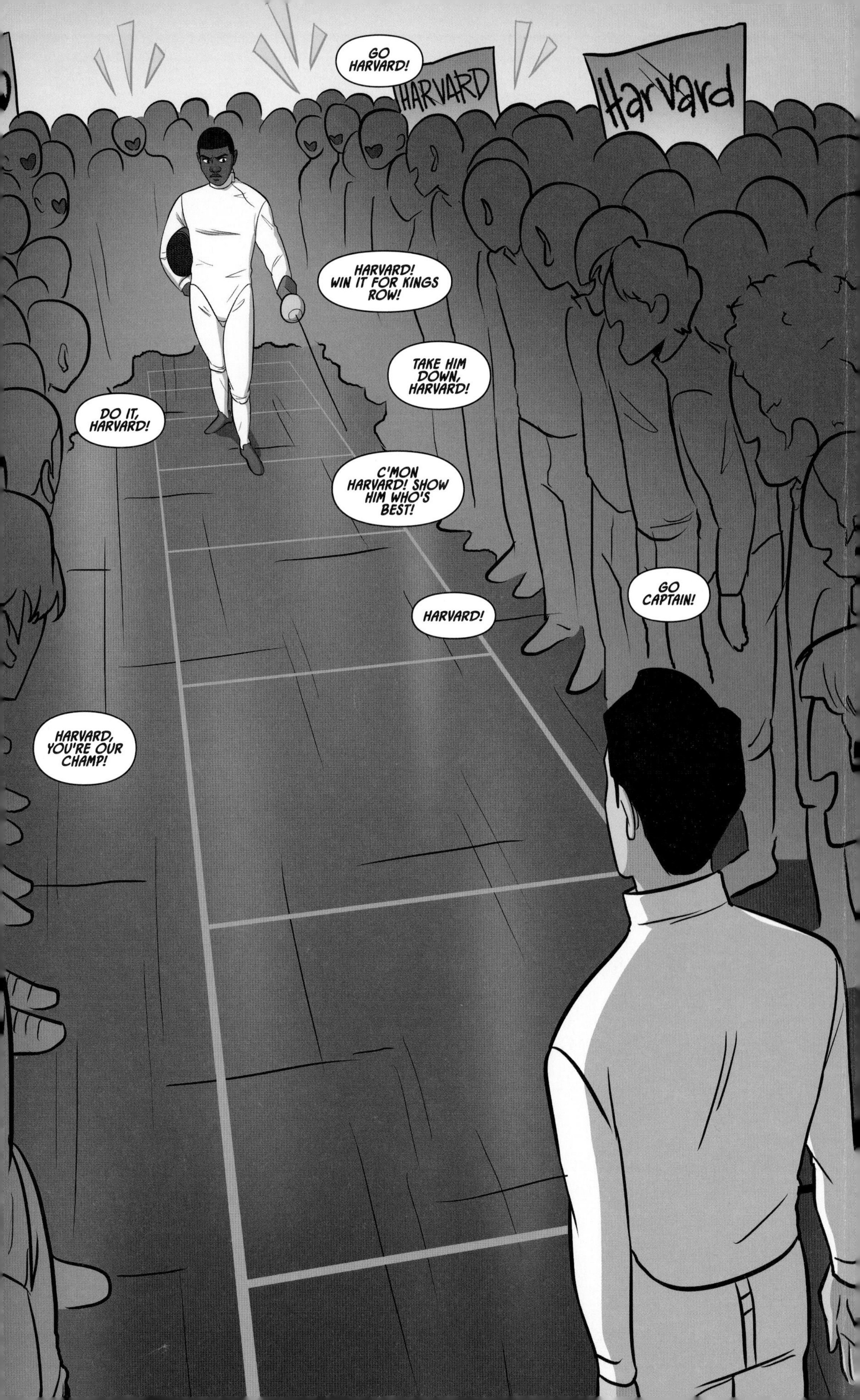
HARVARD
Harvard
GO HARVARD!
HARVARD! WIN IT FOR KINGS ROW!
TAKE HIM DOWN, HARVARD!
DO IT, HARVARD!
C'MON HARVARD! SHOW HIM WHO'S BEST!
GO CAPTAIN!
HARVARD!
HARVARD, YOU'RE OUR CHAMP!

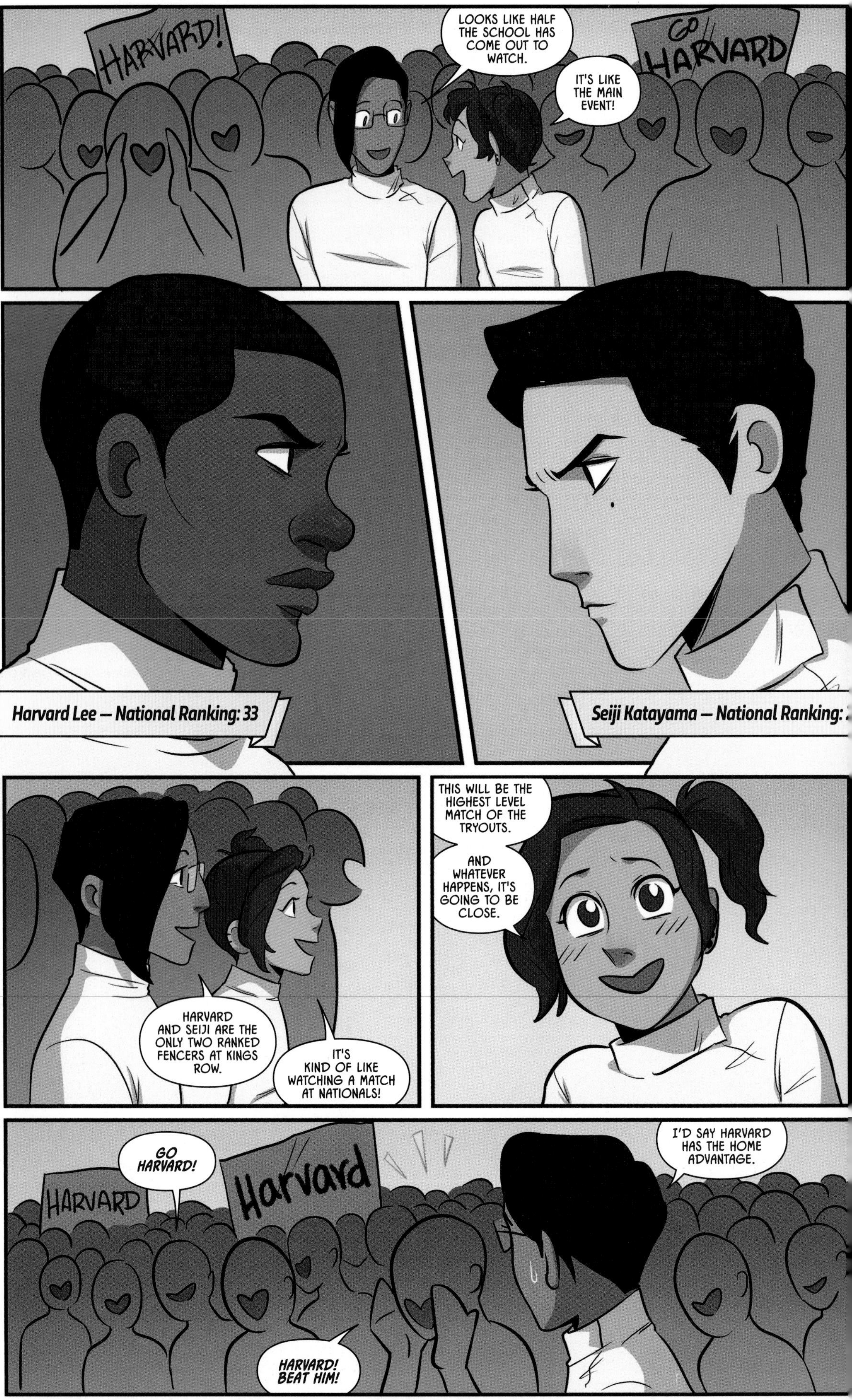
HARVARD!
LOOKS LIKE HALF THE SCHOOL HAS COME OUT TO WATCH.
GO HARVARD
IT'S LIKE THE MAIN EVENT!
Harvard Lee — National Ranking: 33
Seiji Katayama — National Ranking:
HARVARD AND SEIJI ARE THE ONLY TWO RANKED FENCERS AT KINGS ROW.
IT'S KIND OF LIKE WATCHING A MATCH AT NATIONALS!
THIS WILL BE THE HIGHEST LEVEL MATCH OF THE TRYOUTS.
AND WHATEVER HAPPENS, IT'S GOING TO BE CLOSE.
HARVARD
GO HARVARD!
Harvard
I'D SAY HARVARD HAS THE HOME ADVANTAGE.
HARVARD! BEAT HIM!

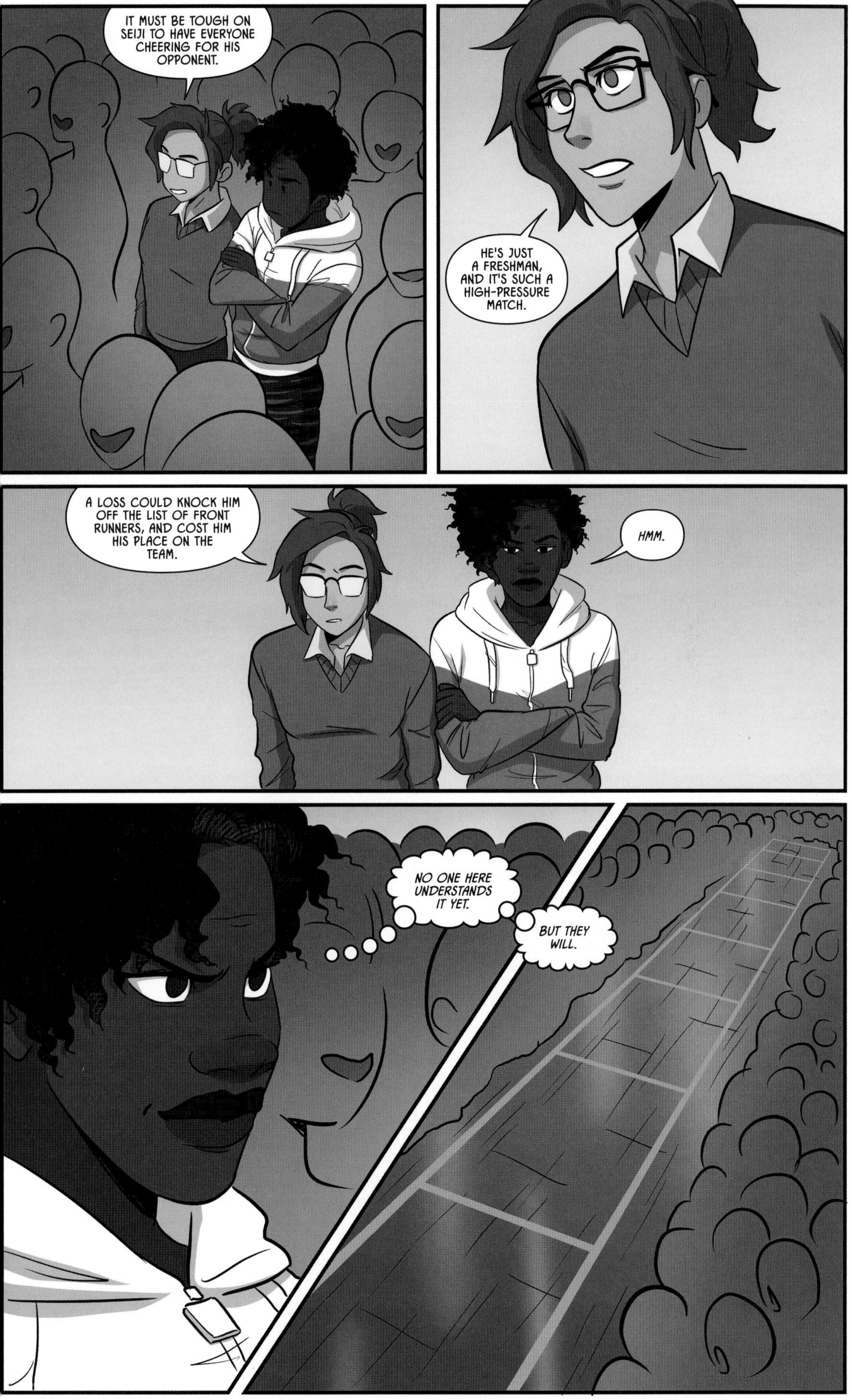
IT MUST BE TOUGH ON SEIJI TO HAVE EVERYONE CHEERING FOR HIS OPPONENT.
HE'S JUST A FRESHMAN, AND IT'S SUCH A HIGH-PRESSURE MATCH.
A LOSS COULD KNOCK HIM OFF THE LIST OF FRONT RUNNERS, AND COST HIM HIS PLACE ON THE TEAM.
HMM.
NO ONE HERE UNDERSTANDS IT YET.
BUT THEY WILL.

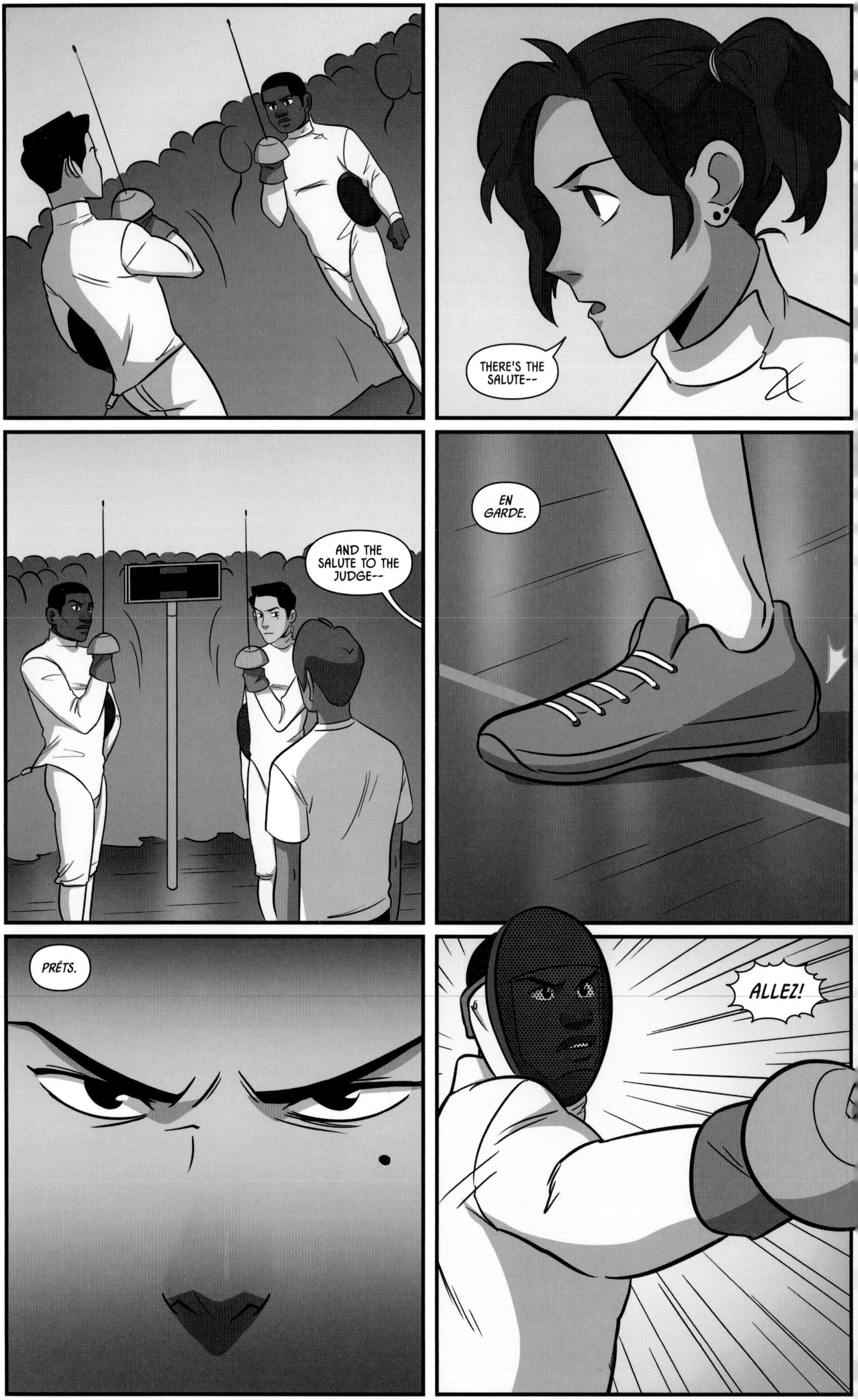
THERE'S THE SALUTE--
AND THE SALUTE TO THE JUDGE--
EN GARDE.
PRÊTS.
ALLEZ!

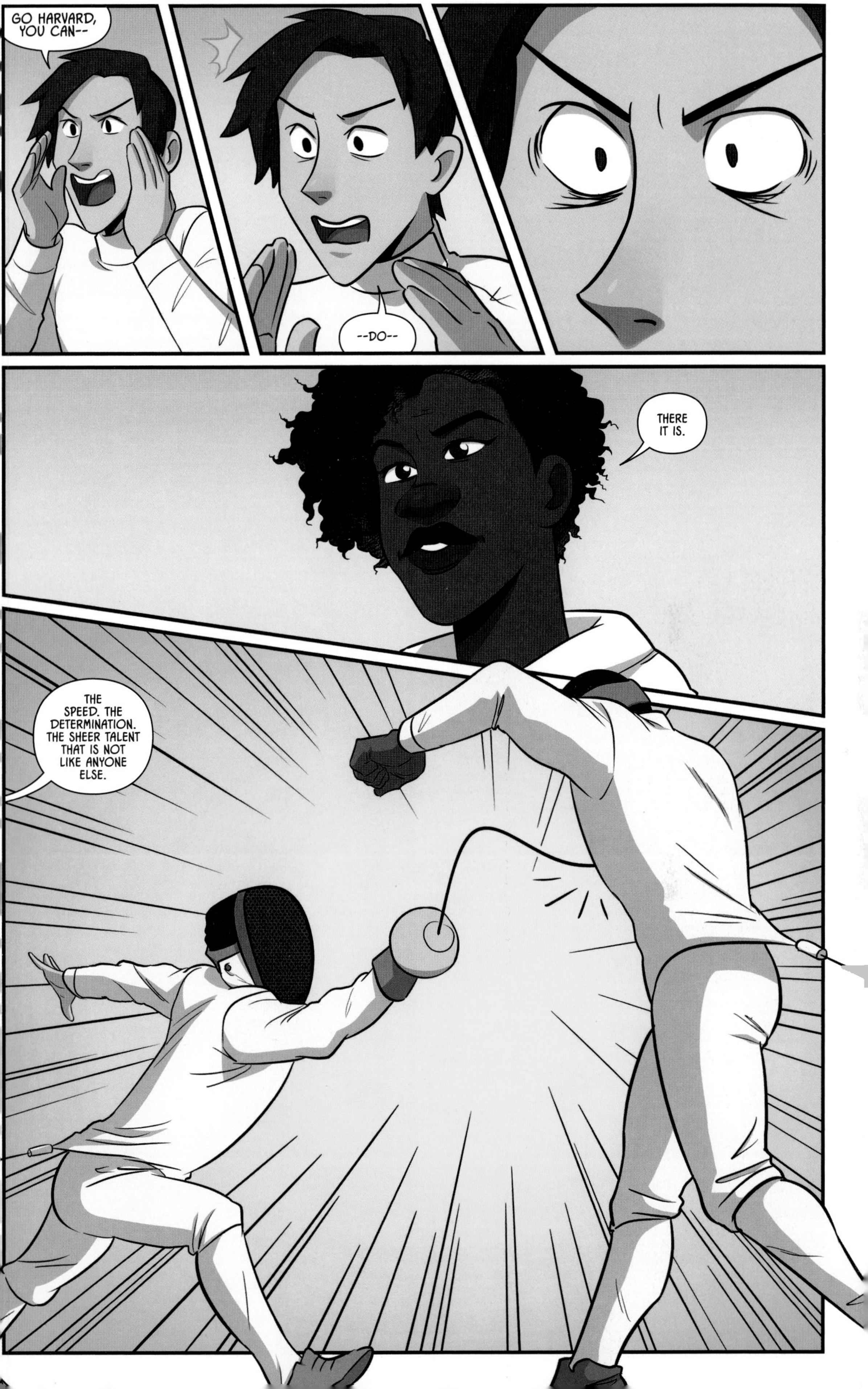
GO HARVARD, YOU CAN--
--DO--
THERE IT IS.
THE SPEED. THE DETERMINATION. THE SHEER TALENT THAT IS NOT LIKE ANYONE ELSE.

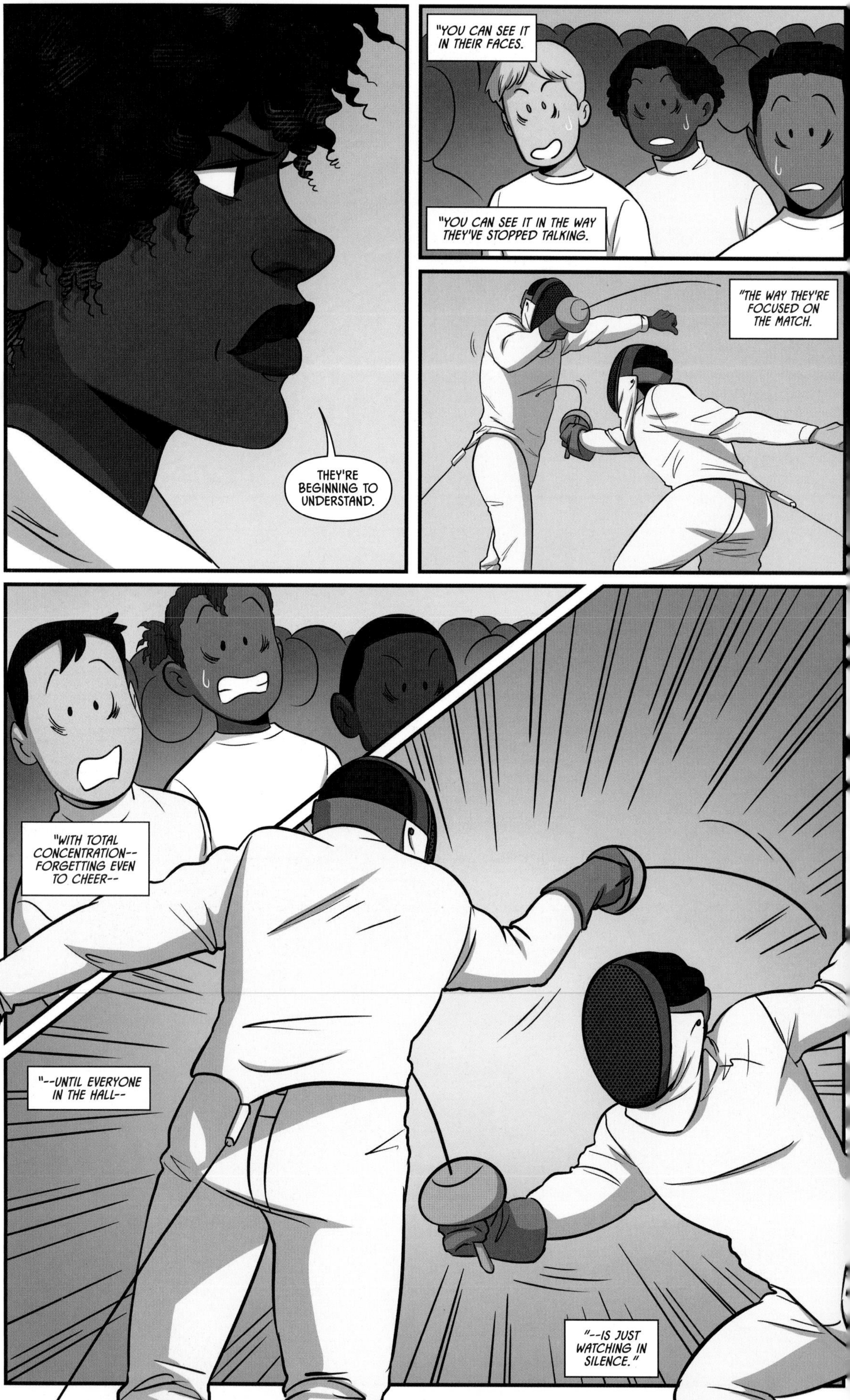
THEY'RE BEGINNING TO UNDERSTAND.
"YOU CAN SEE IT IN THEIR FACES.
"YOU CAN SEE IT IN THE WAY THEY'VE STOPPED TALKING.
"THE WAY THEY'RE FOCUSED ON THE MATCH.
"WITH TOTAL CONCENTRATION-- FORGETTING EVEN TO CHEER--
"--UNTIL EVERYONE IN THE HALL--
"--IS JUST WATCHING IN SILENCE."

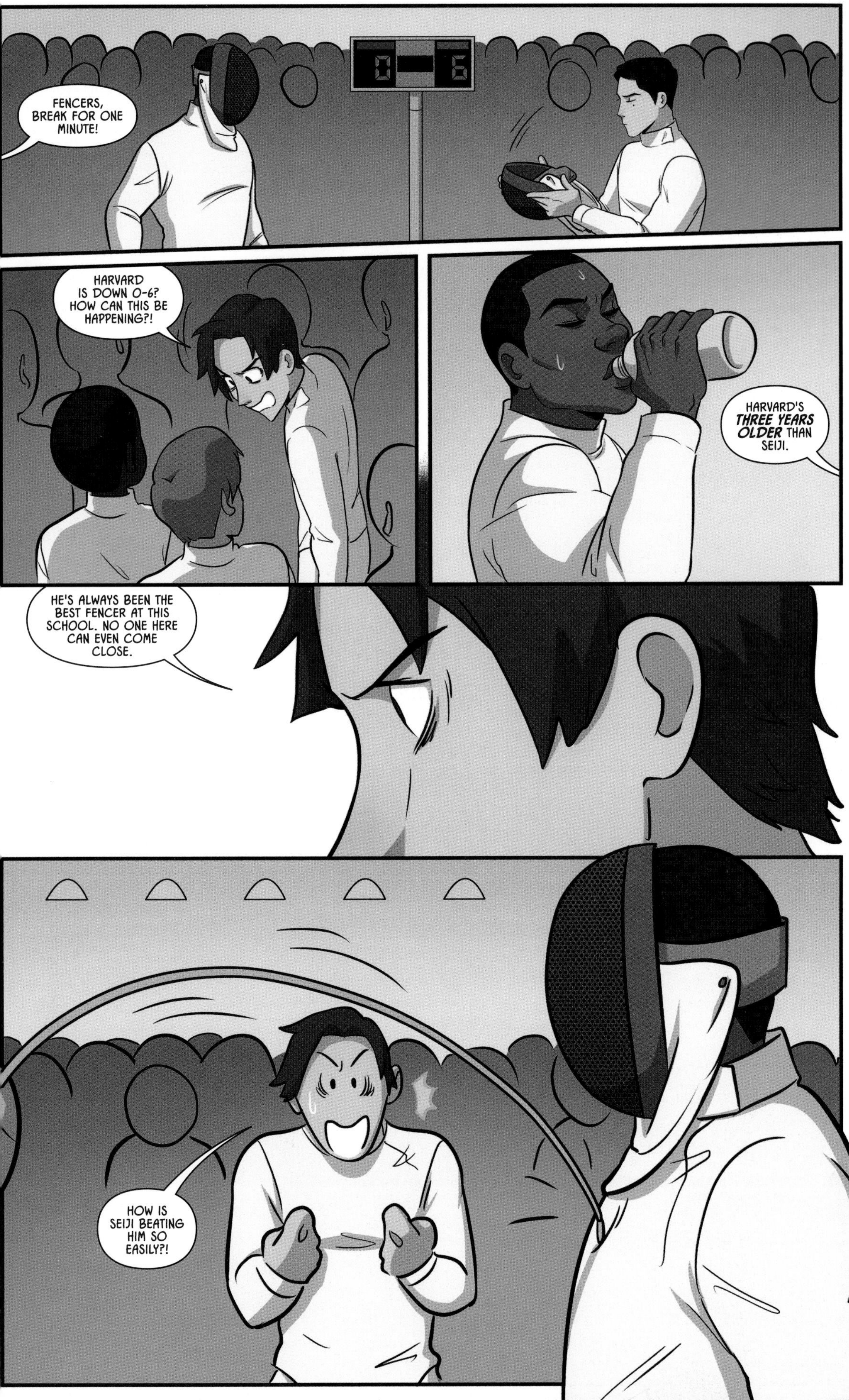
0-6
FENCERS, BREAK FOR ONE MINUTE!
HARVARD IS DOWN 0-6? HOW CAN THIS BE HAPPENING?!
HARVARD'S **THREE YEARS OLDER** THAN SEIJI.
HE'S ALWAYS BEEN THE BEST FENCER AT THIS SCHOOL. NO ONE HERE CAN EVEN COME CLOSE.
HOW IS SEIJI BEATING HIM SO EASILY?!

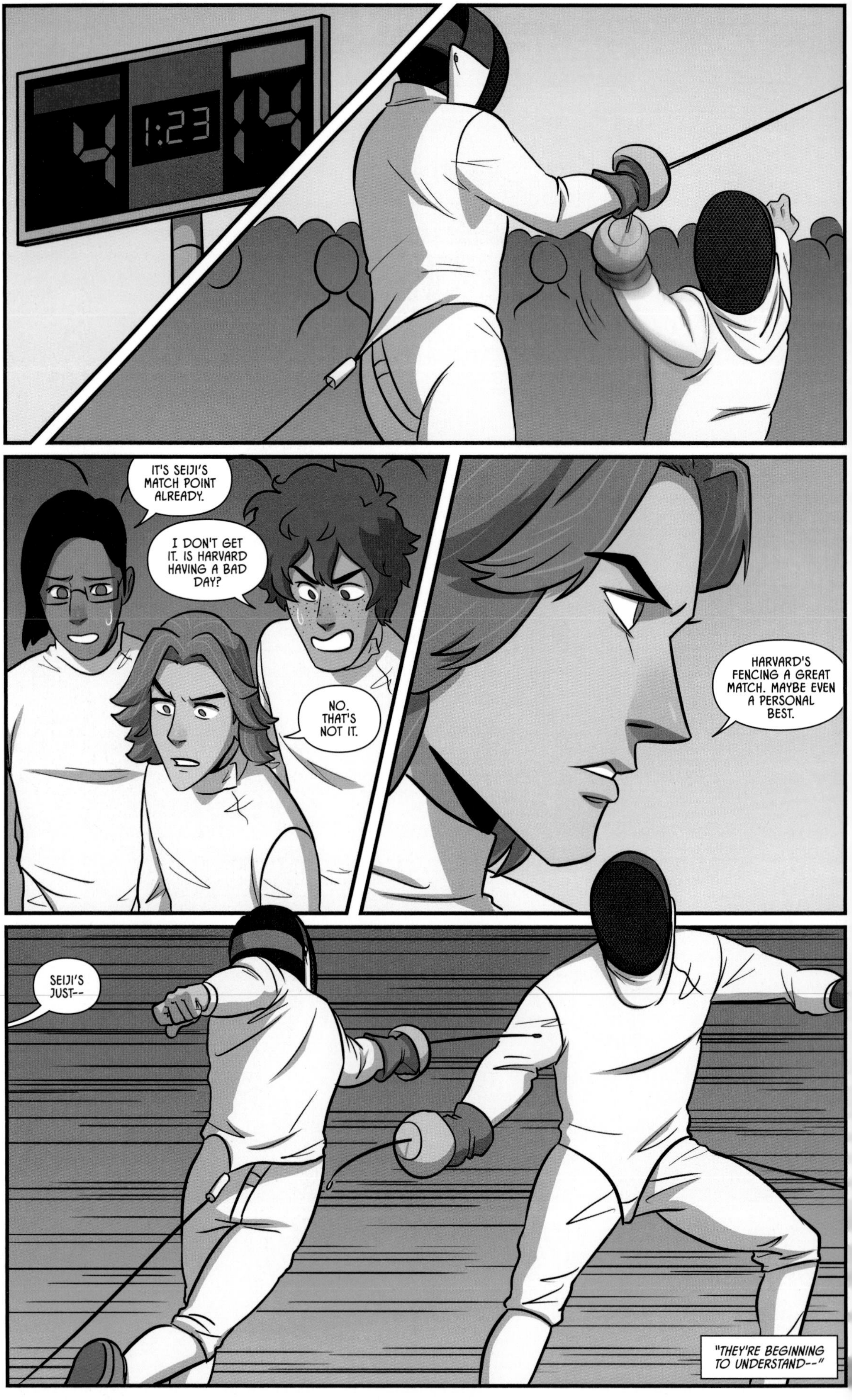
4
1:23
14
IT'S SEIJI'S MATCH POINT ALREADY.
I DON'T GET IT. IS HARVARD HAVING A BAD DAY?
NO. THAT'S NOT IT.
HARVARD'S FENCING A GREAT MATCH. MAYBE EVEN A PERSONAL BEST.
SEIJI'S JUST--
"THEY'RE BEGINNING TO UNDERSTAND--"

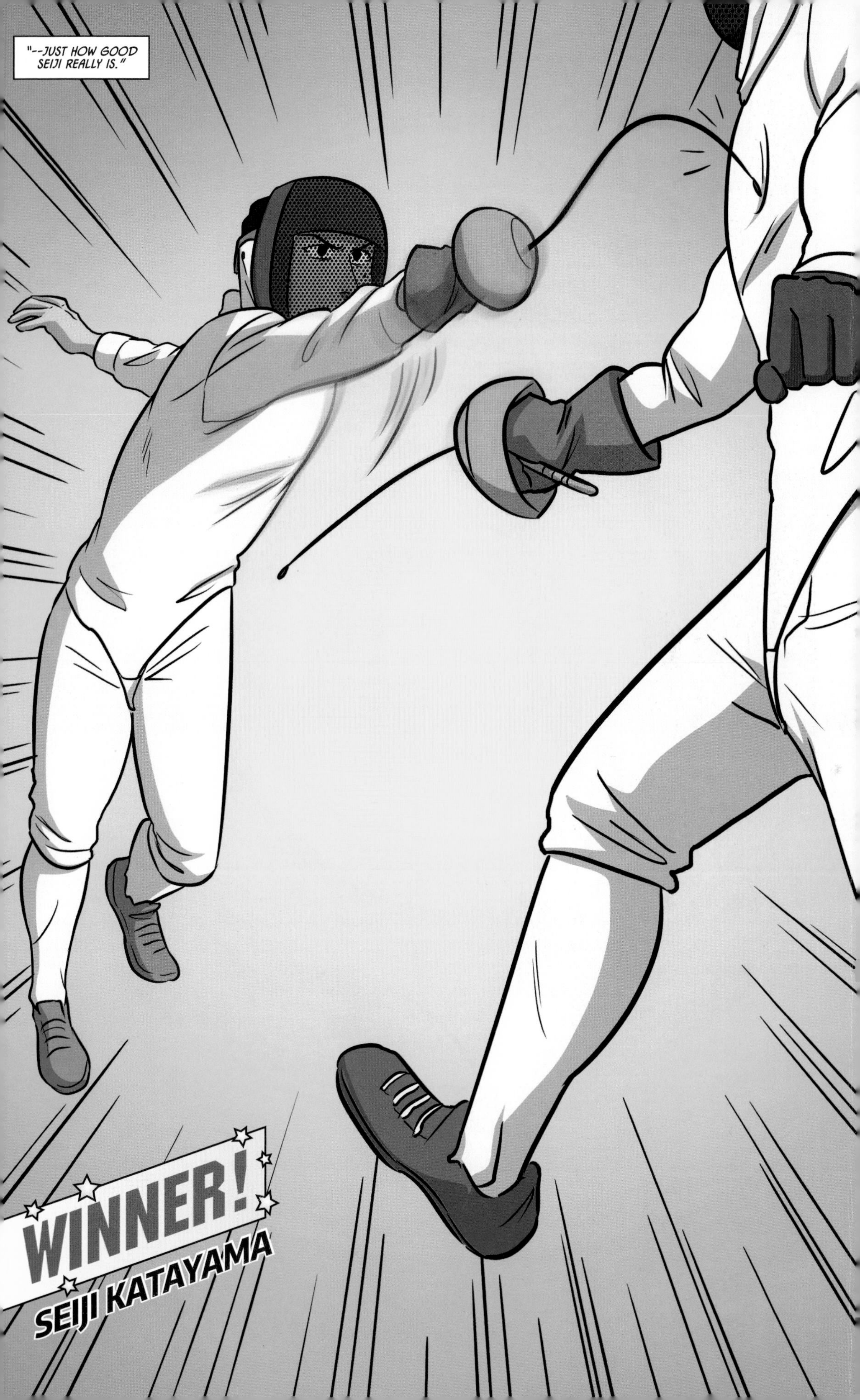
"--JUST HOW GOOD SEIJI REALLY IS."
WINNER!
SEIJI KATAYAMA

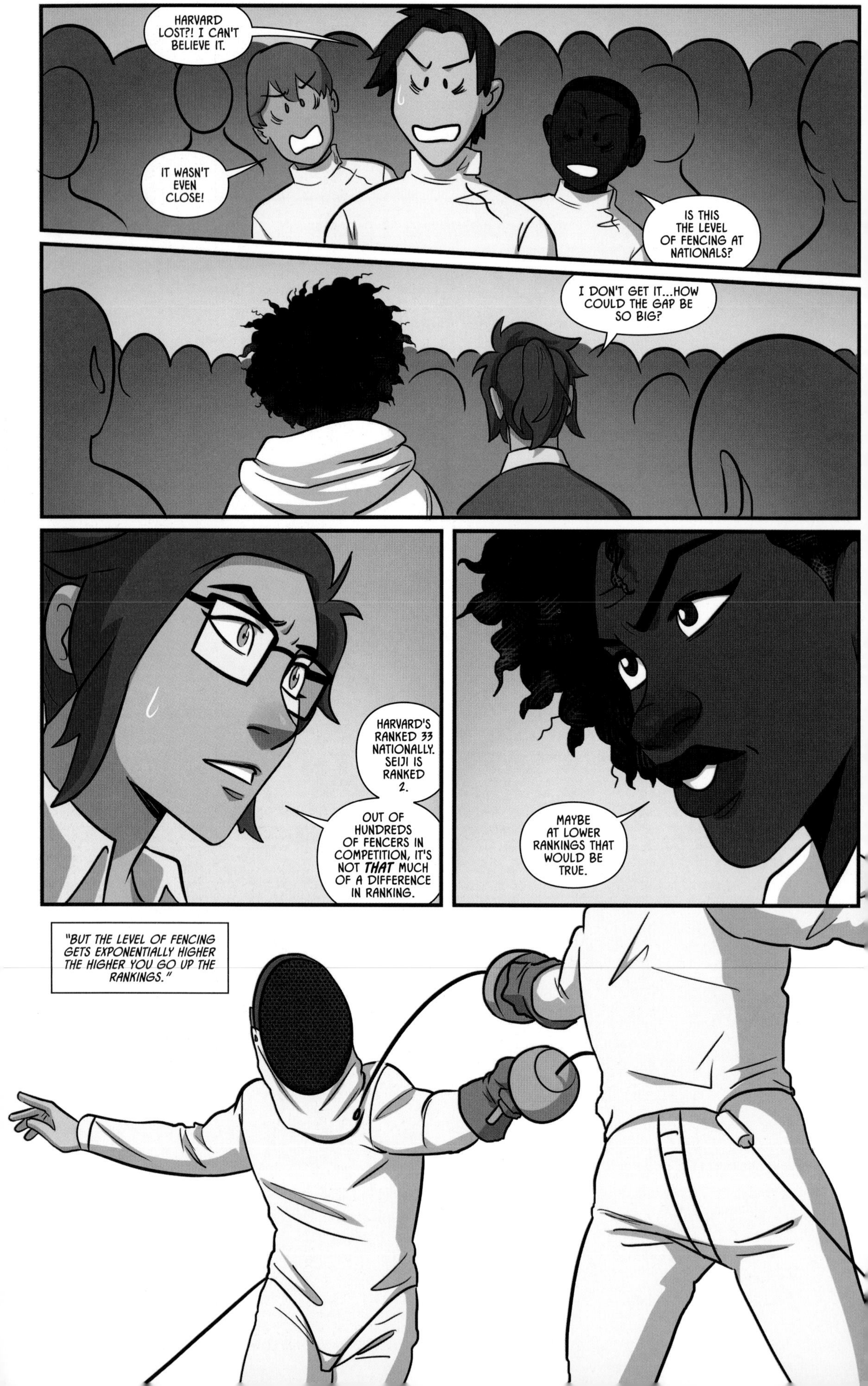
HARVARD LOST?! I CAN'T BELIEVE IT.
IT WASN'T EVEN CLOSE!
IS THIS THE LEVEL OF FENCING AT NATIONALS?
I DON'T GET IT...HOW COULD THE GAP BE SO BIG?
HARVARD'S RANKED 33 NATIONALLY. SEIJI IS RANKED 2.
OUT OF HUNDREDS OF FENCERS IN COMPETITION, IT'S NOT THAT MUCH OF A DIFFERENCE IN RANKING.
MAYBE AT LOWER RANKINGS THAT WOULD BE TRUE.
"BUT THE LEVEL OF FENCING GETS EXPONENTIALLY HIGHER THE HIGHER YOU GO UP THE RANKINGS."

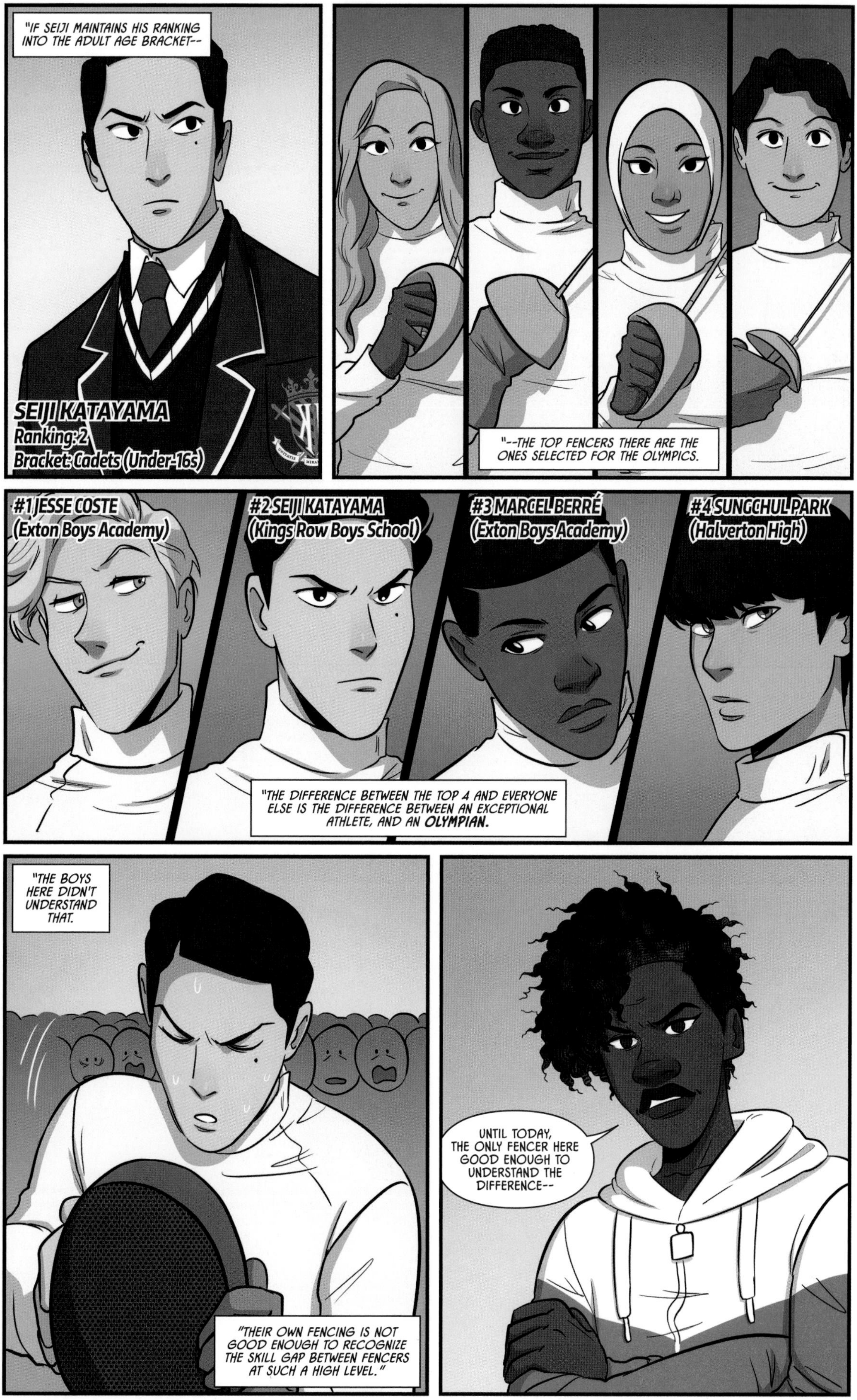
"IF SEIJI MAINTAINS HIS RANKING INTO THE ADULT AGE BRACKET--
SEIJI KATAYAMA
Ranking: 2
Bracket: Cadets (Under-16s)
"--THE TOP FENCERS THERE ARE THE ONES SELECTED FOR THE OLYMPICS.
#1 JESSE COSTE
(Exton Boys Academy)
#2 SEIJI KATAYAMA
(Kings Row Boys School)
#3 MARCEL BERRÉ
(Exton Boys Academy)
#4 SUNGCHUL PARK
(Halverton High)
"THE DIFFERENCE BETWEEN THE TOP 4 AND EVERYONE ELSE IS THE DIFFERENCE BETWEEN AN EXCEPTIONAL ATHLETE, AND AN OLYMPIAN.
"THE BOYS HERE DIDN'T UNDERSTAND THAT.
"THEIR OWN FENCING IS NOT GOOD ENOUGH TO RECOGNIZE THE SKILL GAP BETWEEN FENCERS AT SUCH A HIGH LEVEL."
UNTIL TODAY, THE ONLY FENCER HERE GOOD ENOUGH TO UNDERSTAND THE DIFFERENCE--

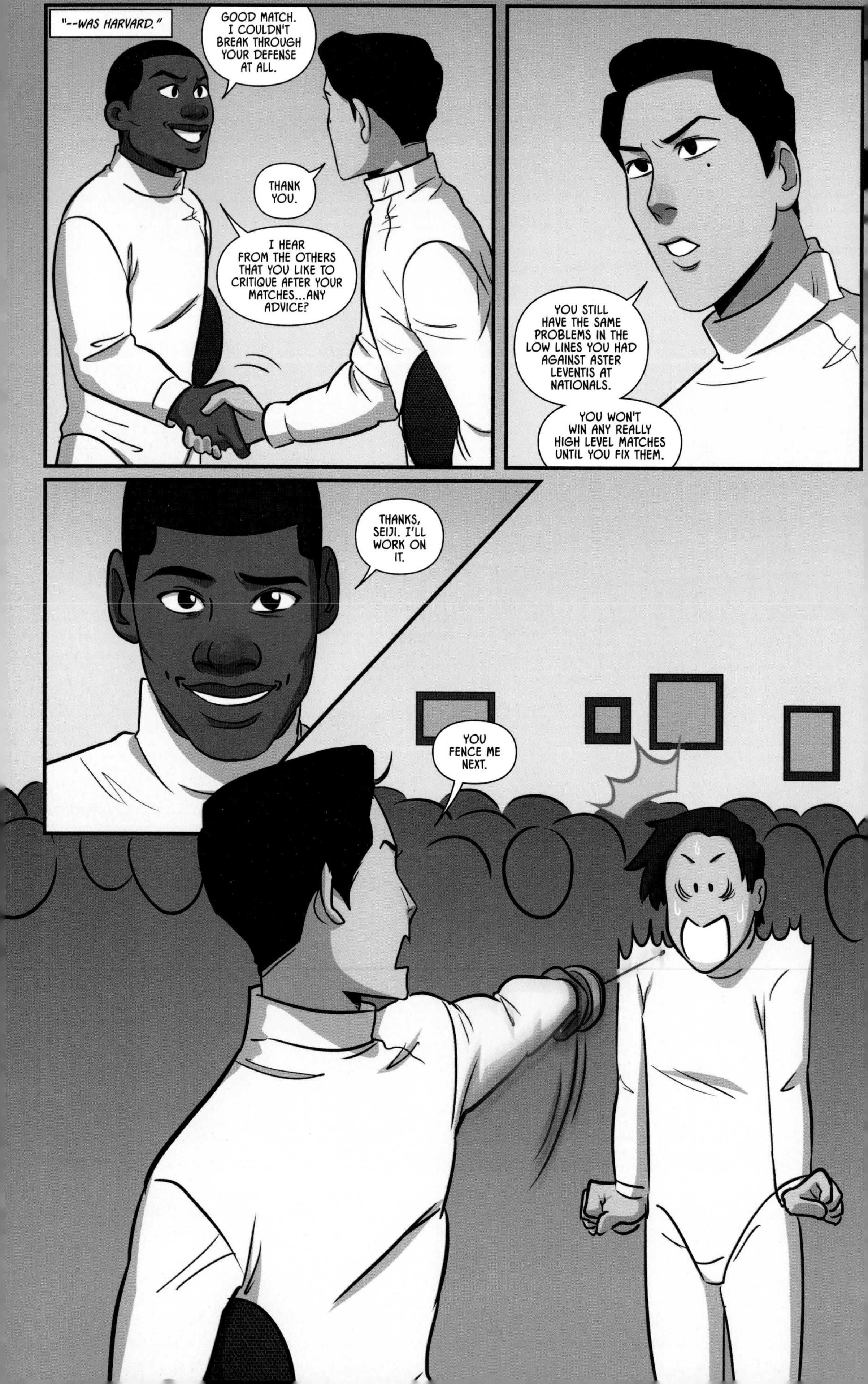
"--WAS HARVARD."
GOOD MATCH. I COULDN'T BREAK THROUGH YOUR DEFENSE AT ALL.
THANK YOU.
I HEAR FROM THE OTHERS THAT YOU LIKE TO CRITIQUE AFTER YOUR MATCHES...ANY ADVICE?
YOU STILL HAVE THE SAME PROBLEMS IN THE LOW LINES YOU HAD AGAINST ASTER LEVENTIS AT NATIONALS.
YOU WON'T WIN ANY REALLY HIGH LEVEL MATCHES UNTIL YOU FIX THEM.
THANKS, SEIJI. I'LL WORK ON IT.
YOU FENCE ME NEXT.

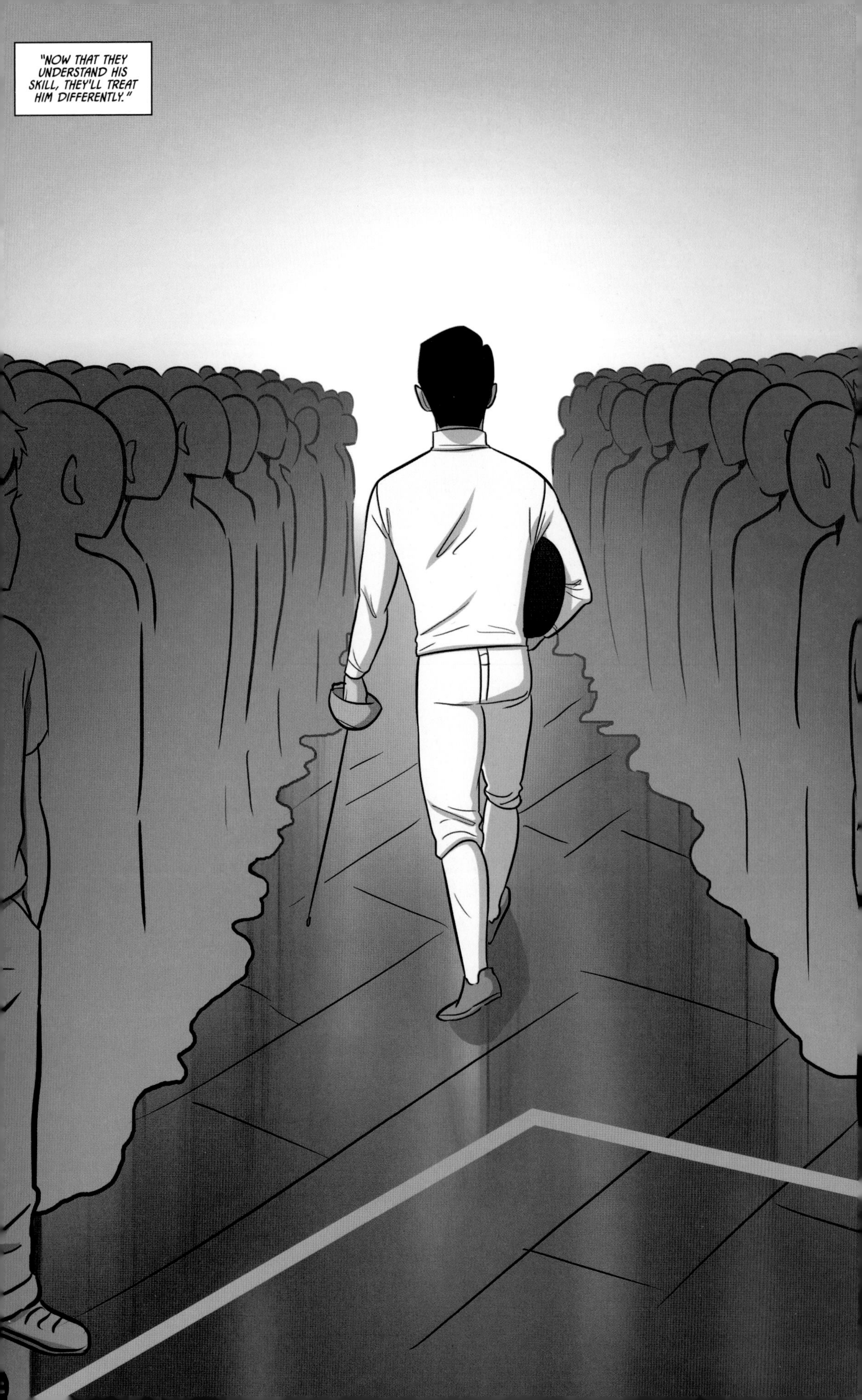
"NOW THAT THEY UNDERSTAND HIS SKILL, THEY'LL TREAT HIM DIFFERENTLY."

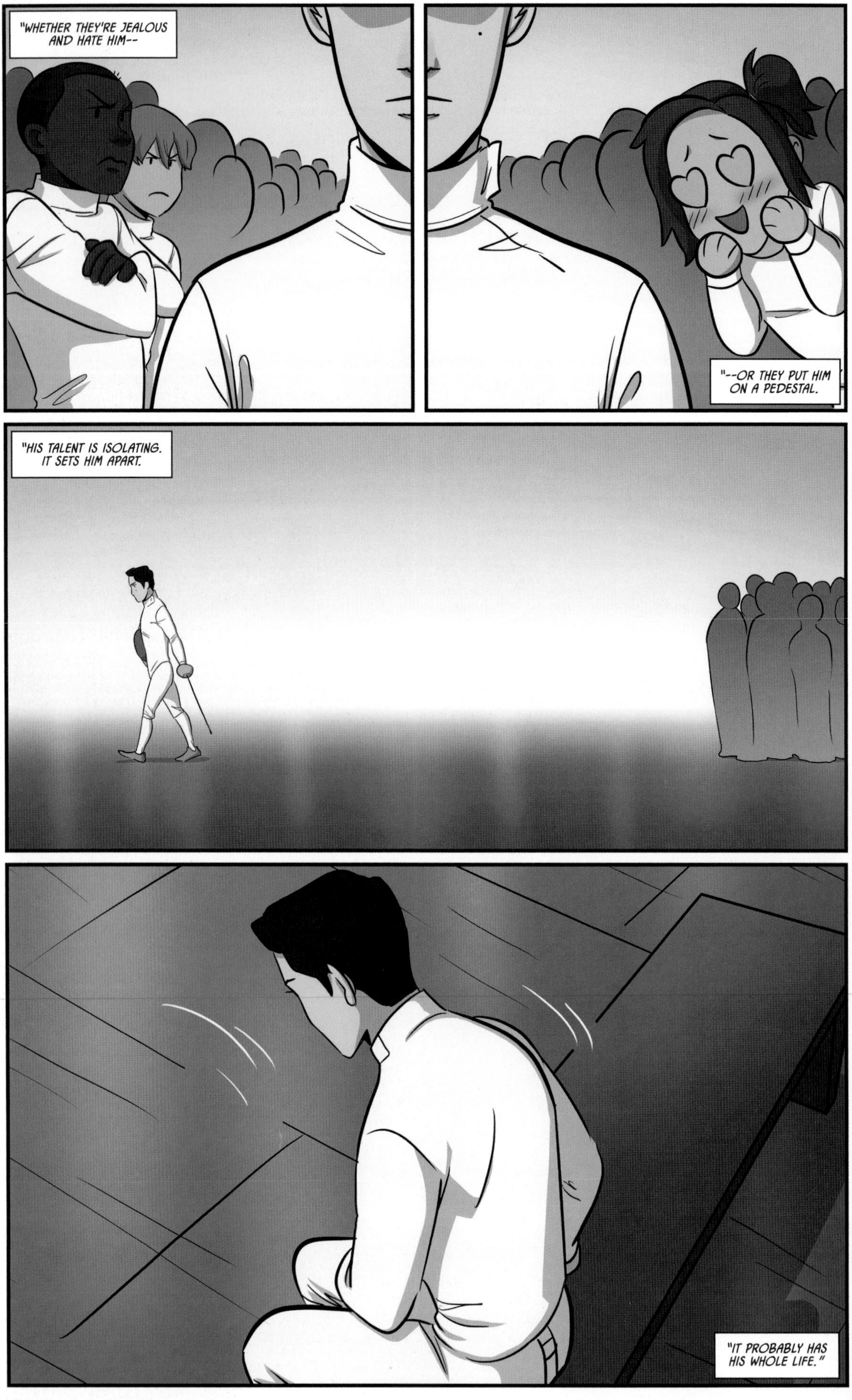
"WHETHER THEY'RE JEALOUS AND HATE HIM--
"--OR THEY PUT HIM ON A PEDESTAL.
"HIS TALENT IS ISOLATING. IT SETS HIM APART.
"IT PROBABLY HAS HIS WHOLE LIFE."

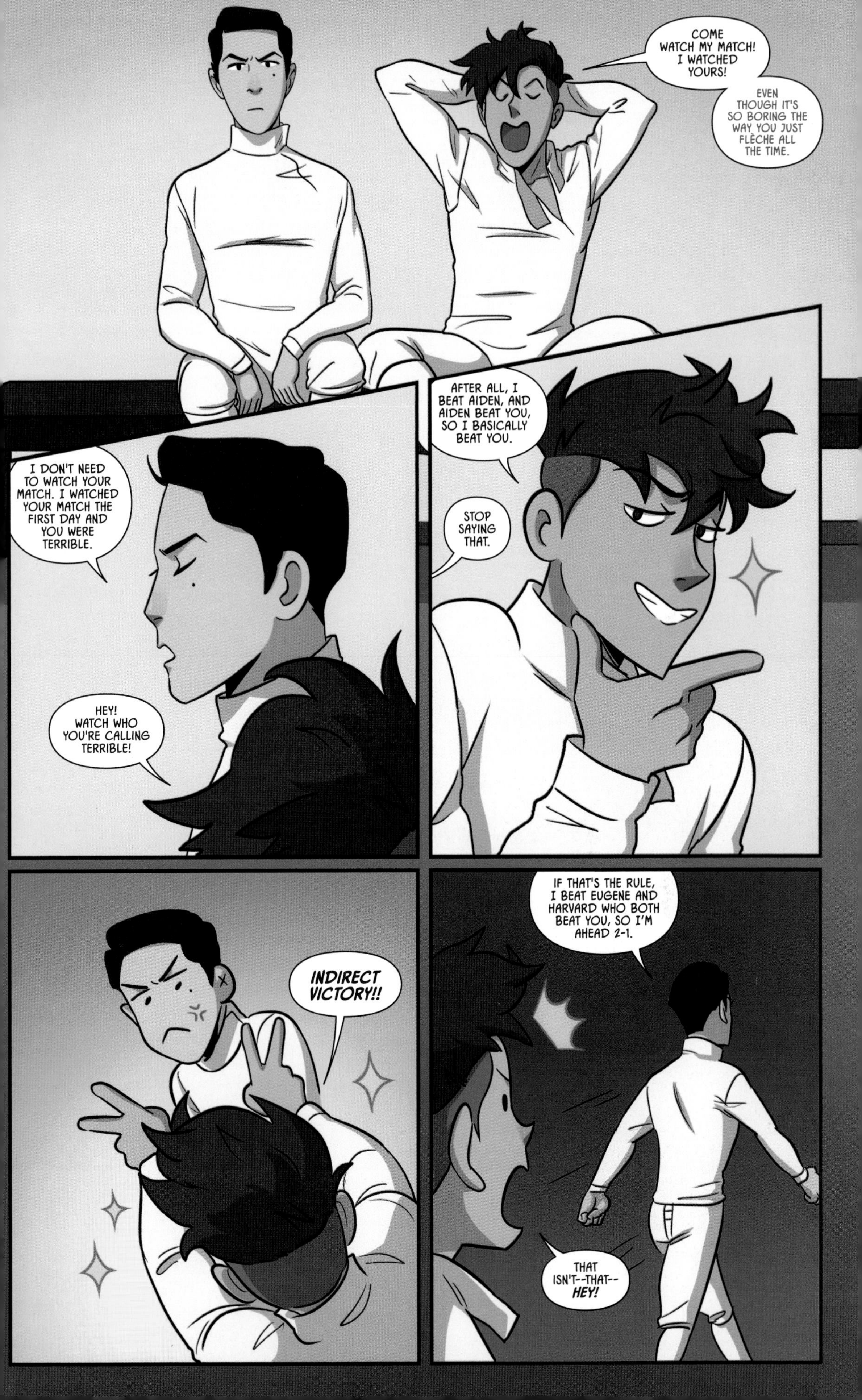

COME WATCH MY MATCH! I WATCHED YOURS!
EVEN THOUGH IT'S SO BORING THE WAY YOU JUST FLÈCHE ALL THE TIME.
I DON'T NEED TO WATCH YOUR MATCH. I WATCHED YOUR MATCH THE FIRST DAY AND YOU WERE TERRIBLE.
HEY! WATCH WHO YOU'RE CALLING TERRIBLE!
AFTER ALL, I BEAT AIDEN, AND AIDEN BEAT YOU, SO I BASICALLY BEAT YOU.
STOP SAYING THAT.
INDIRECT VICTORY!!
IF THAT'S THE RULE, I BEAT EUGENE AND HARVARD WHO BOTH BEAT YOU, SO I'M AHEAD 2-1.
THAT ISN'T--THAT-- HEY!

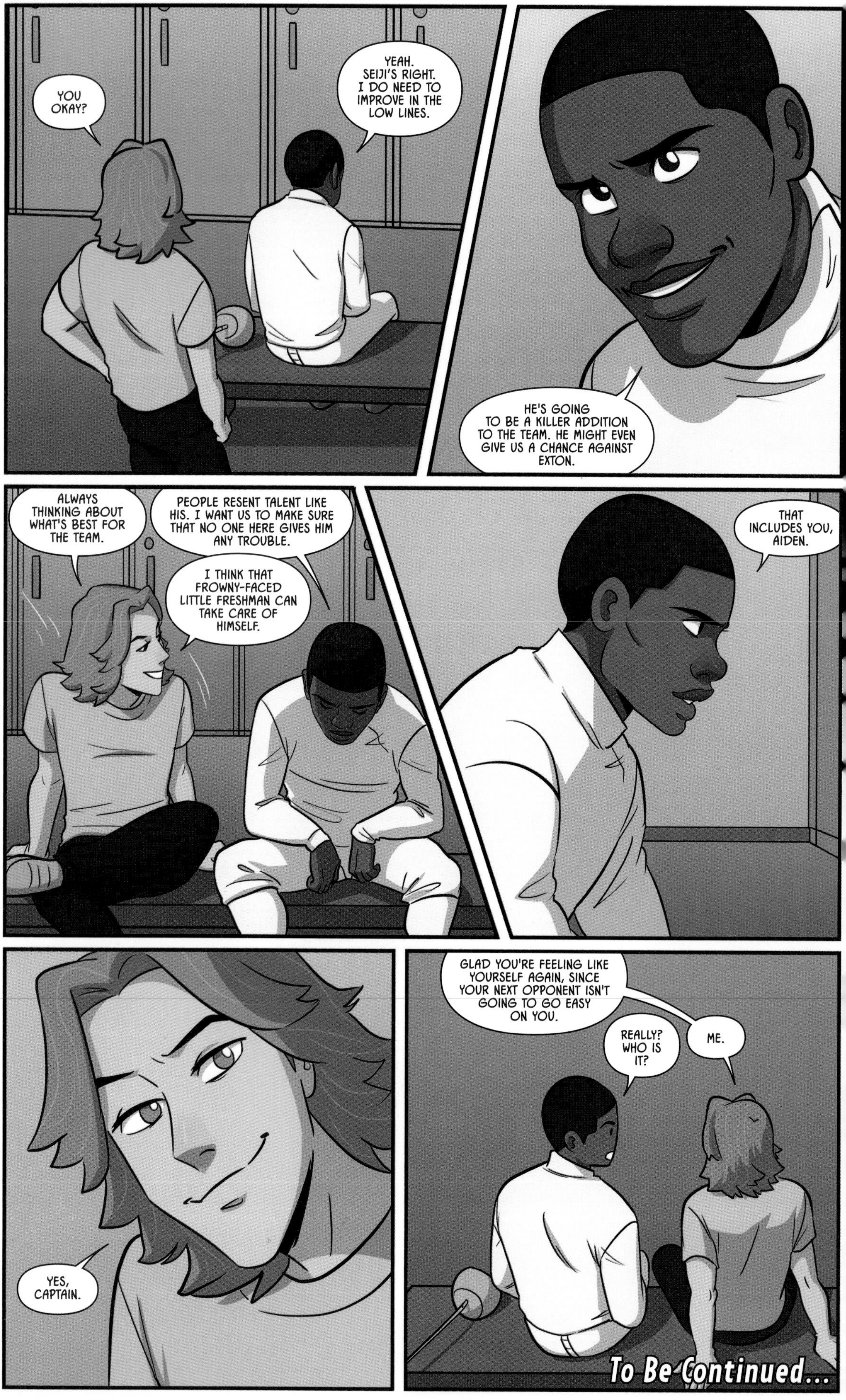
YOU OKAY?
YEAH. SEIJI'S RIGHT. I DO NEED TO IMPROVE IN THE LOW LINES.
HE'S GOING TO BE A KILLER ADDITION TO THE TEAM. HE MIGHT EVEN GIVE US A CHANCE AGAINST EXTON.
ALWAYS THINKING ABOUT WHAT'S BEST FOR THE TEAM.
PEOPLE RESENT TALENT LIKE HIS. I WANT US TO MAKE SURE THAT NO ONE HERE GIVES HIM ANY TROUBLE.
I THINK THAT FROWNY-FACED LITTLE FRESHMAN CAN TAKE CARE OF HIMSELF.
THAT INCLUDES YOU, AIDEN.
YES, CAPTAIN.
GLAD YOU'RE FEELING LIKE YOURSELF AGAIN, SINCE YOUR NEXT OPPONENT ISN'T GOING TO GO EASY ON YOU.
REALLY? WHO IS IT?
ME.
To Be Continued...

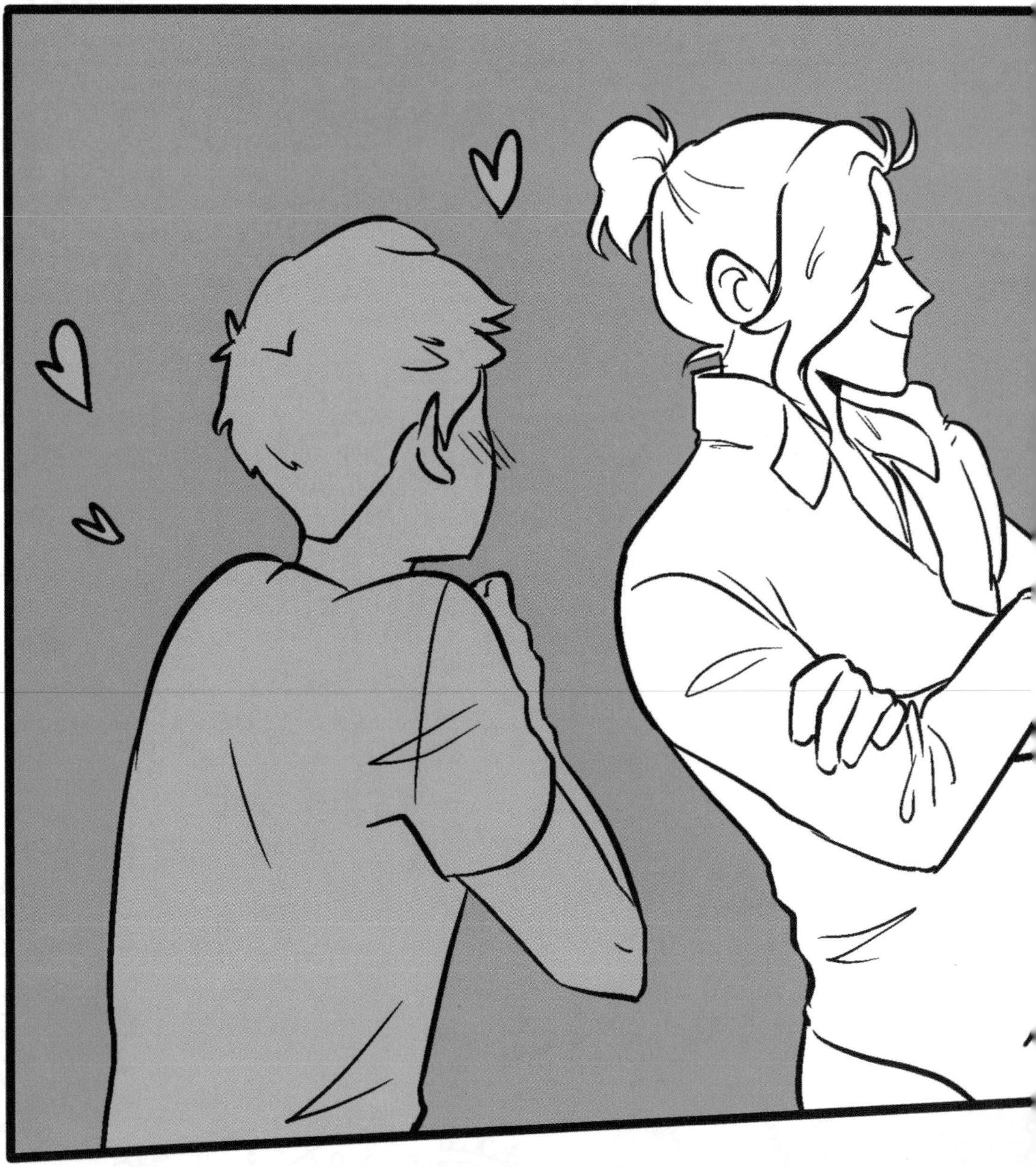

COVER Gallery

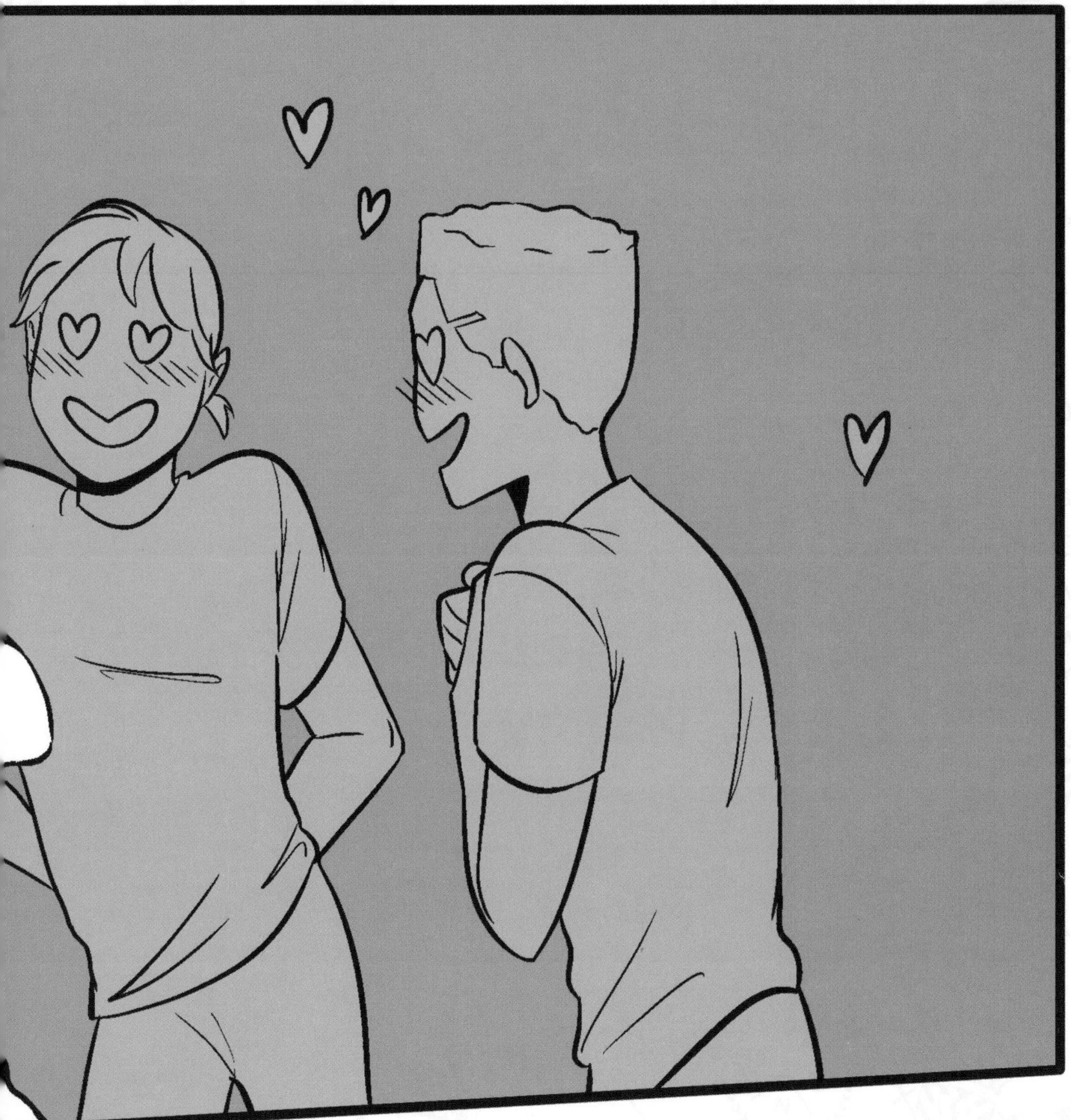

ISSUE 05 COVER BY
Johanna the Mad

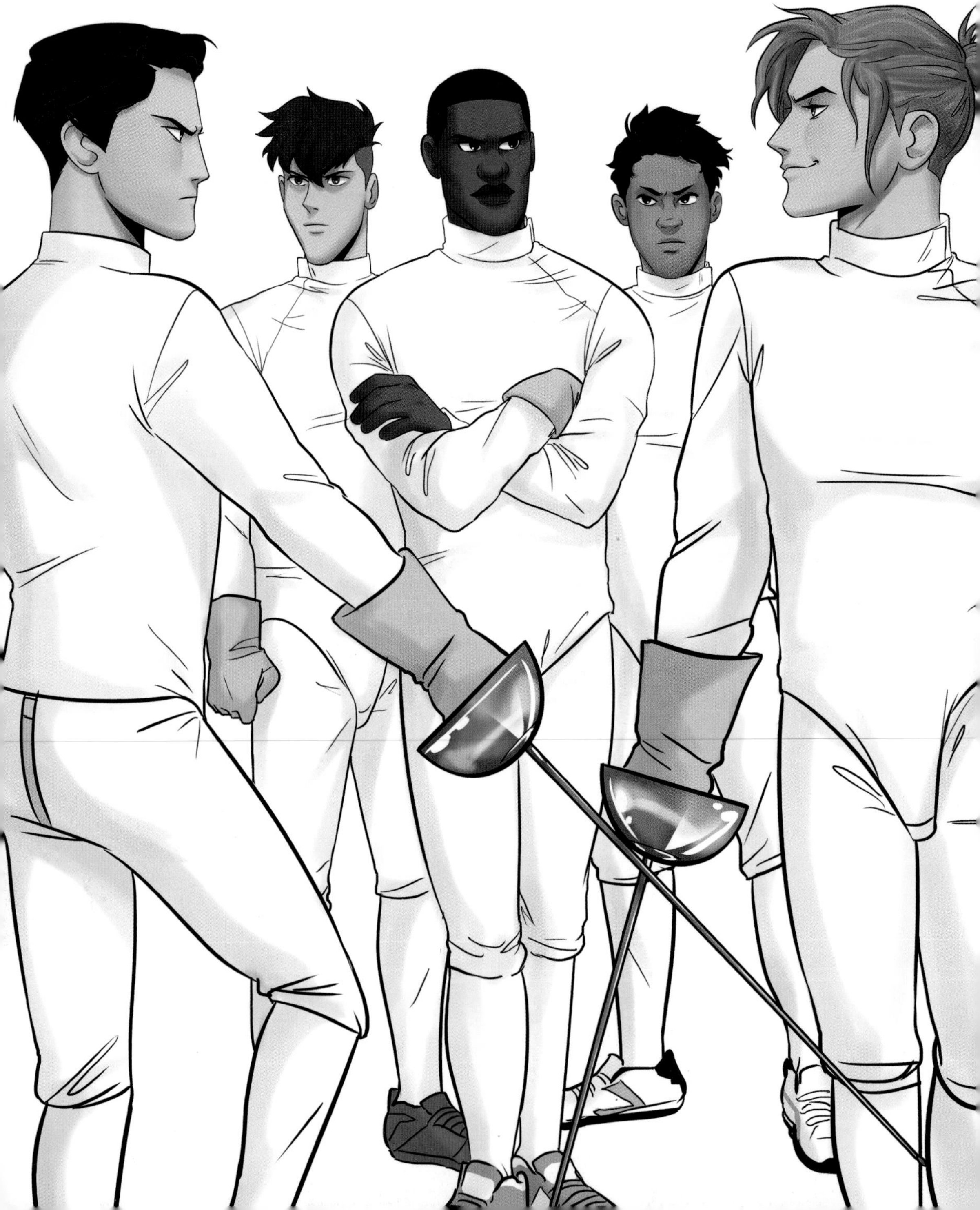

ISSUE 05 UNLOCKED RETAILER VARIANT COVER BY

Shanen Pae

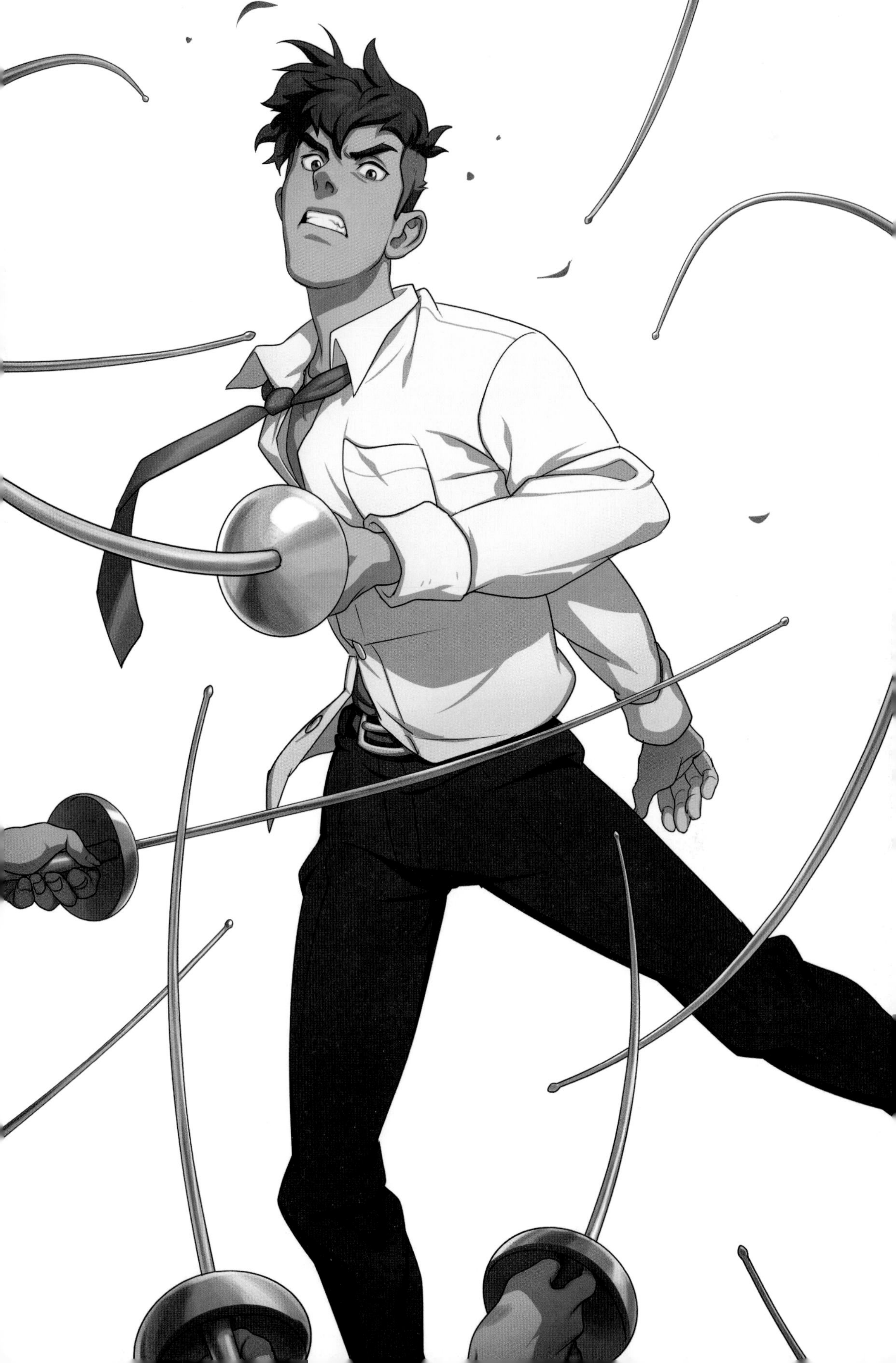

ISSUE 06 COVER BY

Johanna the Mad

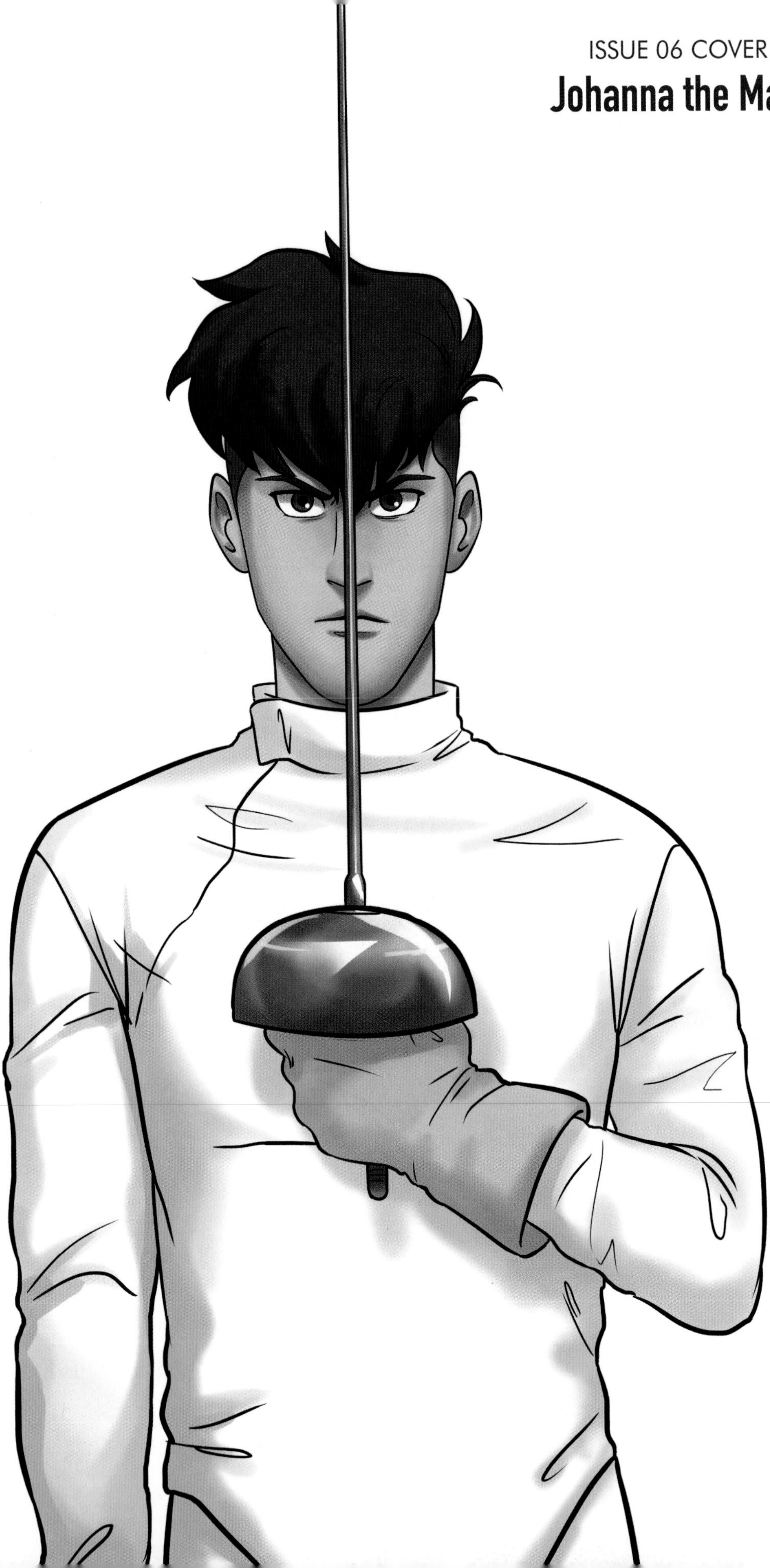

ISSUE 07 COVER BY

HamletMachine

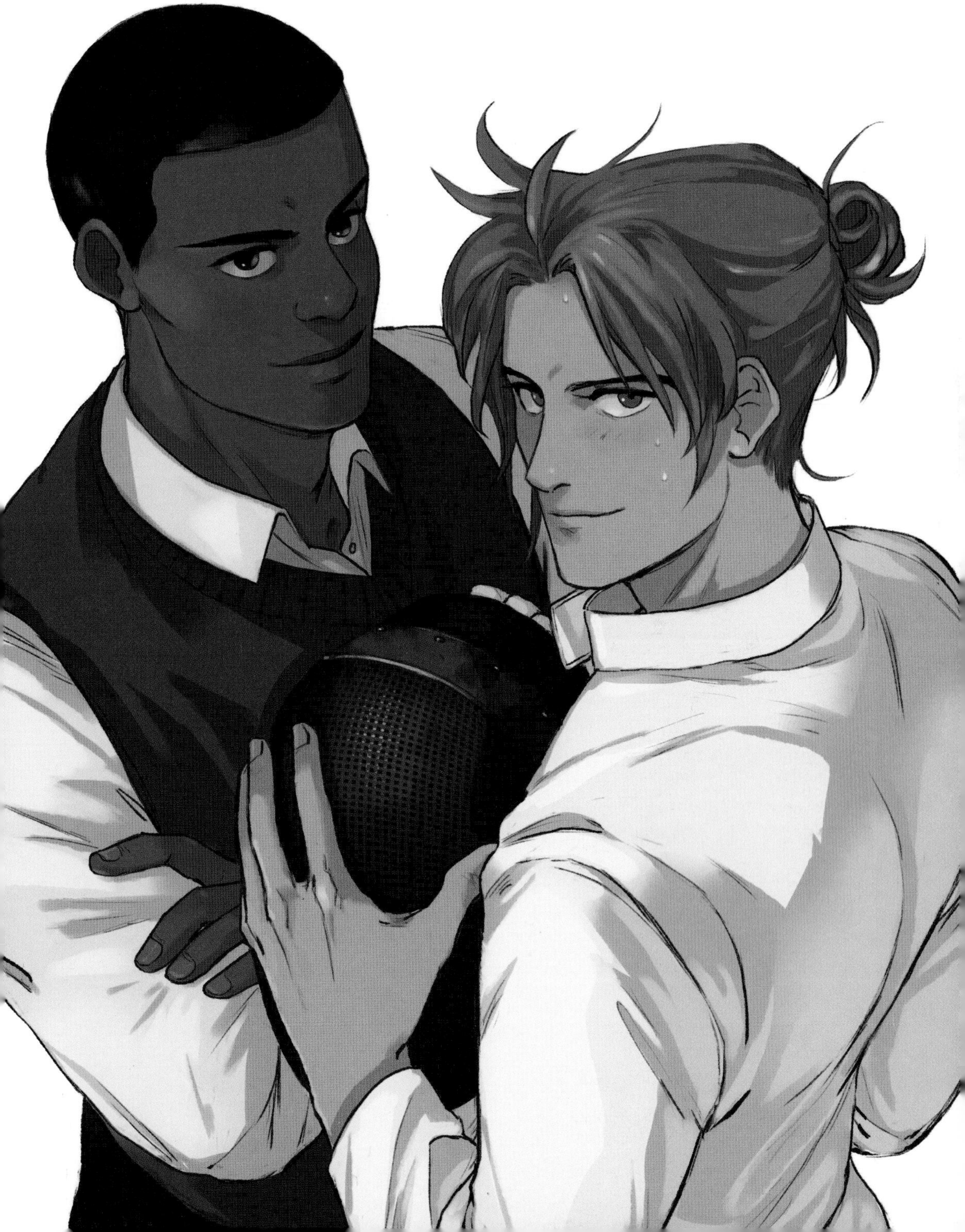

ISSUE 08 COVER BY
HamletMachine

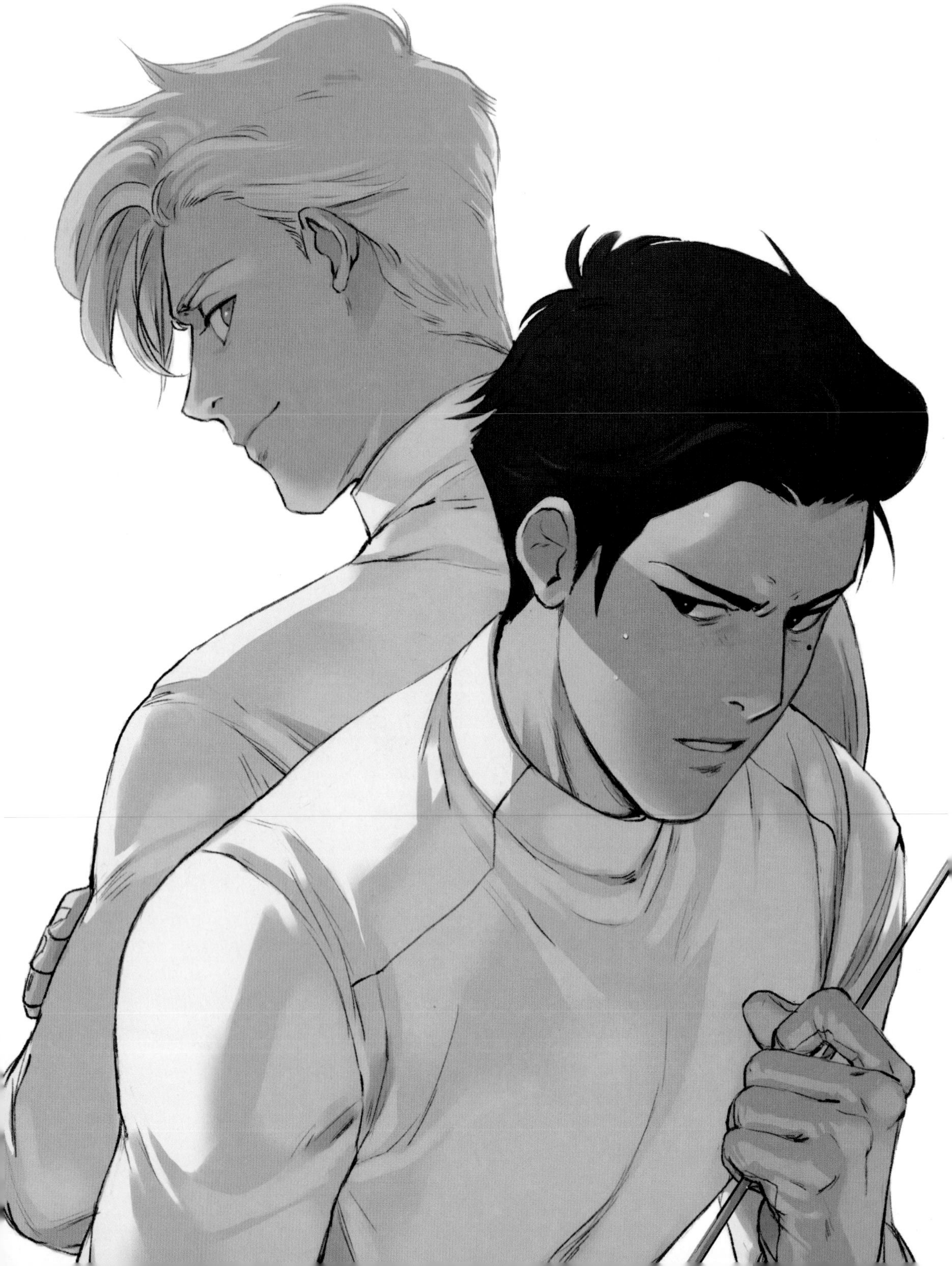

PENCIL PAGES
Gallery

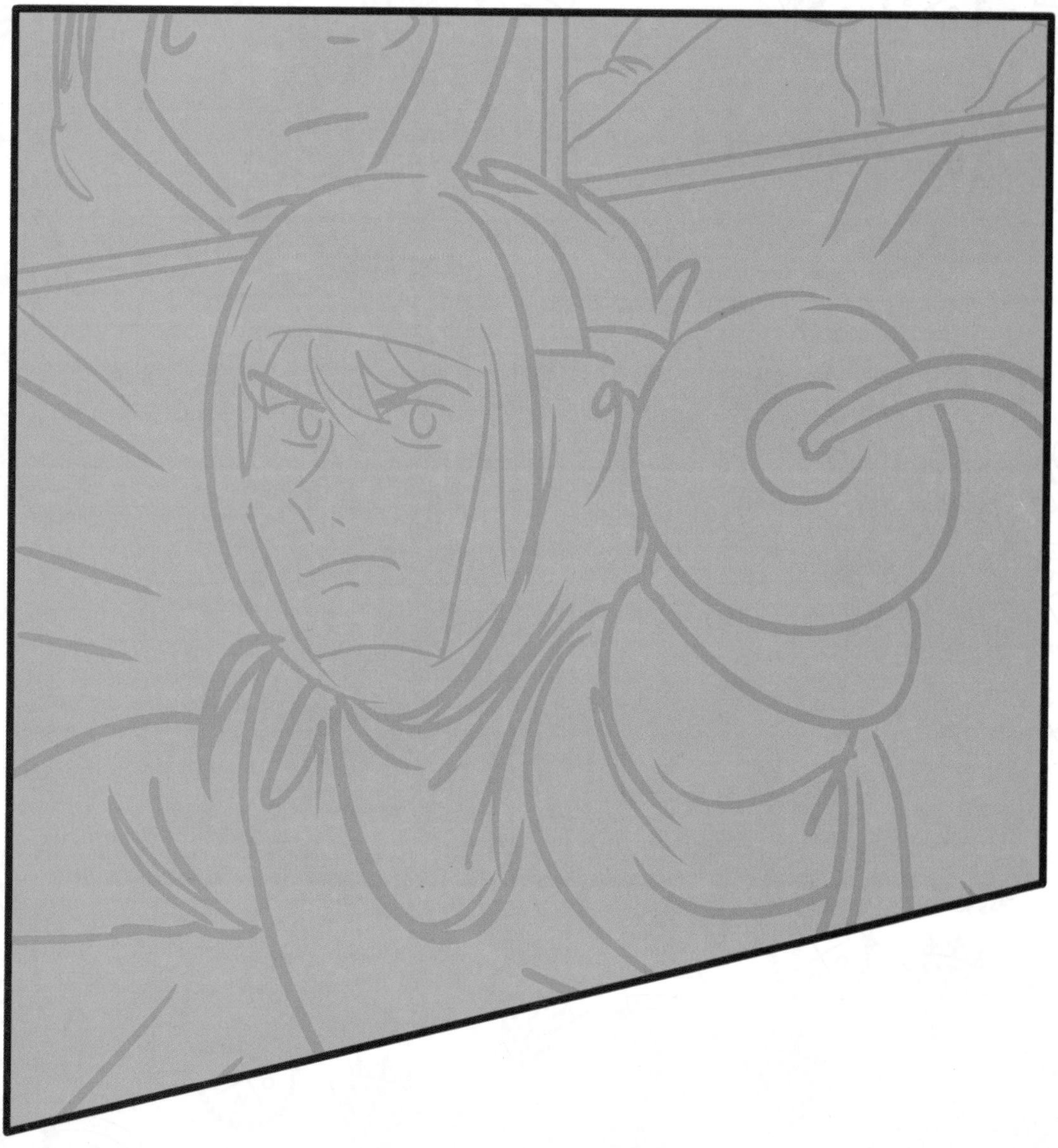

ISSUE 05, PAGE 02

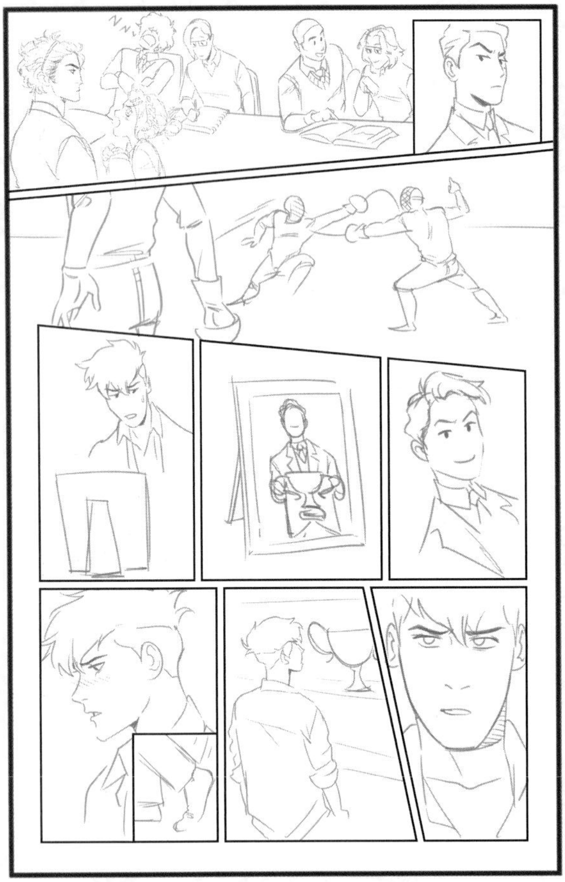

ISSUE 05, PAGE 12

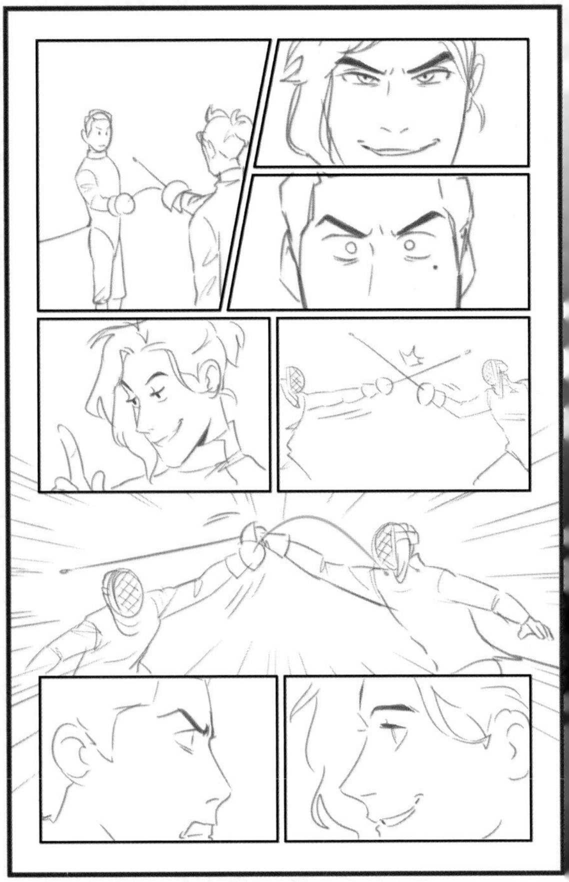

ISSUE 05, PAGE 21

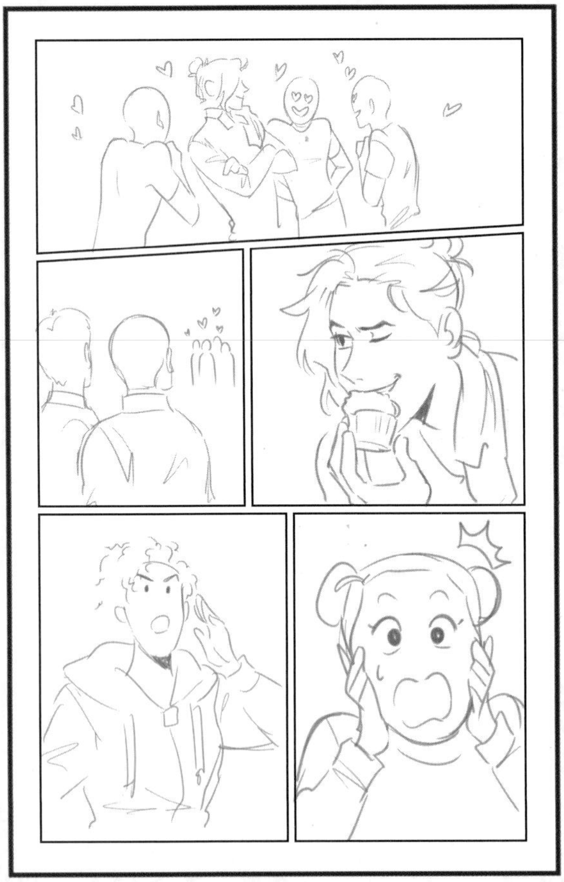

ISSUE 06, PAGE 02

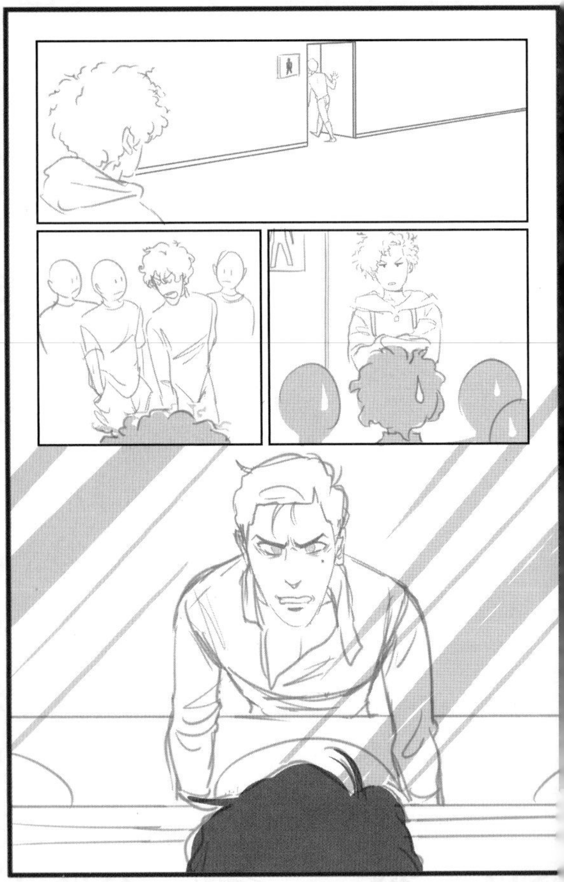

ISSUE 06, PAGE 07

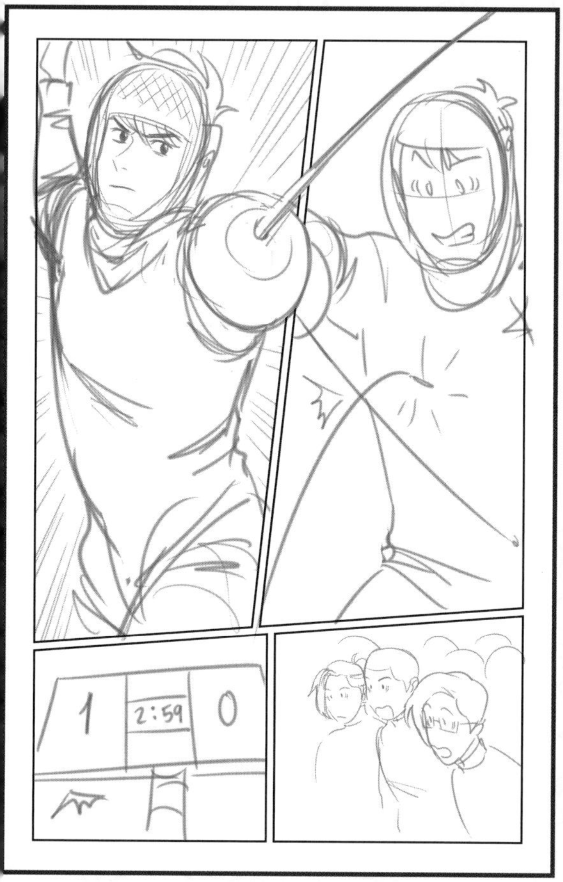

1
2:59
0

ISSUE 06, PAGE 12

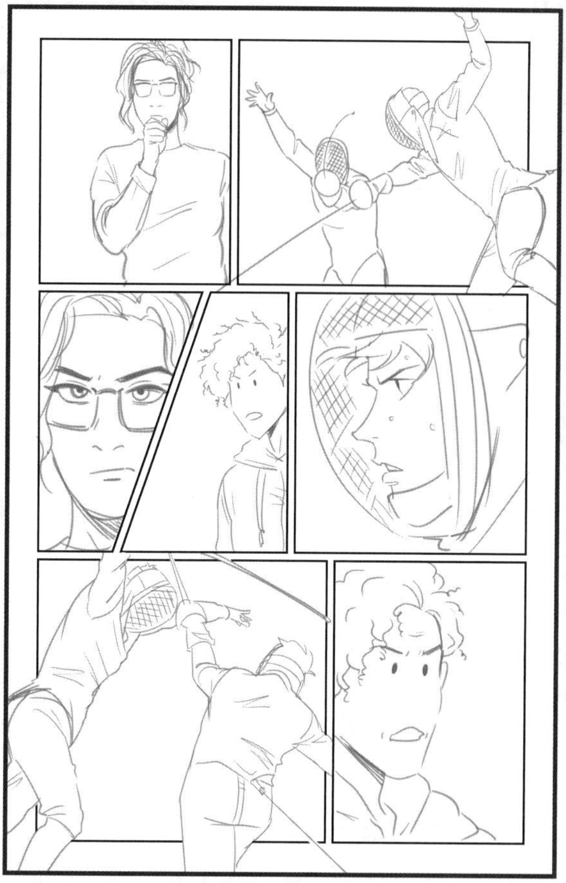

ISSUE 06, PAGE 20

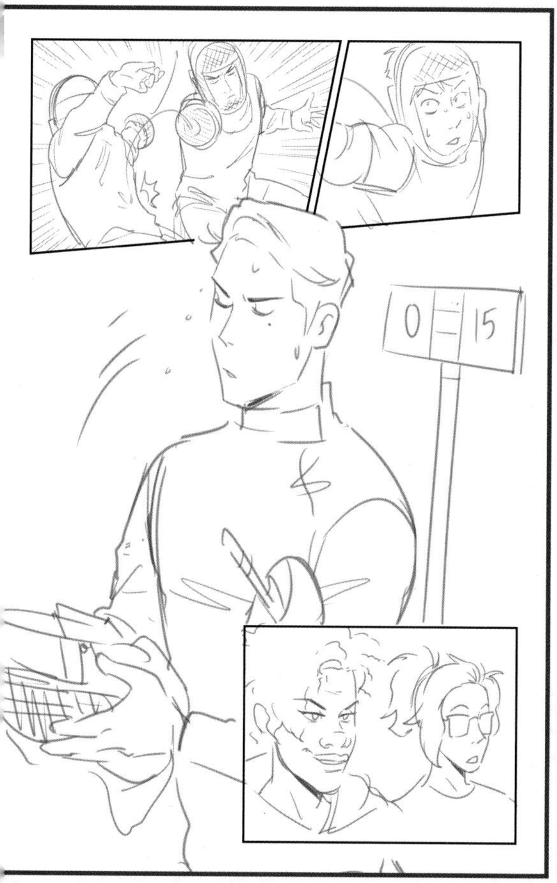

0
15

ISSUE 07, PAGE 04

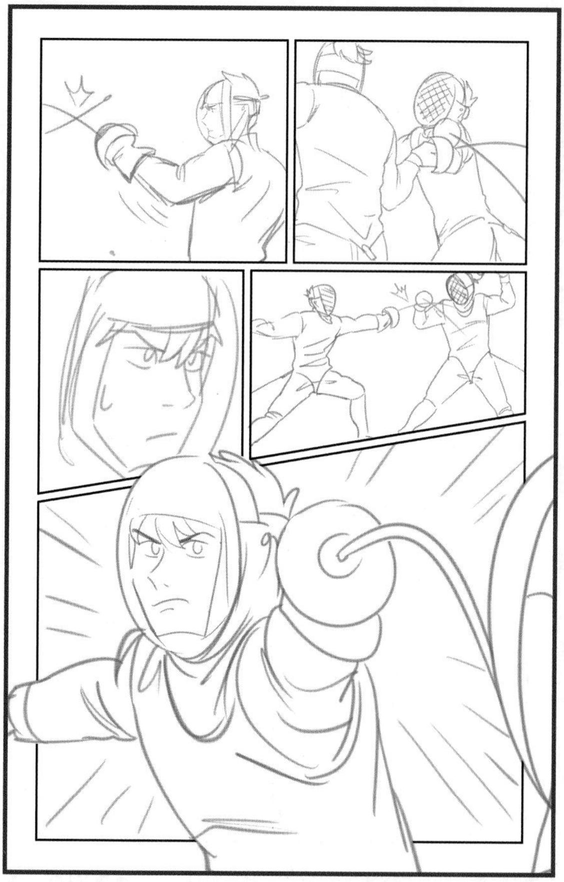

DISCOVER **ALL THE HITS**

STEVENSON · ELLIS · WATTERS · ALLEN
LUMBERJANES
BEWARE THE KITTEN HOLY
NEW YORK TIMES BESTSELLING SERIES

GIANT DAYS
VOLUME ONE

RIBON • FISH • PEER
SLAM!
VOLUME ONE

Hope Larson • Brittney Williams • Sarah Stern
GOLDIE VANCE
Volume One

THE BACKSTAGERS

TYSON HESSE'S
DIESEL
IGNITION

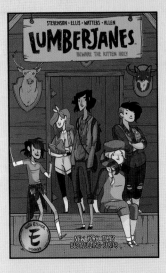

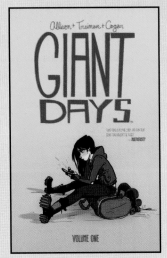

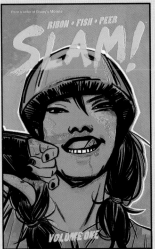

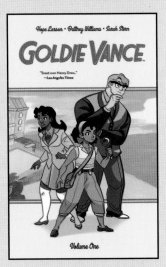

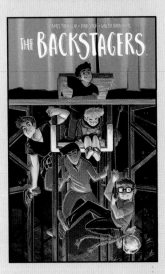

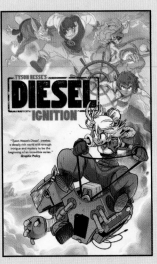

Lumberjanes
Noelle Stevenson, Shannon Watters, Grace Ellis, Brooklyn Allen, and Others
Volume 1: Beware the Kitten Holy
ISBN: 978-1-60886-687-8 | $14.99 US
Volume 2: Friendship to the Max
ISBN: 978-1-60886-737-0 | $14.99 US
Volume 3: A Terrible Plan
ISBN: 978-1-60886-803-2 | $14.99 US
Volume 4: Out of Time
ISBN: 978-1-60886-860-5 | $14.99 US
Volume 5: Band Together
ISBN: 978-1-60886-919-0 | $14.99 US

Giant Days
John Allison, Lissa Treiman, Max Sarin
Volume 1
ISBN: 978-1-60886-789-9 | $9.99 US
Volume 2
ISBN: 978-1-60886-804-9 | $14.99 US
Volume 3
ISBN: 978-1-60886-851-3 | $14.99 US

Jonesy
Sam Humphries, Caitlin Rose Boyle
Volume 1
ISBN: 978-1-60886-883-4 | $9.99 US
Volume 2
ISBN: 978-1-60886-999-2 | $14.99 US

Slam!
Pamela Ribon, Veronica Fish, Brittany Peer
Volume 1
ISBN: 978-1-68415-004-5 | $14.99 US

Goldie Vance
Hope Larson, Brittney Williams
Volume 1
ISBN: 978-1-60886-898-8 | $9.99 US
Volume 2
ISBN: 978-1-60886-974-9 | $14.99 US

The Backstagers
James Tynion IV, Rian Sygh
Volume 1
ISBN: 978-1-60886-993-0 | $14.99 US

Tyson Hesse's Diesel: Ignition
Tyson Hesse
ISBN: 978-1-60886-907-7 | $14.99 US

Coady & The Creepies
Liz Prince, Amanda Kirk, Hannah Fisher
ISBN: 978-1-68415-029-8 | $14.99 US

BOOM! BOX™

AVAILABLE AT YOUR LOCAL COMICS SHOP AND BOOKSTORE
To find a comics shop in your area, visit www.comicshoplocator.com
WWW.**BOOM-STUDIOS**.COM